MW00366073

Borderless Wars

In 2011, Nasser al-Awlaki, a terrorist on the U.S. "kill list" in Yemen, was targeted by the CIA. One week later, a military strike killed his son. The following year, the U.S. Ambassador to Pakistan resigned, concluding he was undermined by CIA-conducted drone strikes of which he had no knowledge or control. The demands of the new, borderless "gray area" conflict have cast civilians and military into unaccustomed roles with inadequate legal underpinning. As the civilian Department of Homeland Security defends the United States against increasing cyber threats and armies of civilian contractors work in paramilitary roles in conflict areas, appropriate roles in wartime and legal boundaries of war demand clarification.

In this book, former Under Secretary of the U.S. Air Force Antonia Chayes examines gray areas in counterinsurgency, counterterrorism, and cyber warfare. Her innovative solutions for role definition and transparency offer new approaches to a rapidly evolving civil-military-legal environment.

Antonia Chayes, former Under Secretary of the U.S. Air Force, is Professor of Practice of International Politics and Law at the Tufts University Fletcher School of Law and Diplomacy. The author of numerous articles and coauthor of *The New Sovereignty*, Chayes has served on several government commissions and on the board of United Technologies Corporation. Wife of the late Abram Chayes, she is the mother of Eve, Sarah, Angelica, Abigail, and Lincoln, and she has nine grandchildren and one great-grandchild.

Borderless Wars

Civil Military Disorder and Legal Uncertainty

ANTONIA CHAYES

*Fletcher School of Law and Diplomacy,
Tufts University*

CAMBRIDGE
UNIVERSITY PRESS

CAMBRIDGE
UNIVERSITY PRESS

32 Avenue of the Americas, New York, NY 10013-2473, USA

Cambridge University Press is part of the University of Cambridge.

It furthers the University's mission by disseminating knowledge in the pursuit of education, learning, and research at the highest international levels of excellence.

www.cambridge.org
Information on this title: www.cambridge.org/9781107521506

' First published 2015

Printed in the United States of America

A catalog record for this publication is available from the British Library.

Library of Congress Cataloging in Publication Data
Chayes, Antonia Handler, 1929– author.
Borderless wars : civil military disorder and legal uncertainty / Antonia Chayes, Tufts University Fletcher School of Law and Diplomacy.
pages   cm
Includes bibliographical references and index.
ISBN 978-1-107-10934-6 (hardback) – ISBN 978-1-107-52150-6 (pbk.)
1. Military law – United States.   2. Terrorism – Prevention – Law and legislation – United States.   3. Civil-military relations – United States.   4. Asymmetric warfare.   5. Civil war.   6. Cyberspace operations (Military science)   I. Title.
KF7209.C47   2015
322.'50973–dc23   2015007702

ISBN 978-1-107-10934-6 Hardback
ISBN 978-1-107-52150-6 Paperback

To the memory of Abram Chayes, whose path I still follow, and to our five children: Eve, Sarah, Angelica, Abigail, and Lincoln. The mutual support they have shown makes the "too hard" possible.

Contents

Foreword

As the Commander of all NATO global operations from 2009 to 2013, I was often asked what kept me awake at night. The answer is a single word: cyber. In this brilliant new book, renowned lawyer, scholar, security practitioner, and professor Antonia Chayes provides some very real ideas to deal with the looming tower of cyber security.

But this book does not stop with cyber issues. It is distinctive for its originality in making connections that others have not made. It is distinctive in its clarity in explaining to an audience concerned with current and emerging security issues that their focus must be not just on who is winning or losing but on how, in the long run, civilians and military must work together to deal with the irregularity of warfare, and the legality of all the actions taken to combat it. This is an ambitious, creative, and incredibly timely examination of three critical areas of national security policy that exist in "the gray" between war and peace. Ultimately, it is a primer on the profound national security challenges and responsibilities the United States faces in the twenty-first century. Despite its strength, the world's most powerful state still wrestles with a very real set of formidable and complex threats. Modern threats combine rigid ideology, agile technology, and global discontent in ways that have not only disturbed and destabilized bureaucracies and militaries but also call into question the validity and adequacy of legal frameworks, domestic and international. Chayes has chosen to explore a particular kaleidoscope of campaigns – counterinsurgency, counterterrorism, and cyber warfare – that the American government has undertaken to do battle in this murky terrain that is modern-day war making.

Chayes blends a rich review of the existing scholarship with an incisive examination of the current doctrine, law, and policy to give the reader a clear, detailed sense of what is working, what is not, and which questions must still be asked and answered. She weaves deftly between domestic legal and political concerns and questions of international jurisprudence and geopolitics. Uninhibited by standard siloed thinking on matters of war, peace, and politics, Chayes moves seamlessly from the heights of grand strategy and guiding principles to the arenas occupied by policy makers and lawyers and right down into the field where soldiers, NGOs, firms, and militants operate. Her expertise as a legal scholar with high-level experiences in the public and private sectors affords her the ability to speak to all levels of concern with authority and ease. This particular vantage point further allows her to frame and reframe insurgency, terrorism, and cyber warfare as civil, military, criminal, public, and private in turn. Scholars, policy makers, military officers, journalists, and the like must grapple with each paradigm in earnest in order to understand these threats in their entirety.

Chayes does not stop with critical analysis but goes further, offering a number of recommendations that reflect an exhaustive understanding of the "state of the art" but remain digestible and actionable at the same time. Her critiques and suggestions reflect an urgent, well-learned set of beliefs: first, after a decade of war and loss, this is a moment for real reflection about why the most powerful military in the world still struggles on the battlefield against unconventional warriors. It is a moment when the law must catch up to events on the ground if the United States is to maintain the legitimate respect of its peers and those populations whose hearts and minds it seeks to win. And it is a moment when imagination and collaboration must be harnessed in order to conceive of and respond to threats that heretofore did not exist in their present forms.

This is a book that deserves the widest distribution and attention in the hands of global leaders. It will make an enormous positive difference in our approach.

Admiral James Stavridis USN
Dean, The Fletcher School, Tufts University;
Supreme Allied Commander of NATO, 2009–2013

Acknowledgments

My heartfelt thanks to Sarah Chayes for her tough and uncompromising efforts in editing this manuscript. I could hear her tough voice in the marginal comments saying, "Mom – did you know that … ?" Once in a while, she even wrote "good."

I had extraordinary research assistants. My thanks to Jennifer Keene, who probed, questioned, researched, and helped me write for more than two years – her thinking helped shape this book. I call her the "tooth fairy" because she would often work late at night, and the next morning I would find a section changed and adequately footnoted. Sasha Giller did the same on the cyber section – probing, researching, suggesting, and questioning. He was another tooth fairy. Meg Guliford has helped me unstintingly with precision and enormous energy. My special thanks to Brian Kelly and the editors of the Harvard *National Security Law Journal*, Rebecca Cress, Aaron Blacksberg, Chris Kimmel, Abby Colella, and Daniel Isenberg, for their work on the cyber section. Sasha Pippenger helped me early on as I thought through the drone issues.

My thanks to my colleagues who read and commented most helpfully, including Sulmaan Khan, Dipali Mukhopadhyay, Mary Ellen O'Connell, Cecile Aptel, Herbert Lin, Eileen Babbitt, and Richard Shultz, as well as John Herfort, my nephew. And both my daughter Eve Lyman and my cousin Ellen Handler Spitz gave me the artistic ideas for the cover.

I am grateful also to members of my civ-mil class, especially Artin Afkhami and Momtuz Baloch, whose early comments helped the analysis along.

Introduction

Liber Scriptus proferetur
In Quo totum continetur
Unde mundus judicetur

The Written Book shall be brought
In which all is contained
Whereby the world shall be judged

Dies Irae from the Requiem Mass

"Are you saying that a U.S. citizen targeted by the United States in a foreign country has no constitutional rights?" demanded Judge Rosemary Collyer of the Federal District Court of the District of Columbia on July 19, 2013. Facing her was Brian Hauck, a deputy assistant attorney general. "How broadly are you asserting the right of the United States to target an American citizen? Where is the limit to this?"

Then the judge answered her own question: "The limit is the courthouse door."[1]

The case was a civil action against four officials, including General David Petraeus, then Director of the Central Intelligence Agency (CIA), and Leon Panetta, then Secretary of Defense.[2] The father of

---

[1] Scott Shane, "Judge Challenges White House Claims on Authority in Drone Killings," *The New York Times*, July 20, 2013, http://www.nytimes.com/2013/07/20/us/politics/judge-challenges-white-house-claims-on-authority-in-drone-killings.html (accessed September 28, 2014).

[2] The two additional defendants in the case of al-Awlaki v. Panetta included the Commander of U.S. Special Operations Command, Admiral William H. McRaven, United States Navy, and the Commander of the Joint Special Operations Command,

Anwar al-Awlaki brought the lawsuit. A terrorist leader of al-Qaeda in the Arabian Peninsula, al-Awlaki had been a master propagandist who allegedly inspired the mass shootings at the U.S. army base at Fort Hood, Texas, in 2009, and masterminded an attempted attack on an American airplane. His son was killed accidentally two weeks later in a drone strike against Samir Khan, a publicist in the same al-Qaeda offshoot.

Although Judge Collyer, a George W. Bush appointee who also sits on the Foreign Intelligence Surveillance Court, ultimately dismissed the case in April 2014,[3] the lawsuit raised fundamental legal issues that have been the subject of ongoing debate regarding how U.S. laws are construed.

The judge's remarks also raised much broader issues about the nature of contemporary warfare and the changes in the roles of the military vis-à-vis the many different civilian actors with whom it works. This shift in roles has been especially dramatic since 9/11. Along with senior civilian leadership, Congress at the policy level, and diplomats and aid workers at the operational level, many more civilians are now relevant in any discussion of civil-military relations. They include the CIA in a paramilitary role;[4] almost every U.S. federal government agency and many agencies at state and local levels; the U.S. courts; and a growing army of civilian contractors, many of whom are ex-military currently performing quasi-military roles. And, of course, both civilians and military must work with the people in the host country in which the conflict is taking place, including officials, security forces, and ordinary citizens. Civil-military relations – the focus of this book – have become increasingly blurred in the attempt to adapt to festering gray area conflict situations.

The security situation the United States and its allies have been facing continues to be fraught with multiple simultaneous conflicts.

Lieutenant General Joseph Votel, United States Army. Admiral McRaven retired from military service in September 2014, and General Votel was promoted and assumed command of USSOCOM in September 2014.

[3] Al-Aulaki v. Obama 727F.Supp2d 201(D.D.C. 2010); Charlie Savage, "Judge Dismisses Suit against Administration Officials over Drone Strikes," *The New York Times*, April 4, 2014, http://nyti.ms/1egGT9K (accessed September 28, 2014). 727 F. Supp. 2d 1 (D.D.C. 2010).

[4] Some observers in the United States and elsewhere regard intelligence officials as part of the military even when their agency is civilian.

Some are ongoing disputes, others are reshuffled semi-wars, and some represent new outbreaks of violence. These conflicts are not usually traditional wars. Very few involve attempts at state-on-state conquest as typified by Saddam Hussein's invasion of Kuwait in 1990. More often, these wars fall within a spreading inkblot between war and peace. Some are internal conflicts that often destabilize historical boundaries. Some end up obliterating historical boundaries. Often combatants on one side of a conflict are not traditional soldiers in uniform, but are non–state actors – insurgents or terrorists – even though sometimes they serve as proxies for a state, as do militias in Iraq. It is the threat of widespread terrorism that has captured the continuing attention of western democracies. These gray area conflicts are the stage for this book.

Ironically, while in 2012 the number of large-scale killings in violent conflicts decreased, pervasive volatility has been growing.[5] As Alex de Waal, Executive Director of the World Peace Foundation argues, stability is now more elusive than it was in the past: "More effort than ever is invested in peace, and peace agreements are larger and more complicated than ever before, but they seem not to bring peace."[6] But while many analysts and scholars focus on peace-building, little attention is being paid to the confused evolution of civil-military relations within the United States and its allies, and its impact on the very peace being sought. Significant and confusing changes impinge on classic democratic notions of civilian control of the military and on the behavior of both civilians and military. In response to the demands of the irregularity and pervasiveness of the gray area of conflict – not war/not peace – both civilians and military have been cast into unaccustomed roles. The classic notion of a civil-military dyad is no longer sufficient as a model: there are many actors who perform both civil and military functions,

---

[5] Human Security Research Group, *Human Security Report 2013: The Decline in Global Violence: Evidence, Explanation, and Contestation* (Vancouver: Human Security Press, 2013), 12, http://www.hsrgroup.org/docs/Publications/HSR2013/HSRP_Report_2013_140226_Web.pdf (accessed October 2, 2014).

[6] Alex de Waal, "Framework of the 'Political Marketplace'" (lecture, World Peace Foundation seminar "The Political Marketplace: Analyzing Political Entrepreneurs and Political Bargaining with a Business Lens," June 12–13, 2014), http://sites.tufts.edu/reinventingpeace/files/2014/10/Political-Marketplace_de-Waal.pdf (accessed March 24, 2015).

including allies in a coalition, contractors, police, and host nation officials. It is not clear in the United States and Europe who the relevant civilians are or should be; and who, in addition to uniformed soldiers, is or should be performing military roles. Moreover, the U.S. military, at least, has undertaken perceived traditional civilian roles of reconstruction and rehabilitation of war-torn societies. Perhaps most important, military leadership has been induced into the realm of policy, and is now making strategic choices and practicing diplomacy at least as often as it fights battles. In this evolving context, the dialogue among civilians and military seems unplanned and ad hoc, with success often dependent on personal chemistry.

The blurred lines of authority, moreover, are further confused by the lack of adequate legal underpinnings, both domestic and international, to govern this new, fractured conflict environment. Existing law may not apply to evolving conditions, or it may fail to add clarity to role distribution. International rules – including customary law, treaty law and legal principles – are being stretched to fit new situations, but unfortunately, laws – particularly international treaties – are not infinitely elastic, nor are they easily rewritten. In other instances, there is a legal void. The current fit is awkward and not reassuring to the public. American domestic legislation, even laws written after 9/11, do not offer adequate guidance about what actions are permissible, or for those actions permitted by law, who should act. Executive powers have been increased, but oversight has not matched that expansion. The secrecy surrounding legal justification has magnified both confusion and public unease.

This book examines three different contemporary sets of issues within the gray area between war and peace: (1) counterinsurgency; (2) counterterrorism, in particular targeted killing; and (3) cyber attacks and cyber warfare. Each area presents some novel issues at both policy and operational levels that are not addressed adequately by the current legal frameworks. In each case, just as with nuclear weapons in the 1940s,[7] legal change lags behind a rapidly evolving operational environment. Complex new rules are hard to adopt and slow to be widely accepted, if they are accepted at all. In

---

[7] Nuclear weapons were first tested by the Soviet Union in 1949; the first arms control agreement was the Limited Test Ban Treaty of 1963.

each area, the book addresses what may have aggravated difficult situations, and what measures might improve effectiveness.

This book does not explicitly address issues arising from the exponential development of the military industrial complex ("the iron triangle"[8]) over the past dozen years. That complex can better be described as an agglomeration of power among military, industrial producers, and Congress, rather than as a confusion of roles among the actors. Nor does it discuss lobbyists or political groupings trying to increase the military budget. Lobbyists and interest groups have become part of the "rough and tumble" of American politics, but their contribution to the current divisiveness now may be a distraction from congressional attention to novel and complex security issues.

How the United States and Its Allies Have Adapted to "Gray Area" Conflict

These three issue areas – counterinsurgency, counterterrorism, and cyber attacks – illustrate the attempt, especially by the United States, to adapt to the new gray area that lies between peace and war. Terrorism is by no means new. But its pervasiveness and geographic spread have not been seen before. Conventional wars ultimately do end, even if sporadic violence continues for a time. But in recent years, when one region seems to be stabilized for a while, another geographic gray area seems to emerge, often destabilizing its neighbors, just as the war in Syria has deepened the political-sectarian strife in Iraq.[9] New crises confront a different set of decision makers, and their approaches are often as ahistorical as they are foolishly optimistic.

Although the history of warfare before the twenty-first century does offer important insights, the parallels are not fully examined, even when they might be useful as reference points for action

---

[8] Hugh Heclo, "Issue Networks and the Executive Establishment," in *The New American Political System*, ed. Anthony King (Lanham, MD: American Enterprise Institute Press, 1978).

[9] Dexter Filkins, "What We Left Behind," *The New Yorker*, April 28, 2014, http://www.newyorker.com/magazine/2014/04/28/what-we-left-behind (accessed September 27, 2014).

against today's multiple and relentless outbreaks of violence. The United States has not developed enduring criteria to indicate when it may be useful for great powers to intervene in another country with or without force. The changing landscape of violent conflict may render static criteria unhelpful, but ongoing historic analysis of the motivations for intervention and nonintervention can be an important guide. Fear of a terrorist threat to the homeland has been the most powerful motivating factor since 9/11. Metastasizing insurgencies have also been a factor, even when they do not pose a direct threat to the homeland. American responses to the pervasive, spreading areas of violence also stem from altruistic impulses to assist suffering civilians or to grasp a perceived opportunity to help forge a democratic government. Many earlier decisions to intervene or exercise restraint were based on a simpler Cold War calculus about potential Soviet response in the twentieth century.

Recent interventions have raised both international and domestic legal issues with international political repercussions. They have also resulted in unforeseen and negative consequences. Unfortunately, the aftermaths of such interventions, as in Iraq, Afghanistan, and Libya, have demonstrated a continuation of the spreading violence with no end in sight.

The experience suffered during the UN operation in Somalia in October 1993 (UNISOM II), when television broadcasts showed the bodies of dead American soldiers being dragged through the streets of Mogadishu, inoculated America against intervention for a number of years. That event, it is argued, contributed to the decision to withhold support for a possible UN response to the genocide in Rwanda in 1994.[10] It certainly shaped Presidential Decision Directive 25 that limited American participation in the UN's expanded peacekeeping operations to those that affected the vital interests of the United States. President Obama struck a similar note twenty years later at the West Point commencement in May 2014: "The United States will use military force, unilaterally if necessary, when our core interests demand it – when our people are threatened, when our livelihoods are at stake, when the security

---

[10] Samantha Power, *A Problem from Hell: America and the Age of Genocide* (New York: Harper Collins, 2002), 374–375.

of our allies is in danger."[11] War fatigue, lack of success, and the stirring of public opinion by terrorist atrocities do not provide useful guidance for anything as crucial as a decision to intervene in a conflict or to offer or withhold military support. Even less rational are responses based on unrelated domestic political issues that at least in the United States include the time in an election cycle, the nature of congressional support for the executive branch at a given moment, and competing priorities.

Past Civil-Military Models Are Not Helpful

Perhaps in part because of this lack of a consistent rational methodology for deciding whether or when to intervene, and because of the variety of motivations that may drive such decisions, recent interventions and crisis responses have produced an improvised rearrangement of civil-military roles. The pervasive threat of terrorism has not been fully digested. And where forces have intervened, the importance of reconstruction efforts have also contributed to the blurring of civil-military roles.[12] No model has yet emerged that provides for the kind of deep cooperation and systematic planning among civilian and military leaders that the new characteristics of today's gray area conflicts require. Without such collaboration, role definition at the operational level, in turn, seems to develop reactively, or on a personal basis. In many cases, the relationships are not tailored to the situation, and are far less effective than had they been well thought through. The off-budget and widespread use of civilian contractors is a further problem. They affect command and control and skew the entire incentive system, even though they may be needed to fill unexpected demand.

The classic model of "objective" civilian control of a professional military insulated from politics was never realistic. Created by Samuel Huntington, the theory required that civilian leadership

---

[11] President Barack H. Obama (speech, United States Military Academy, West Point, NY, May 28, 2014), White House official website, http://www.whitehouse.gov/the-press-office/2014/05/28/remarks-president-united-states-military-academy-commencement-ceremony (accessed October 2, 2014).

[12] Gabriella Blum, "The Fog of Victory," *European Journal of International Law* 24, no. 1 (2013): 391–421.

dominate policy, and operations be controlled by the military to effect the policy choices made. Operationally, the Huntington model would suggest a sequence of a policy decision to intervene, followed by combat operations managed by a professional military, ending with a peace agreement, after which civilians at the operational level would enter the scene to rebuild the society.[13] Yet that neat separation did not even characterize the post–World War II narrative, in which the allied military forces were needed and employed to rebuild both Europe and Japan.[14]

Even combat operational choices may have crucial political consequences. The documented lessons from the Vietnam War made that clear.[15] The ambiguity about new gray area warfare should have alerted policymakers to the need for deep and continuing collaboration and dialogue among civilians and military in both planning for intervention and execution thereafter. But any recognition on the part of policymakers that is revealed in after-the-fact reflections on current conflicts has not led to new systems or new models.

Counterinsurgency

Counterinsurgency (also known as COIN), the first area examined in this book, has as its central premise the protection of the civilian population. Its slogan – "clear, hold, build" – suggests a sequence, but further examination of the doctrine implies that the military might have to help rebuild a society while still fighting a war. Counterinsurgency thrusts the military into exposed positions among the population – a phenomenon widely illustrated in film and commentary. But reality on the ground has demanded that the tasks of reconstruction often be undertaken while fighting continues. Civilians are not adequately trained, nor, in most cases, are they willing to face such dangers. The military is therefore called upon to fill a critical void in the reconstruction efforts – a necessity that can often

---

[13] Samuel P. Huntington, *The Soldier and the State: The Theory and Politics of Civil-Military Relations* (Cambridge, MA: Harvard University Press, 1957), 84.

[14] Carl J. Friedrich, *American Experiences in Military Government in World War II* (New York: Rinehart & Co., 1948).

[15] Robert Komer, *Bureaucracy Does Its Thing: Institutional Constraints on U.S.-GVN Performance in Vietnam*, RAND Institute, http://www.rand.org/pubs/reports/R967.html (accessed October 8, 2014).

exacerbate the unequal budgets and authorities between military and civilian agencies. And when the military has stepped in to fill that void, resentment has developed among civilians about role usurpation. A parallel resentment has developed among military about being forced to assume roles they feel they are neither prepared nor equipped to fill on top of their often staggering combat duties.

No satisfactory model has been proposed to meet these demands. This book's extended discussion of counterinsurgency examines some of the highly exacting conditions for success that will be required if the doctrine is ever to be relied on in the future. Yet no policymaker has yet admitted failure, nor fully articulated the problems with the concept.

Counterinsurgency raises no serious issues of international or domestic law, so long as the laws of occupation are complied with in relevant situations. The doctrine may actually be more demanding than international humanitarian law rules on avoiding civilian casualties. But a lack of positive legal guidance perpetuates the confusion and resentment that have riddled attempts to implement the doctrine. No legal provision has been made that would create a process to tailor appropriate roles to a given situation. It is possible that no legal framework that created civil-military processes, such as planning, intensive training, and practice, would be sufficient to overcome bureaucratic inertia, turf hoarding, or failings of personal chemistry. However, as Chapter 3 discusses, the Goldwater-Nichols Act,[16] which mandated inter-service cooperation among the military, actually reduced the wasteful rivalry that had existed earlier. Although legislation is suggested for the United States, this book acknowledges the difficulties of obtaining it and recommends a multifaceted "saturation approach" that might help, should counterinsurgency efforts be mounted again.

Counterterrorism
In the case of targeted killing, a major element in U.S. counterterrorism (CT) policy, the CIA performs military roles along with the

---

[16] Goldwater-Nichols Department of Defense Reorganization Act of 1986, 10 U.S. Code 111, http://www.govtrack.us/congress/bills/99/hr3622 (accessed October 15, 2014).

military. The high level of secrecy makes it hard to tell whether cooperation or chaos best characterizes this civilian-military relationship. The current respective roles of the CIA and the military may be a sensible adaptation to emerging situations, but to the public it appears a bureaucratic cow path followed in different directions to deal with each situation as it arises – or perhaps even a way to avoid legal and public responsibility. Covert civilian action seems politically simpler and quicker, but the lack of transparency has frayed public confidence. If advanced planning for role allocation has occurred, it has not been articulated, nor has adequate oversight been made apparent. The question of "blowback" – whether widespread targeted killings encourage the spawning of new armies of terrorists while eliminating existing individuals – is also raised.

Targeted killing, as well as other aspects of counterterrorism, raise some of the most contentious issues of domestic and international legality, making the blurred civilian-military lines even more troublesome. The analysis in this book reviews, but does not enter into, the ongoing vigorous debate that has been raging in the press, blogs, scholarly journals, and reports by legal experts and policy analysts about the legality of this technique. The ambiguity of characterizing terrorism as "war" or "something less" – even within a single speech by President Obama – raises serious questions of fact and law. Different legal rules apply in wartime, both internationally and domestically. International law has a set of rules under both customary law, treaties and general principles for wartime behavior. The president has greater powers under the U.S. Constitution, Article II, during war than in other circumstances.

Challenges under international law have been made as to whether Article 51 of the UN Charter plausibly permits the United States to meld a collection of Islamic terrorist organizations into a single, worldwide actor that can be attacked in many different, seemingly unrelated sovereign states indefinitely. These issues are analyzed in Chapter 8, along with legal doctrines and interpretations that have been relied on by the U.S. government that a global, non-international armed conflict exists, which would permit the United States to strike the enemy wherever it presents a threat. This line of analysis also extends the right to attack without permission if a nation is unwilling or unable to respond to a threat. These interpretations are not shared by allies and may be altered over time with new situations and different policymakers.

Targeted killing also raises important legal issues under domestic law. Although the 2001 Authorization for the Use of Military Force (AUMF)[17] has been considered sufficient to justify the Osama bin Laden raid and even strikes against terrorist cells in Yemen, it has more recently been used to justify attacking terrorists that have little relationship to the original al-Qaeda, as well as organizations created long after 9/11. Supporting facts for this extension of the mandate have not been forthcoming. The rise of ISIS (the Islamic State in Iraq and Syria, or the Islamic State)[18] raises the linkage issue even more sharply, as al-Qaeda has explicitly disavowed any connection with ISIS.[19] The Obama administration recognized legal shortcoming by introducing legislation in February 2015 to create a new mandate that expands the AUMF to include ISIS and associated forces in an approach that led to criticism without passage.[20] Finally, one of the most contentious domestic legal issues has been whether the assassination by drone strikes of U.S. citizens, such as Anwar al-Awlaki, in a non-war zone constitutes an unconstitutional denial of due process. The years of secrecy, followed by piecemeal and reluctant legal clarification, have only intensified domestic and international questions about the role of civilian covert action in counterterrorism – especially in light of past American abuses.

---

[17] Authorization for the Use of Military Force, Pub. L. No. 107–40, § 2(a), 115 Stat. 224, 224 (2001), http://www.gpo.gov/fdsys/pkg/PLAW-107publ40/pdf/PLAW-107publ40.pdf (acccessed March 24, 2015).

[18] Also known as ISIL (The Islamic State of Iraq and the Levant) or Daesh (the Arabic word for ISIS).

[19] Liz Sly, "Al Qaeda Disavows Any Ties with Radical Islamist ISIS Group in Syria, Iraq," *The Washington Post*, February 3, 2014, http://wapo.st/1gGHZlA (accessed September 26, 2014).

[20] https://www.whitehouse.gov/sites/default/files/docs/aumf_02112015.pdf. See critique of the bill by Professor Jack Goldsmith, "The Administration's Hard to Fathom Draft AUMF in Lawfare," February 12, 2015, http://www.lawfareblog.com/2015/02/the-administrations-hard-to-fathom-draft-aumf/ (accessed March 22, 2015).

Cyber Attacks and Cyber Warfare

Cyber attacks, representing the third type of gray area conflicts explored in this book, present a different set of civil-military issues. In the United States, the civilians involved in dealing with intrusions into the cyber world are more diverse than those in the other two cases. Both civilians and military are needed to cope with this gray area of potential warfare. In the United States, many federal agencies bear some measure of responsibility for cyber defense, as Chapter 11 describes. Moreover, offices that deal with cyber exploitation and attacks are found in state and local government as well as at the federal level. The Department of Homeland Security (DHS) has responsibility for the vast civilian infrastructure that is held in private hands, while the currently combined National Security Agency (NSA)/Cyber Command deals with potential military threats. But clear lines will be difficult to maintain in ambiguous situations. Moreover, as large as DHS has grown, budget disparities between the purely civilian DHS and the NSA/Cyber Command skew civil-military relationships into another novel pattern.

As the cyber discussion attempts to develop, the variety of current and possible cyber attacks stretches the concept of gray area warfare into new dimensions. A cyber event may represent an act of espionage, or it may be a precursor to a physical attack that could lead to bodily harm. If an attack were to be made on a nuclear plant, military involvement is certainly to be expected. The magnitude and impact of a cyber attack might cause disruption that approximates a kinetic attack. But a major and disruptive intrusion into privately held infrastructure is initially ambiguous. It may be difficult to identify exactly when an "attack" has taken place, who perpetrated the act, whether retaliation is legal and necessary, and, if so, what response is appropriate and proportionate.

The multiple offices that deal with potential cyber attacks throughout the American state and local governmental system require a degree of coordination and practice that did not exist when natural disasters occurred, such as Hurricane Katrina. American interagency and intergovernmental cooperation to cope with even natural disasters is in its infancy. Some improvement was seen in collaboration a few years after Katrina with the less harmful

Deepwater Horizon oil spill. But the public cannot evaluate the outcomes of the many simulations designed to train departments, agencies, and the private sector to deal with a cyber attack – whether the ability to collaborate in the face of a cyber emergency exhibits growing strengths or not.

The area of potential cyber war is characterized, as counterinsurgency is, by a lack of legal guidance. Neither international law nor domestic American law for cyber attacks and cyber warfare has been developed. As in the case of targeted killing, the characterization of an event as an act of war or as something else might trigger different legal rules. A series of creative attempts have been made to bring cyber attacks under the umbrella of existing international and domestic legal doctrines, but the effort has not been very satisfactory. Thus far, only by relying on analogy have answers been provided.

Domestically, the U.S. Congress has rejected every proposed law, however undemanding, that would clarify civil-military roles. Instead, Congress has left the allocation to executive action. Internationally, issues of verification have impeded any notion of regulation, although some rudimentary cooperation agreements provide a bare beginning. Chapters 12 and 13 examine current efforts, observing, however, that international regulation is not politically realistic so long as offensive capabilities continue to be considered nationally useful.

Conclusion

Clarity and effectiveness in civil-military relations are the sinew and connective tissue of security policy. The quality of that relationship seems to significantly affect both strategic assessments of action to be considered and policy execution. The three areas examined in this book – counterinsurgency, counterterrorism, and cyber attack – indicate that far more structure and consciousness is needed than the impromptu role allocation made in response to an immediate, current threat. Constant, open, deliberative discourse and civil-military planning are necessary to create new models of civil-military relations that meet emerging needs. And the new relationships will require legal underpinning that is more than a distortion of doctrine developed at other times to meet other needs.

While many scholars and diarists have examined how civil-military relations have worked in specific historic and current situations, more general theories have not yet examined the strains and shifts in situations that hover between war and peace. What is needed is greater clarity in role definition as novel security situations arise in such environments. But a more rational and sensible role definition in turn depends on careful discourse and planning among civilian and military leadership – as well as international collaboration – so that the response to new situations is not improvised. And the process must be made more transparent to the public to gain the necessary support for action or legislative change. Clarity in role definition also requires clarifying and articulating existing legal underpinnings and working toward developing a sound legal basis where it is absent, both domestically and internationally. Democracies live under the rule of law with the expectation that governmental relationships are subject to law. But where the law lacks relevance or clarity – where analogies can be stretched unpersuasively to cover novel situations – that expectation is thwarted.

2

Civil-Military Relations

From Theory to Policy

In gray area warfare, traditional models of civil-military relationships do not explain realities for the populations of the democratic
west or their host-nation allies; nor do they provide useful guidance
for policymakers. It is therefore unsurprising that the responses
to novel and rapidly changing forms of warfare are improvised
adjustments that often lead to uncomfortable civil-military relations. The classic Huntington model, rational and elegant in
form, posited essentially sequential operations: civilians control
the formulation of policy; thereafter, the military executes military operations based on that policy. Then, after fighting subsides,
civilian agencies assume responsibility for institutional rebuilding. Yet even after World War II, American and European allied
civilian governments proved unequal to the task of reconstructing European institutions; the bulk of institutional reconstruction
was performed by the military.[1] As one contemporaneous scholar
observed,

The real difficulty with military government operations ... was not so much
lack of civilian control, as it was inadequate presentation of the civilian
government viewpoint on the higher levels of the military hierarchy. There
were civilians (or civilians in uniform) located in G-5 [planning] staffs of
theater headquarters, the War Department Civil Affairs Division and elsewhere. But few of them had had major governmental experience ... Policy

[1] George C. S. Benson and Mark de Wolfe Howe, "Military Organizational
Relationships," in *American Experiences in Military Government in World War II*,
ed. Carl J. Friedrich (New York: Rinehart, 1948), 52–69.

directives, often inadequate, were sometimes contradictory; moreover, staff supervision was almost completely absent.[2]

Japan, which was different in tone, was under the firm hand of General Douglas MacArthur, the Supreme Commander for the Allied Powers in the Pacific.[3]

Samuel Huntington's classic civil-military relations model – that of civilian "objective control" over a professional military far removed from politics – was an aspiration and an inspiration. His model envisioned a professional officer corps removed from politics but ready to execute the articulated policy of civilian leadership: "The essence of objective civilian control is the recognition of autonomous military professionalism."[4] Military professionals, he argued, possess expert knowledge about the management of violence; when civilian leaders have decided on a course of action, they should rely on their military for operational and tactical decisions and action.

Even Huntington realized that his model was an ideal that could not be fully realized in the United States. The Constitution had bifurcated war powers between the president and Congress, thus providing an opportunity for political interference and maneuvering by the military that was not available in western parliamentary democracies, where objective control could be more fully realized.[5] The chief danger that Huntington chose to guard against was the politicization of the military in a democratic society.

The model was then, and is now, valued in its idealized form for transitional as well as established democracies. It was not a model suitable for analyzing autocracies where the military is certainly under civilian control but serving the ends of dictatorship. Nor did his model deal with a military engaged in lucrative business,

---

[2] Ibid., 53.
[3] Arthur D. Bouterse, Philip H. Taylor, and Arthur A. Maas, "American Military Government Experience in Japan," in *American Experiences in Military Government in World War II*, ed. Carl J. Friedrich (New York: Rinehart, 1948), 318–354.
[4] Samuel P. Huntington, *The Soldier and the State: The Theory and Politics of Civil-Military Relations* (Cambridge, MA: Harvard University Press, 1957), 83.
[5] Ibid.; 85 U.S. Constitution, Art. I(8) (congressional war powers), Art. II (presidential power), http://www.archives.gov/exhibits/charters/constitution.html (accessed September 8, 2014).

as in China or Egypt. It did not attempt to protect against military takeover or excess influence in governance of the kind witnessed in Pakistan, Egypt, and many sub-Saharan African countries.

Although the Huntington model has managed to survive many theoretical and factual questions for more than a half-century, it was challenged at the time by the sociologist Morris Janowitz, who argued that the military was not a breed apart, but rather a reflection of the larger society and how that society operated. Based on extensive questionnaires, autobiographies, and interviews, Janowitz concluded that insulation was impossible and unwise. He argued that many aspects of society, especially developments in organizational management, characterized military organizations as well as civilian corporate life, including the use of persuasion, team building, and the coordination of specialized functions. He stated: "A large segment of the military establishment resembles a civilian bureaucracy insofar as it deals with problems of research, development and logistics." Later, Janowitz observed: "In fact, the central concern of commanders is no longer the enforcement of rigid discipline, but rather the maintenance of high levels of initiative and morale." According to him, civilian-military connections – professional and political alike – could be harnessed for improved decision making.[6]

More recently, Peter Feaver, who has both theoretical knowledge and policy experience in civil-military relations, has suggested a more flexible but still fully rational model of the interaction between civilian and military institutions by positing the relationship as one of principal and agent, between civilian leadership and its military "armed servants."[7] Like Huntington, he holds civilian leadership responsible for policy formation and the military for policy execution. The key to Feaver's analysis of the civil-military "problematique" is the delegation of "the societal protection function to specialists and institutions responsible for violence." Civilians may monitor the military effectively and cooperatively or intrusively. The military may "work" (i.e., cooperate to execute policy) or

---

[6] Morris Janowitz, *The Professional Soldier: A Social and Political Portrait* (New York: The Free Press, 1971), 7–13.

[7] Peter D. Feaver, *Armed Servants: Agency, Oversight, and Civil-Military Relations* (Cambridge, MA: Harvard University Press, 2003).

"shirk," which in Feaver's parlance does not mean "goofing off," but rather exercising the flexibility to perform unenthusiastically, delaying compliance, or even evading civilian requirements.[8] As with Huntington, Feaver's model of civilian leadership is simplified to a unitary entity, not a bargaining process among civilian leaders. Also, as with Huntington, operations follow policy sequentially.[9]

These models have practical application: NATO enlargement policy has drawn on both the Huntington and Feaver models. But NATO has demanded something more: "democratic civilian control."[10] The insistence on an underlying democratic form of government makes it clear that professionalism and insulation of the military are not sufficient to qualify aspirants for admission into NATO. NATO enlargement policy also assumes governmental stability and strength. Democratic civilian control implies noninvolvement on the part of the military in domestic politics – consistent with Huntington's theory. Admission requirements also include democratic control of the size, structure, and budget of the military as well as control of foreign and security policy.[11] Although NATO does not explicitly require nations to mirror the United States or western Europe, such pressure is implicit. NATO, in formulating these requirements, is not only guarding against a lapse into autocracy, but is also concerned with the possibility of military aggressiveness to preserve a communist, autocratic past.[12] Even with these

---

[8] Political scientists' focus of agency differs from that of lawyers somewhat, in that the latter is concerned with legal responsibility of agents' actions, and the former is concerned with performance.

[9] Aaron Friedberg, *In the Shadow of the Garrison State: America's Anti-Statism and its Cold War Grand Strategy* (Princeton: Princeton University Press, 2000).

[10] North Atlantic Treaty Organization, *Study on NATO Enlargement*, September 2, 1995, ch. 5, http://www.nato.int/cps/en/natolive/official_texts_24733.htm (accessed October 7, 2014).

[11] Andrew Cottey, Tim Edmunds, and Anthony Forster, "Democratic Control of Armed Forces in Central and Eastern Europe: A Framework for Understanding Civil-Military Relations in Post-Communist Europe" (working paper, Economic and Social Research Council, 1999), ftp://budgie6.ethz.ch/dcaf/ssap/ev_civil-military_relations.pdf (accessed October 10, 2014).

[12] Mary Elise Sarotte, "A Broken Promise: What the West really told Moscow about NATO expansion," *Foreign Affairs*, September/October 2014, http://www.foreignaffairs.com/articles/141845/mary-elise-sarotte/a-broken-promise (accessed March 29, 2015).

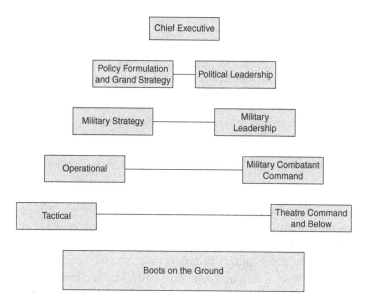

FIGURE 2.1. The Classical Model.

additional requirements, civil-military roles and the distribution of power can be visualized as a pyramid (Figure 2.1), in the manner of both Huntington and Feaver.

Within a decade after publication of Huntington's seminal book, *The Soldier and the State*, the Vietnam War exposed a far messier, more intertwined process of decision making. "Accidental" civil-military theorists emerged, making the complexity unmistakable. Robert Komer, a defense official, wrote a widely circulated 1972 report to the Defense Advanced Research Projects Agency, *Bureaucracy Does Its Thing: Institutional Constraints on U.S.-GVN Performance in Vietnam.*[13] Among his many insights in discussing the difficulties in changing strategy in the Vietnam War was an analysis of bureaucratic resistance to change among civilians and military at both national and theatre levels.

[13] Robert Komer, *Bureaucracy Does Its Thing: Institutional Constraints on U.S.-GVN Performance in Vietnam* (Santa Monica: RAND, 1972), http://www.rand.org/content/dam/rand/pubs/reports/2005/R967.pdf

Komer argued:

One form of institutional constraint typical of organizational behavior – bureaucratic inertia – is strongly evident here. A hallmark of bureaucracy is reluctance to change accepted ways of doing things. Bureaucrats prefer to deal with the familiar. It is more comfortable and convenient to continue following tested routines ... So whether private or public, civilian or military, organizations typically like to keep operating the way they are operating, and to shift only slowly in response to changing situations. And the more hierarchical and disciplined they are – and military organizations are almost archetypes – the greater the built-in institutional obstacles to change.[14]

Although bureaucratic behavior had been discussed theoretically before, Komer applied such thinking specifically to civil-military relations in the conduct of the Vietnam War with a degree of detail that made its applicability undeniable. Moreover, he underscored the complexity of civil-military relations by emphasizing the importance of host nation civilians and especially, the legitimacy and effectiveness of the host nation government, together with the role of the nation's military in executing policy.[15] Komer also understood how important a role both domestic and international politics played in decision making.[16]

In 1971, Graham Allison, then a young scholar, wrote about governmental processes in relation to the Cuban Missile Crisis. He offered insights relevant to, though not specifically addressing, civil-military complexities by developing three models of government decision making. His "Model II" paralleled Komer's insights:

[G]overnments perceive problems through organizational sensors. Governments define alternatives and estimate consequences as their component organizations process information; governments act as these organizations enact routines. Government behavior can therefore be understood ... less as deliberate choices and more as outputs of large organizations functioning according to standard patterns of behavior.[17]

Although the insights of such accidental civil-military theorists were not directed at the Huntington-Janowitz debate, they represent

---

[14] Ibid., 65.
[15] Ibid., 128.
[16] Ibid., 128.
[17] Graham T. Allison, *Essence of Decision: Explaining the Cuban Missile Crisis* (Boston: Little, Brown and Company, 1971), 67.

an implicit rejection of Huntington's elegant rational model.[18] That model simplifies civil-military relations into a dyad. In recognizing patterns of organizational behavior and the many actors involved in decision making, the accidental civil-military theorists implicitly make the case for extended dialogue and discussion between civil and military leadership in the process of both planning and execution of foreign and security policy. Otherwise, the complexity they have exposed is likely to defeat sound policy.

The need for interchange between civilian and military was discussed by the scholar Claude E. Welch, Jr., when, in a series of comparative case studies published in 1976, he argued that "civilian control ... is more a set of relationships than an individual event.... Civilian control is a matter of degree. All armed forces participate in politics in various fashions.... Any military has an impact on [a nation's] political system."[19] The very issue of whether a proposed operation is feasible – a strategic assessment – has always involved a technical, professional judgment, whether solicited or not. Unfortunate consequences have followed when broad military advice is not sought or ignored.[20]

Likewise, as Eliot Cohen has explained more recently, civilian leadership must attend to the political consequences of major military moves.[21] The idea of sequencing the roles of civilian leadership and military execution simply does not work.

Policy and military decision making are necessarily intertwined, as analysts and those who have been in positions of civilian or military leadership have come to recognize (see Figure 2.2).[22]

---

[18] There were other more explicit contemporaneous critics writing in the civil-military tradition who argued that military professionalism in Latin America increased the risk of military takeover. See Alfred Stepan, *Rethinking Military Politics: Brazil and the Southern Cone* (Princeton: Princeton University Press, 1988).

[19] Claude E. Welch, Jr., *Civilian Control of the Military: Theory and Cases from Developing Countries* (Albany: State University of New York Press, 1976), 1–2.

[20] See Risa Brooks, *Shaping Strategy: The Civil-Military Politics of Strategic Assessment* (Princeton: Princeton University Press, 2008).

[21] Eliot Cohen, "The Unequal Dialogue: Theory and Reality of Civil Military Relations and the Use of Force," in *Soldiers and Civilians: The Military Gap and American National Security*, ed. Peter Feaver and Richard Kohn (Cambridge, MA: MIT Press, 2001), 436.

[22] See Richard K. Betts, *American Force: Dangers, Delusions, and Dilemmas in National Security* (New York: Columbia University Press, 2012); Robert S. McNamara, *In Retrospect: The Tragedy and Lessons of Vietnam* (New York: Vintage Books, 1996);

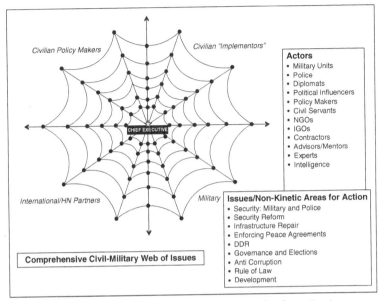

Civilian Policy Makers

Civilian "Implementors"

CHIEF EXECUTIVE

Actors
• Military Units
• Police
• Diplomats
• Political Influencers
• Policy Makers
• Civil Servants
• NGOs
• IGOs
• Contractors
• Advisors/Mentors
• Experts
• Intelligence

International/HN Partners

Military

Issues/Non-Kinetic Areas for Action
• Security: Military and Police
• Security Reform
• Infrastructure Repair
• Enforcing Peace Agreements
• DDR
• Governance and Elections
• Anti Corruption
• Rule of Law
• Development

Comprehensive Civil-Military Web of Issues

FIGURE 2.2. More Complex Reality. (My thanks to Jamie deCoster for this depiction of complexity.)

The national security policy responsibilities of senior civilian leaders do not stop with a decision to intervene in a conflict, or to withdraw once entered. Especially in this era of irregular warfare, civilian leaders still need to monitor and gauge the political and foreign policy impacts of strategic and even tactical measures in an ongoing confrontation. As Cohen points out:

If the normal theory of civil-military relations is suspect, what have been the successful practices of the past? To begin with, effective war statesmen have acted well beyond the minimal roles assigned to them by the normal theory of civil-military relations, viz. the setting of purpose, the approval of action, and the termination of conflict. Success in the waging of war seems to have been accompanied by a great deal of crossing of the civil-military gap by politicians probing, testing, haranguing, and manipulating their military subordinates about technical matters as well as strategic ones.[23]

and Gordon Goldstein, *Lessons in Disaster: McGeorge Bundy and the Path to War in Vietnam* (New York: Times Books, 2008).

[23] Cohen, "The Unequal Dialogue," 439.

Further along in the same article, after reviewing historic moments of civilian leadership – including the actions of Lincoln, Clemenceau, and Churchill – Cohen states:

When it comes to the use of force, however, the heart of sound civil-military relations remains now, as in the past, an unequal dialogue. The imperatives of politics and of military professionalism invariably, and appropriately, tug in opposite directions; inevitably too, professional judgments require scrutiny rather than unthinking acceptance.[24]

Conversely, the military, particularly in the gray areas, necessarily assumes some political, diplomatic, or other classically civilian functions that seem alien to their training and disposition. In fact, there has been an increasing awareness that military leaders are in fact exercising a diplomatic policy role, particularly in the Regional Command structure that was set up following the Goldwater-Nichols legislation of the 1980s.[25] As Dana Priest observed: "Long before September 11, the U.S. government had grown increasingly dependent on its military to carry out its foreign affairs. The shift was incremental, little noticed ... The military simply filled a vacuum left by an indecisive White House, and atrophied State Department, and a distracted Congress."[26] Subsequent developments have clarified the need for both civilian and military leaders to recognize their intertwined roles, even though ultimate civilian control is maintained, and to engage in a dialogue that produces sound policy.

The volume of essays *"American Civil-Military Relations*, edited by Suzanne C. Nielson and Don M. Snider of the U.S. Military Academy (West Point) in 2009, probes deeply both the enduring nature of Huntington's legacy and the value of his critics in light of subsequent events. In one of the book's most insightful articles, Richard K. Betts states:

One could make the case that for ideal integration of objectives, strategy and operations, civilians and military should be equally conversant in each others' [sic] terms of reference and should participate equally at all stages.

---

[24] Ibid., 457.

[25] Goldwater-Nichols Department of Defense Reorganization Act of 1986, 10 U.S. Code 111, 1985, http://www.govtrack.us/congress/bills/99/hr3622 (accessed December 12, 2014).

[26] Dana Priest, *The Mission: Waging War and Keeping Peace with America's Military* (New York: W. W. Norton, 2004), 14.

In the end, however, few would deny that there is some level of high politics at which soldiers should be silent, and some level of tactical specificity or micromanagement where civilians should keep their hands off.[27]

Thus, even though the ideal of military policy detachment and subservience has proven to be unworkable, scholars need to explore and help develop useful and usable new patterns. U.S. and NATO leadership have yet to respond effectively to the complexity of continuing irregular warfare, either with newly developed theoretical structures or adequate policies for enduring civil-military relations. Current responses to insurgencies and terrorism, such as counterinsurgency and targeted killing, and to cyber attacks require more line-crossing among civil and military relations than classic theory permits. These adjustments are necessary, given the nature of the hybrid problems that have arisen. But hasty adjustments that are neither fully debated nor given adequate legal underpinning will not lead to optimum performance by either the military or the needed civilians.

---

[27] Richard K. Betts, "Are Civil-Military Relations Still a Problem?," in *American Civil-Military Relations: The Soldier and the State in a New Era*, ed. Suzanne C. Nielsen and Don M. Snider (Baltimore: The John Hopkins University Press, 2009), 36.

3

The Counterinsurgency Dilemma

What passing-bells for these who die as cattle?
Only the monstrous anger of the guns.
Only the stuttering rifles' rapid rattle
Can patter out their hasty orisons.

Wilfred Owen, "Anthem for Doomed Youth"

The widespread terrorist attacks in the early part of the twenty-first century and the evolving responses to those attacks changed not only the security environment but also the relationship between civilian and military responses to terrorism. Approaches dubbed "counterinsurgency" and "counterterrorism" have been dominant at different times since September 11, 2001.[1] Both approaches have blurred the lines between tasks that have traditionally been military and those that have been civilian. And in both counterinsurgency and counterterrorism, the division of responsibility between civilians and military lacks a clear legal basis, although the role issues and legal problems differ. The absence of firm legal underpinnings impedes the civilian-military cooperation necessary for mission success. Legal clarity is no panacea for lack of policy clarity, but it might improve some problems of role definition and confusion.

Twenty-first-century counterinsurgency represents a radical adaptation of recent U.S. war-fighting strategy and tactics, as well as a revival of an approach that had been developed in the past but abandoned. It upended traditional notions of civilian control

---

[1] For the readers' clarity, I do not use the abbreviations COIN for counterinsurgency or CT for counterterrorism.

and civil-military relations. As a strategy, it is not new. It was and remains a radical departure not only from General Westmoreland's use of massive force in Vietnam but also from the Powell-Weinberger doctrine of overwhelming force of the 1980s and 1990s. Because of the need for a militarily weaker enemy to rely on the population, counterinsurgency doctrine focused on winning over that population, rather than on actions only aimed at destroying the enemy. This approach fired the U.S. imagination after the publication of the *U.S. Army/Marine Corps Counterinsurgency Field Manual (FM 3–24)* in 2005.[2] But it promised more than it could deliver. Many of the difficulties that counterinsurgency had encountered in the past were neither confronted nor addressed. Unsurprisingly, its brand of counterinsurgency has proven very difficult to implement.

Never an exclusively American phenomenon, counterinsurgency strategy has a rich history. It had been advocated, applied, and described even before the days of the post–World War II Malayan Emergency and the French war against Algerian independence.[3] The British had employed a counterinsurgency strategy starting in the mid-nineteenth century in Waziristan, the "land of Bin Laden."[4] In 1961, David Galula, a Tunisian-born French military officer and

[2] *The U.S. Army/Marine Corps Counterinsurgency Field Manual* (Chicago: University of Chicago Press, 2007), 3–24. According to Stephen Biddle, the field manual was downloaded from the internet more than 2 million times by 2008. Amazon sales figures show that more than 500,000 copies have been sold. "The New Army/Marine Corps Counterinsurgency Field Manual as Political Science and Political Praxis," *Perspectives on Politics* 6 (June 2008): 347–360.

[3] For an analysis of earlier counterinsurgency campaigns including Malaya, Cambodia, and Algeria, see David Galula, *Counterinsurgency Warfare: Theory and Practice* (New York: Frederick A. Praeger, Inc., 1964); Andrew M. Roe, *Waging War in Waziristan: The British Struggle in the Land of Bin Laden, 1849–1947* (Lawrence: University Press of Kansas, 2010), 60–122; John A. Nagl, *Learning to Eat Soup with a Knife: Counterinsurgency Lessons from Malaya and Vietnam* (Chicago: University of Chicago Press, 2002); Frank Kitson, *Low Intensity Operations: Subversion, Insurgency and Peacekeeping* (Harrisburg: Stackpole Books, 1971); Roger Trinquier, *Modern Warfare: A French View of Counterinsurgency* (New York: Praeger, 1964); Robert M. Cassidy, "Back to the Street without Joy: Counterinsurgency Lessons from Vietnam and Other Small Wars," *Parameters* 34, no. 2, (July 2004): 73–83; and Alistair Horne, *A Savage War of Peace: Algeria 1954–1962* (New York: NYRB Classics, 2006).

[4] Roe, *Waging War in Waziristan*. For a fuller historic view, see Peter Hopkirk, *The Great Game: The Struggle for Empire in Central Asia* (New York: Kodasha International, 1990).

scholar, explored the characteristics of several insurgencies, including Vietnam, and provided detailed advice for waging a counterinsurgency campaign.[5] But although counterinsurgency was advocated during the Vietnam War by both the U.S. Marines and civilians and called "the other war" by President Lyndon Johnson- it was treated as secondary to General Westmoreland's war of attrition, so-called "search and destroy."[6] Despite every effort to keep a counterinsurgency strategy going in parallel with the war of attrition, the former did not flourish as a full alternative until it was too late to matter. "Pacification," as counterinsurgency was called then, only gained a strategic foothold as the war was winding down, when General Creighton Abrams replaced General Westmoreland as Commander of the Military Assistance Command Vietnam (MACV).[7] In *Bureaucracy Does Its Thing*, Robert Komer denied that there was an actual policy confrontation between counterinsurgency and traditional war-fighting approaches, but he observed that "almost every element which might logically be regarded as part of a counterinsurgency-oriented strategy was called for repeatedly and tried (often several times) on at least a small scale. Compared to the conventional U.S./GVN [government of South Vietnam] military effort, however, [those efforts] were always 'small potatoes.'"[8]

Nevertheless, despite its frustrating history of implementation during the Vietnam War, counterinsurgency strategy seemed suited to address the conflicts of the early twenty-first-century that have been increasingly fought against and among nonstate actors – a phenomenon described by Rupert Smith as "war amongst the people."[9]

---

[5] Galula, *Counterinsurgency Warfare*, 3–16.
[6] Robert Komer, *Bureaucracy Does Its Thing: Institutional Constraints on U.S.- GVN Performance in Vietnam*, RAND Institute, http://www.rand.org/pubs/ reports/R967.html (accessed October 8, 2014), 92.
[7] James McAllister, "Who Lost Vietnam?: Soldiers, Civilians, and U.S. Military Strategy," *International Security* 35, no. 3 (2010): 95–123.
[8] Komer, *Bureaucracy Does Its Thing*, 128, 129.
[9] In his book *The Utility of Force*, Rupert Smith distinguishes the "old paradigm" of sequential "industrial war" – or "peace-crisis-war-resolution, which will result in peace again" and where military action is the deciding factor – from today's "continuous crisscrossing between confrontation and conflict," which involves "war amongst the people." This new paradigm is characterized by increased kinetic

The appropriate means for such wars, Thomas X. Hammes argued, involve "fourth-generation" warfare that "uses all available networks – political, economic, social, and military – to convince the enemy's political decision makers that their strategic goals are either unachievable or too costly for the perceived benefit."[10]

Sarah Sewall, in her introduction to the *U.S. Army/Marine Corps Counterinsurgency Field Manual*, also noted how radically counterinsurgency differs from the more traditional approach to war fighting: the focus is not enemy-centric; rather, the civilian *is* the mission. "The civilian population is the center of gravity – the deciding factor in the struggle. Therefore, civilians must be separated from insurgents to insulate them from insurgent pressures and to deny the insurgent 'fish' the cover of the civilian 'sea.'"[11]

Counterinsurgency adds tasks that used to be essentially civilian in nature in an environment where civilians, for the most part, could not function. Komer again describes the "unifying thread" among counterinsurgency advocates in Vietnam:

First was their emphasis on the primacy of political over military aims in the Vietnam conflict. They saw the greatest need as being to protect and win over the population on which the insurgency fed, rather than to destroy the organized insurgency forces. This view often took the form of stressing the need to build a viable and responsive local government. It also underlay the stress on winning the hearts and minds by providing a more attractive alternative to Viet Cong rule. Land reform, rural aid programs, anticorruption measures, administrative decentralization and representative government were seen as tools to this end.[12]

action within communities, a change in the ends and strategies of fighting, new uses for old weapons, the intractability of conflicts, and the increasing role of nonstate actors. Of the new paradigm, Smith writes: "Rather than war and peace, there is no predefined sequence, nor is peace necessarily either the starting or the end point: conflicts are resolved, but not necessarily confrontations." Rupert Smith, *The Utility of Force* (New York: Vintage, 2007), 18–19.

[10] Thomas X. Hammes, *The Sling and the Stone: On War in the 21st Century* (St. Paul: Zenith Press, 2006), 2.

[11] Sarah Sewall, Introduction to *U.S. Army/Marine Corps Counterinsurgency Field Manual* (Chicago: University of Chicago Press, 2007), xxv.

[12] Komer, *Bureaucracy Does Its Thing*, 128. See also David Kilcullen, *Counterinsurgency* (Oxford: Oxford University Press, 2010), 2. According to Kilcullen, the "art" of counterinsurgency "is to develop specific measures, tailored to the environment, to suppress a particular insurgency and strengthen the resilience of a particular threatened society and government."

Conventional state-on-state conflicts fought by armies were replaced by asymmetric warfare fought by irregular forces and civilians. Counterinsurgency was developed as a strategy to defeat such warfare. It was not possible to fight Sunni ex-military and irregulars with traditional strategies in Anbar Province in Iraq, so another strategic option, such as counterinsurgency, was needed.[13] But that does not imply that counterinsurgency uses manpower more economically – that is, less "blood" for perhaps more "treasure." Instead, it is quite the opposite. Counterinsurgency actually increases the hazards of ground warfare for soldiers. Furthermore, by incorporating reconstruction into the war-fighting strategy, counterinsurgency necessarily adds to the number of "boots on the ground" that are needed. It is a long-range strategy – not one that implies an early exit. But although the adoption of counterinsurgency caused a dramatic turnaround in Iraq after 2007,[14] it failed to address the longer-range political and social problems that resurfaced in violent civil conflict. Its application in Vietnam, as in Iraq and Afghanistan, focused more on village-level tactical efforts than on overarching issues of government legitimacy and effectiveness. While counterinsurgency alone cannot be held responsible for the subsequent events in Iraq, these events raise questions about civil-military relations at all levels within such a context, and the effectiveness of implementing counterinsurgency in such a highly fraught political climate as Iraq turned out to be.

In theory, counterinsurgency is as applicable to today's conflicts as it was to Vietnam. Any military intervention to prevent the spread of terrorism or insurgencies is unlikely to succeed if not supported by the people. And one key to lack of support is the conviction that the host government fails to serve its people. The array of issues that might require intervention into the political and civic arenas is broad. But it takes a long time for interveners to understand the

---

[13] Richard H. Shultz, Jr., *The Marines Take Anbar: The Four-Year Fight Against Al Qaeda* (Annapolis: Naval Institute Press, 2013).

[14] Dave Dilegge, "The Four Phases of the U.S. Counterinsurgency Effort in Iraq," *Small Wars Journal* (blog), March 18, 2007, http://smallwarsjournal.com/blog/the-four-phases-of-the-us-counterinsurgency-effort-in-iraq (accessed October 9, 2014). See also Shultz, Jr., *The Marines Take Anbar: The Four Year Fight Against Al Qaeda, 2013*.

issues and to find effective responses. The depth of understanding of the local political and social structure; the political will to take on their structural problems; the time and cost of commitment, and domestic trade-offs that a counterinsurgency strategy requires makes it questionable whether the doctrine will be put into practice effectively in the near future. Yet some version may be necessary to counter ongoing irregular wars. Unfortunately, somehow over time, the pitfalls are forgotten. The same goals are attempted and the same mistakes are often repeated. Perhaps had counterinsurgency strategy been fully implemented in Vietnam, some of the obstacles and requirements for success would have been more apparent now.[15]

---

[15] Komer, *Bureaucracy Does Its Thing*, xii.

4

Civil-Military Implications

The Demands of a Counterinsurgency Strategy

Stringent conditions must be fulfilled in order for the counterinsurgency approach to achieve a modicum of success. These conditions, without adequate domestic legal direction, put immense pressure on civil-military relations at all levels. These conditions include: (1) a host government in which most of the population can have, or build trust; (2) the ability to handle at least some simultaneity of kinetic action and peacebuilding/nation building without degrading either task; (3) a high degree of functionality (in terms of both resources and human capacity) in the intervener's civilian institutions; (4) the ability of civilians and military to collaborate effectively, requiring a more evolved model of civil-military relations; (5) interveners' political and military willingness to accept high danger for both military and civilian officials; and (6) persistence over a long period of time.[1]

A Host Government That Can Begin to Build Trust

Counterinsurgency requires a credible and visible alternative to an insurgency: "[T]he real battle is for civilian support for, or acquiescence to, counterinsurgents and local authorities."[2] This support or acquiescence only comes, however, if the counterinsurgents and

---

[1] I am grateful to Sarah Sewall for these conditions, many of which were developed in my classes in which she was a guest lecturer.
[2] Sarah Sewall, introduction to *U.S. Army/Marine Corps Counterinsurgency Field Manual* (Chicago: University of Chicago Press, 2007), xxv.

local authorities can show capability and willingness to provide for the population's basic needs, to assure the population's reasonable security, and to help in the longer-term effort to provide justice and stability. These are not easy requirements even in a more traditional post-conflict environment, but they are far more demanding in the gray area between war and peace. The first assumption is that there is even a government with which to work. If the interveners have toppled an existing government, or find a collapsed government or only local powers of varying strengths, the task is questionable from the beginning. Depth of knowledge about the local culture and local needs is required before the interveners can help the population create a government on which it can rely. Too often over the past few decades, western countries, and especially the United States, have attempted to create a "mirror image" of their ideal model of a western democracy quickly, down to the last detail of a new constitution and elections. But the formalities were accomplished without regard for the nature of the government installed or in power, as well as the lack of support within the population. This was partly the case in Vietnam.[3] Unfortunately, neither Iraq nor Afghanistan reflected a lesson learned.[4]

It has become increasingly evident that it is impossible to gain the trust of the population when the host government and local authorities are infested with corruption, are unrepresentative, or lack the competence or will to pursue population-centric goals. This is a problem both military and civilian interveners face. In 2009, International Security Assistance Force (ISAF) Commander General Stanley McChrystal issued counterinsurgency guidance to ISAF troops in Afghanistan that included these words: "Confront corrupt officials. Protecting the people requires protection from physical harm, corruption, and abuse of power. With your Afghan counterparts work to change corrupt behavior that adversely affects the people and the mission. If the behavior does not change, demand the Afghan higher

---

[3] Robert Komer, *Bureaucracy Does Its Thing: Institutional Constraints on U.S.-GVN Performance in Vietnam*, RAND Institute, http://www.rand.org/pubs/reports/R967.html (accessed October 8, 2014), x.

[4] See James H. Lebovic, *The Limits of U.S. Military Capability: Lessons from Vietnam and Iraq* (Baltimore: Johns Hopkins University Press, 2010).

leadership take appropriate action."[5] By then, however, "the Afghan higher leadership" was so entrenched in what Sarah Chayes describes as "a structured, mafia-esque system in which money flows upward via purchase of office, kickbacks, or 'sweets' [petty bribes], in return for permission to extract resources ... and protection in case of legal or international scrutiny" that it would have taken a significant shift in focus and priorities at every level to implement McChrystal's guidance. In the end, neither alliance civilian leadership nor ISAF could muster the political will required to enforce this imperative. The guidance was not implemented.[6]

As the UN reported in February 2013, the cost of corruption in Afghanistan rose to an estimated $3.9 billion in 2012, with 50 percent of the population forced to pay at least one bribe to a public official.[7] Media-reported 2013 figures may well have been underestimated. The United States and the international aid community continued to back this "government by crime syndicate" seemingly unaware of the driving role corruption played in fueling the insurgency. Standard operating procedures, particularly among civilian agencies that should have taken the lead, made it difficult to envision a different approach. Civilian policy makers responsible for

[5] International Security Assistance Force, *ISAF Commander's Counterinsurgency Guidance*, August 2009, http://www.nato.int/isaf/docu/official_texts/counterinsurgency_guidance.pdf (accessed October 9, 2014). It is notable that the *Counterinsurgency Field Manual* does not deal with the broad problem of corruption.

[6] Working Group on Corruption and Security, *Corruption: The Unrecognized Threat to National Security*, Carnegie Endowment for International Peace, June 2014, http://carnegieendowment.org/files/corruption_and_security.pdf (accessed October 17, 2014); Sarah Chayes, "Government by Crime Syndicate," *Los Angeles Times*, September 25, 2011, http://articles.latimes.com/2011/sep/25/opinion/la-oe-chayes-corruption-20110925 (accessed October 10, 2014); Sarah Chayes, *Thieves of State: Why Corruption Threatens Global Security* (New York: W. W. Norton, 2015), ch. 3–5.

[7] "UN: Cost of Afghan Corruption Rose Sharply Last Year to 3.9 Billion USD, with Half the Population Paying a Bribe," *RAWA News*, February 7, 2013, http://www.rawa.org/temp/runews/2013/02/07/un-cost-of-afghan-corruption-rose-sharply-last-year-to-3-9-billion-usd-with-half-the-population-paying-a-bribe.html#ixzz2KM47gf5Z (accessed October 3, 2014). See also Matthew Rosenberg, "With Bags of Cash, C.I.A. Seeks Influence in Afghanistan," *The New York Times*, April 28, 2013, http://www.nytimes.com/2013/04/29/world/asia/cia-delivers-cash-to-afghan-leaders-office.html (accessed October 3, 2014).

developing legal institutions – known by the shorthand, "rule of law" – in Afghanistan did not take sufficient measures to curb the corrupt government that was increasingly distrusted by the people, even as they made some local efforts to create legal institutions.[8] Worse, the actions that spoke the loudest were the regular payments by the CIA to President Karzai, his half-brother Ahmed Wali, and other corrupt government officials for their assistance, which undercut any expressed concerns about government corruption.[9] U.S. leadership, in Afghanistan as elsewhere, has been reluctant to focus and use its leverage, stating its respect for sovereignty and fearing that it would appear colonialist in its interventions. There may be some wisdom in the words of Lakhdar Brahimi that the "UN is not always equipped to provide relevant advice on how reforms should be carried out" and urging that UN missions "should adhere to the idea of a light footprint.".[10] But when the United States, with its large "footprint" in both military forces and economic projects, has failed to help curb a host government's deeply corrupt behavior that harms its people, the message was that America condoned that behavior.[11] This was certainly the impression given when the prosecution of Mohammed Zia Salehi, alleged, with others, to have absconded with funds from the Kabul bank in Afghanistan, was terminated.[12] Understanding just how and when an intervener can best exercise leverage would have required a deeper civil-military

[8] Carol Wang, "Rule of Law in Afghanistan: Enabling a Constitutional Framework for Local Accountability," *Harvard International Law Journal* 55 no. 1 (Winter 2014): 211–249,http://www.harvardilj.org/wp-content/uploads/2014/03/HILJ_55-1_Wang .pdf (accessed April 17, 2015).

[9] Dexter Filkins and Mark Mazzetti, "Karzai Aide in Corruption Inquiry Is Tied to C.I.A.," *The New York Times*, August 25, 2013, http://www.nytimes .com/2010/08/26/world/asia/26kabul.html?pagewanted=all (accessed October 6, 2014).

[10] Lakhdar Brahimi, "State Building in Crisis and Post-Conflict Countries" (speech, 7th Global Forum on Reinventing Government, Vienna, Austria, 2007), http:// unpan1.un.org/intradoc/groups/public/documents/un/unpan026305.pdf (accessed October 22, 2014).

[11] Chayes, *"Thieves of States: Why Corruption Threatens Global Security,"* 135–140.

[12] Ibid, 140–144, 154–155. Sarah Chayes, "The Afghan Bag Man: The Foiled Arrest That Explains American Failure in Afghanistan" *Foreign Policy*, May 4, 2013, http://www.foreignpolicy.com/articles/2013/05/03/the_afghan_bag_man (accessed November 24, 2014).

dialogue at several levels of the decision-making process than the one that actually took place.

In Iraq, both international civil and military leaders failed to recognize the importance of institutionalizing a role for the Sunnis in the Nouri al-Maliki government. Beginning in 2003, shortly after the fall of Saddam Hussein's Ba'athist regime, the U.S. policy of de-Ba'athification sought to purge politicians and civil service members belonging to the Ba'ath party – a party strongly linked to Sunni Saddam Hussein's repression of the Shia majority.[13] That policy was made by U.S. defense department civilians who did not understand the implications of this process for future sectarian relations.[14] While Nouri al-Maliki, a Shia Muslim, may have appeared to be a reasonable choice for prime minister in 2006, his leadership, coupled with the lingering resentment of de-Ba'athification, served to heighten tensions between the Shia majority and the Sunni minority in Iraq.[15] Many unsolved problems were masked by the seeming success of General Petraeus' counterinsurgency strategy. Ethnic separation had reduced violence, but its causes were not fully addressed.[16] The leadership of the Sunni Awakening Councils, although nurtured and supported by the United States, had already been turning against jihadists.[17] It is ironic that Anbar province, once a poster child for counterinsurgency, had so deteriorated that it was the first area to succumb to ISIS in 2014. As Iraqi Sunnis increasingly experienced

---

[13] Miranda Sissons and Abdulrazzaq al-Saiedi, *A Bitter Legacy: Lessons of De-Baathification in Iraq*, International Center for Transitional Justice, May 2013, http://ictj.org/publication/bitter-legacy-lessons-de-baathification-iraq (accessed October 10, 2014).

[14] Thomas E. Ricks, *FIASCO: The American Military Adventure in Iraq* (New York: The Penguin Press, 2006), 158–165.

[15] Emma Sky, *The Unraveling: High Hopes and Missed Opportunities in Iraq* (New York: Public Affairs, 2015), chapters 18, 19; Stephen Wicken, *Iraq's Sunnis in Crisis*, Institute for the Study of War, May 2013, http://www.understandingwar.org/report/iraqs-sunnis-crisis (accessed October 11, 2014).

[16] See Nils B. Weidmann and Idean Salehyan, "Violence and Ethnic Segregation," *International Studies Quarterly* 75 (2013): 62.

[17] Gian Gentile, *Wrong Turn: America's Deadly Embrace of Counterinsurgency* (New York: The New Press, 2013); Emma Sky, *Iraq in Hindsight: Views on the US Withdrawal*, Center for New American Security, December 2012, http://www.cnas.org/files/documents/publications/CNAS_IraqInHindsight_Sky_o.pdf (accessed April 14, 2015), Sky, *The Unraveling*, chapter 10.

the repression of their interests by the central government, they had little incentive to support it – and every incentive to support those who fight against it. Before the United States left Iraq in 2011, and long before the deep ISIS incursions into Sunni territory, the United States should have realized that al-Maliki's sectarian exclusions would lead to problems. Moreover, corruption was also a problem in Iraq early on, with the son of al-Maliki taking cuts from reconstruction contracts.[18] And after the ISIS onslaught in 2014, the new prime minister, Haider al-Abadi, found the army riddled with corruption, including 50,000 "ghost soldiers" – soldiers who did not exist but were listed on the payroll.[19]

It takes depth of understanding and clarity of purpose for the interveners to learn how much and what kind of leverage will be effective to help foster a government that can build trust and attain legitimacy in the eyes of its people. There is a delicate balance between helping the population achieve a trustworthy and legitimate government and heavy-handed approaches that will be resented by the host country's population. Yet without exercising sufficient leverage to ensure a modicum of fairness in a host-country government's treatment of its people, it may be impossible for it to gain their trust – a hard-and-fast requirement of counterinsurgency theory.

Indeed, the support of counterinsurgents often reduces host nation officials' sense of accountability to their own population – they know that because of unrelated security imperatives, the interveners are likely to support them no matter how they behave toward their people. And because the population understands this relationship and sees the interveners as crucial to the government's survival, it will hold the interveners responsible for the government's misconduct.

There is no formula for how to deal with a host government during an intervention, but every effort must be made to develop

[18] Dexter Filkins, "What We Left Behind," *The New Yorker*, April 2014, http://www.newyorker.com/magazine/2014/04/28/what-we-left-behind (accessed April 18, 2015).

[19] Loveday Morris, "Investigation Finds 50,000 'Ghost' Soldiers in Iraqi Army, Prime Minister Says," *The Washington Post*, November 30, 2014, http://www.washingtonpost.com/world/middle_east/investigation-finds-50000-ghost-soldiers-in-iraqi-army-prime-minister-says/2014/11/30/d8864d6c-78ab-11e4-9721-80b3d95a28a9_story.html (accessed December 25, 2014).

consensus between the interveners and the population. And that takes clarity of policy and responsibility. In 1972, Robert Komer wrote: "Who was responsible for conflict management of the Vietnam war? The bureaucratic fact is that below Presidential level everybody and nobody was coping with it in the round."[20] Recall that General Westmoreland had argued that to make counterinsurgency work, the Vietnamese government had to take major responsibility. But in that case, just as in Afghanistan and Iraq, the United States was unprepared to exercise the leverage it had over the government to change its practices to better serve the people. Nor was the United States prepared to admit that without a government on whom the people could rely, counterinsurgency would fail.[21]

The Ability to Handle at Least Some Simultaneity of Kinetic Action and Peacebuilding/Nation Building without Degrading Either

Simultaneity of reconstruction and kinetic action is not necessarily ubiquitous in recent counterinsurgencies, but in both Iraq and Afghanistan, there have been geographic areas and times where "fighting" and "building" have indeed been going on side by side.[22] Counterinsurgency doctrine contemplates simultaneity without addressing the inherent pitfalls, nor does it address the fact that a simultaneous counterterrorism campaign, as was the case in Afghanistan, further raised the bar for success. Counterterrorism, involving overt and covert military action, as discussed in Chapter 6,

---

[20] Komer, *Bureaucracy Does Its Thing*, 73. See also Dale Andrade and Lt. Col. James H. Milbanks, "CORDS/PHOENIX: Counterinsurgency; Lessons from Vietnam for the Future," *Military Review* (March–April 2006): 9-23.

[21] Stephen Biddle makes the same observation commenting on American reluctance to engage in "coercive bargaining," in: "Review Symposium: The New US Army/ Marine Corps Counterinsurgency Field Manual as Political Science and Political Praxis," *Perspectives on Politics* 6, no. 2 (June 2008): 347–360: 348.

[22] Sarah Chayes argues: "In both Afghanistan and Iraq there was a long period of NON-simultaneity. The AQ mop-up operations were marginal geographically, and the real problem was the refusal of the U.S. to allow nation building simultaneously with that CT [counterterrorism] effort. If the government is contested enough to provoke an insurgency, it will require rebuilding, while fighting is going on. My problem is we never really gave the state-building agenda the focus it needed." Sarah Chayes, in discussion with the author, October 2013.

implies an increase in civilian casualties, the destruction of property, cultural violations, and the undermining of counterinsurgency's focus on civilian needs.[23] The adverse impact on the population and dealing with wide resentment make it difficult to win "hearts and minds."

In Afghanistan, much of the resentment built up over time as counterterrorism operations continued without the benefits the population expected from the intervention. The resentment came to be focused on the military interveners, who seemed to be killing innocent civilians in the service of a government whose actions were also seen to harm civilians. While popular dissatisfaction, complaints, and growing resentment should be an urgent subject of military and diplomatic consideration, that discussion seems to occur on an ad hoc basis, where personalities, not systems, encourage frank dialogue.[24]

Counterinsurgency's emphasis on building trust and stability means an emphasis on reconstruction – traditionally considered a civilian task. But the "to-do" list for a war-torn country's reconstruction is daunting. It has included institution-building as well as physical restoration, and it quickly shades into "nation-building." This list of reconstruction tasks could be envisioned as a knotted net. For example, security sector reform (SSR) and disarmament, demobilization, and reintegration (DDR) should not be separable from other peacebuilding and nation-building tasks, and they are certainly not separate from the legitimacy of the central government. The efforts to reintegrate ex-militias and soldiers require educational opportunities, job creation, and the rule of law to support them.[25] But the work itself will fail if it is not responsive to local needs and priorities, but done piecemeal in response to

---

[23] Antonia Chayes, "Chapter VII ½: Is Jus Post Bellum Possible?," *European Journal of International Law* 24, no. 1 (2013): 291–305.

[24] Senior U.S. military commander, in confidential discussion with the author, June 25, 2011.

[25] Brigadier General Ferdinand Irizarry noted that security sector reform itself has required education, rule of law, and many of the other elements of state building. Brigadier General Ferdinand Irizarry (lecture, International Security Studies Program Luncheon Lecture Series, Fletcher School of Law and Diplomacy, Tufts University, Medford, MA, October 23, 2012).

donor needs.²⁶ The tasks are all the more difficult when the host government lacks the background, experience, strength, or intent to function in so many demanding areas.²⁷

How can interveners take on such a magnitude of effort in helping reconstruct an entire nation while fighting a war at the same time? To do so is the premise of counterinsurgency, although in both Iraq and Afghanistan, there have been areas and time periods that were not violent, in which the total reconstruction phase

²⁶ An ongoing study by Andrew Beath, Fotini Christia, and Ruben Enikolopov is assessing counterinsurgency-related development projects in Afghanistan through the National Solidarity Program (NSP). To date, the NSP is one of Afghanistan's most successful development projects; it empowers village-level elected Community Development Councils to identify their community needs and carry out small-scale development projects using modest grants. The study has found that communities that received aid from, or interacted with, the NSP were more likely to have favorable opinions toward the government, NGOs, and foreign military forces as well as a more positive perception of the security environment than those that did not. But these same findings have indicated a lack of success when there was simultaneous kinetic action and ongoing violence. The study has found that while development efforts could prevent the spread of violence in regions that were already relatively secure, "they are not effective in reducing violence in regions already experiencing significant security problems." In other words, regardless of whether development projects are addressing the needs and changing the perceptions of those on the ground, they are not deemed effective as war-winning tactics in those areas where kinetic action is ongoing. Andrew Beath, Fotini Christia, and Ruben Enikolopov, "Winning Hearts and Minds through Development: Evidence from a Field Experiment in Afghanistan" (working paper no. 2011–14, MIT Political Science Department, April 2012); Andrew Beath, Fotini Christia, and Ruben Enikolopov, "Direct Democracy and Resource Allocation: Experimental Evidence from Afghanistan" (working paper no. 2011–6, MIT Political Science Department, October 29, 2013). See also Astri Suhrke, *When Less Is More: The International Project in Afghanistan* (New York/London: Columbia University Press/Hurst, 2011).

²⁷ The tasks have not diminished since the efforts to rebuild post–World War II Germany. But conditions in 1945 were far different from those in any recent conflict. Germany had surrendered unconditionally, and all reconstruction began thereafter. The success of post–World War II Germany remains an ideal. A highly industrialized, educated country that surrenders is not an easily replicable situation, and even then, the effort was assumed primarily by the military – but a very different military. The United States and its allies employed conscription. Civilian-soldiers were appointed laterally when their skills were needed. This is no longer the case. Other than small numbers of civil affairs specialists and reserve officers whose rotation prevents continuity, civilian experts are in short supply, with only several thousand government civilians. Contractors do not have the same policy incentives, nor are they chosen for their nation-building expertise.

could have more easily taken place given a clear understanding of the most crucial priorities, as well as lines of cooperation and delegation to civil actors. The *Counterinsurgency Field Manual* calls for "full-spectrum operations" that entail "simultaneous and continuous combinations of offensive, defensive, and stability or civil support operations."[28] It continues: "Commanders shift the predominant type of operation based on the current situation and their assessment as they shape the operational environment and set the conditions to achieve the end-state."[29]

Counterinsurgency presents a dilemma because the positive dividends of development efforts are too often cancelled out by the negative impact of kinetic action – for example, night raids into houses and bombing – as well as by manifest injustice in distribution of goods and services, or apparent support for a repudiated government. All of these issues must be attended to while fighting continues. Followed to its logical conclusion, doctrine demands that the tools to strengthen and rebuild society after conflict are, in fact, the tools to end conflict. Offense and defense are no longer the sum total of the military's job description.

During the early stages of the Iraq War, then-Colonel H.R. McMaster recognized the problem in a memorandum he wrote to General John Abizaid in which he stated:

Military operations alone cannot defeat an insurgency because only economic development and political action can address most sources of disaffection. If military operations are not conducted consistent with political objectives or occur without economic development, they are certain to alienate the population further, reduce the amount of intelligence available to US and Iraqi security forces, and strengthen rather than weaken the enemy.[30]

Given that rebuilding is part of the counterinsurgency strategy and that kinetic action often still occurs in areas where attempts at rebuilding are going on, it is unsurprising that there is no neat, sequential turnover to civilians to reconstruct infrastructure and

[28] The U.S. Army/Marine Corps Counterinsurgency Field Manual (Chicago: University of Chicago Press, 2007), § 3-0. See also § 3-24.2-118, 3-12, 3-13, 3-17.
[29] Ibid.
[30] Fred Kaplan, The Insurgents: David Patreus and the Plot to Change the American Way of War (New York: Simon & Schuster, 2013), 171.

institutions.[31] The ambiguities have mostly been resolved by the military taking on many of the civilian tasks – even helping build a "rule of law" – among the complex tasks that counterinsurgency demands – without the training or, in many cases, the aptitude or desire to do so.

A High Degree of Functionality (Both of Resources and Human Capacity)

Most discussions of military domination and diplomatic failure on the part of interveners have focused primarily on resource inequality, which remains a daunting obstacle to success. A healthy civil-military relationship requires a more sensible division of labor based on adequate civilian participation. Civilian agencies are at a considerable capacity disadvantage compared to the military, especially in the United States.[32] As a result of anemic resourcing and legal authorities, key civilian agencies often have trouble recruiting and maintaining top talent, thus reinforcing the imbalance. Differences in institutional culture and modes of operation also impact the capabilities of civilians compared to military actors in these types of environments.

As a result of – and compounding – these imbalances, the military has had to assume a wide variety of tasks in counterinsurgency contexts for which civilians may be more experienced. In many cases, officers and soldiers have adapted well despite their lack of training and experience, but institution-building is not a primary job of the military, and often the results have seemed jerry-built. Commanders may call on experts both in and out of service, or attempt to build equivalent civilian capacity through the use of contractors.[33] But

---

[31] Gabriella Blum, "The Fog of Victory" (speech, April 10, 2012). See also Gabriella Blum, "The Fog of Victory," *European Journal of International Law* 24, no. 1 (2013): 391–421.

[32] In 2013, the U.S. Department of State and U.S. Agency for International Development's combined budget totaled approximately 2 percent of the national budget, whereas the Department of Defense's budget totaled approximately 18 percent. Jeffrey Zients, "The 2013 Budget," *The White House Blog*, http://www .whitehouse.gov/blog/2012/02/13/2013-budget-0 (accessed October 13, 2014).

[33] Nina M. Serafino, *Global Security Contingency Fund: Summary and Issue Overview*, Congressional Research Service, January 22, 2013, https://www.hsdl .org/?abstract&did=730672 (accessed October 13, 2014).

such solutions cannot fully bridge the difference, even if particular skills are made available.[34]

Nor has there been governmental unity on the priority of civilian participation in the wars. Both the Secretary of State and the Secretary of Defense had pressed Congress to fund a four-year 2012 pilot "Global Security Contingency Fund," into which each department would contribute for counterinsurgency-related activities, and presumably people to perform them.[35] But Congress failed to provide any additional funding in the FY2012 or FY2013 budgets, and little has been heard of the idea since.[36]

There is also an issue of quality. Lack of civilian resources does not explain all of the shortcomings on the diplomatic side. Civilian officials at the working level are not trained to operate in war environments, and many are unwilling to assume the risk, particularly when career rewards push them in other directions. Moreover, even aside from funding, safety, and career issues, civilian departments lack the capacity for sustained and systematic planning and evaluation. Although one hesitates to generalize, diplomats tend to be oriented toward reporting on local conditions by means of their usual channels, through government-to-government contacts. They are unfamiliar with an environment in which their relationships with ordinary civilians may be more crucial than their relationship with a cabinet minister. They tend to be reluctant to challenge host nation authority, or to exercise their dominant status as an intervener, occupier, or even donor, to leverage needed reform.[37]

---

[34] Simon Chesterman and Chia Lehnardt, eds., *From Mercenaries to Market* (New York: Oxford University Press, 2007). See also Martha Minow, "Outsourcing Power: Privatizing Military Efforts and the Risks to Accountability, Professionalism, and Democracy," in *Government by Contract: Outsourcing and American Democracy*, ed. Jody Freeman and Martha Minow (Cambridge, MA: Harvard University Press, 2009), 110–127.

[35] John Glenn and Jane Kaminski, *A New Pool: The Global Contingency Fund*, U.S. Global Leadership Coalition, February 25, 2011, http://www.usglc.org/2011/02/25/a-new-pool-the-global-contingency-fund/ (accessed October 13, 2014).

[36] Serafino, *Global Security Contingency Fund*, 5. Unfortunately, it appears that this effort was totally defunded by FY 2014. See U.S. Global Leadership Coalition, *Detailed Analysis of International Affairs Funding in Final FY14 Omnibus Appropriations Bill*, January 17, 2014, http://www.usglc.org/downloads/2014/01/FY14-International-Affairs-Budget-Analysis_v3_Jan_23.pdf (accessed April 18, 2015).

[37] Komer, *Bureaucracy Does Its Thing*, 61; Biddle, "Review Symposium," 348.

Many of the tasks that the military undertakes, either because the environment is dangerous or because of a civilian shortage, they struggle to perform well. Soldiers can build roads and dig wells. They can build schools – even turn on the lights. That is not unfamiliar. But the weight of institution-building should be carried by civilians. The hard political choices and tasks involved in the governance end of the effort are perhaps the least susceptible to military implementation. And yet, too often the military have taken those jobs on – from developing a legal system to poppy eradication.

Moreover, in Afghanistan, despite the need for deep collaboration, it has been observed that military and civilian actions existed in "hermetically divided spheres of activity" rather than on a continuum of effort.[38] A lack of joint planning partly explains this "stovepiping." However, the weakness of deliberative interagency dialogue, together with an unwillingness to explore lessons learned from shared experience, explains it more fully – and, as discussed in Chapter 5, there is no legal structure to help define a better, more mutually responsive relationship.

A further serious complication in civil-military relations, and not only in counterinsurgency situations, is the extensive use of private contractors to perform essential governmental functions. The justification for the use of all types of contractors in such wars has been a genuine shortage of government personnel, particularly on the civilian side, and a desire to go "off-budget" on the military side. The further justification for contracting many types of government services was the (perhaps now fading) conviction that greater efficiency and effectiveness could be achieved by private business.[39]

---

[38] Sarah Chayes, "What Vali Nasr Gets Wrong," *Foreign Policy*, March 12, 2013, http://www.foreignpolicy.com/2013/03/12/what-vali-nasr-gets-wrong/ (accessed October 14, 2014).

[39] The President's Commission on Roles and Missions of the Military concluded in 1995 that privatizing many functions would lead to greater efficiency. Department of Defense, *Report of the Commission on Roles and Missions of the Armed Forces*, May 24, 1995, http://www.dod.mil/pubs/foi/operation_and_plans/Other/734.pdf (accessed April 17, 2015). But this is only shown to be true when there is competition. See John Donahue "The Transformation of Government Work: Causes, Consequences and Distortions" in Jody Freeman and Martha Minow, *Government by Contract: Outsourcing and American Democracy* (Cambridge, MA: Harvard University Press, 2009), 45.

Due to a lack of both competition and supervision among contractors, the hoped-for cost savings have rarely been achieved – instead, in some cases, shoddy performance, waste, cost overruns, and corruption have resulted.[40] While contractors have been used extensively in war to provide basic services and construction for the military, within the gray area of not war/not peace – and particularly following 9/11[41] – civilians are increasingly being hired to operate in conflict. The strongest public criticism has been leveled against contractors who are hired to perform a military function in a kinetic environment where incidents generated widespread negative publicity.

Contractors in Iraq performed at least thirty-seven of the cruelly excessive interrogations in Abu Ghraib prison.[42] And in 2007, private security contractors from the U.S. firm Blackwater shot and killed seventeen Iraqi civilians in Nisour Square, Baghdad. The high degree of dependence on such abusive companies was revealed seven years later in 2014, when an investigative report revealed that after the Nisour Square shooting, State Department investigators were sent home because they were disrupting the embassy's

[40] "The Special Inspector for Iraq Reconstruction estimated that waste associated with Iraq relief and reconstruction efforts totaled at least $8 billion. (Special Inspector for Iraq Reconstruction, "Learning from Iraq: A Final Report from the Special Inspector for Iraq Reconstruction", March 2013, at 20.) [Likewise, t]he Commission on Wartime Contracting estimated that between $31 billion and $60 billion was lost to contract waste and fraud in contingency operations in Iraq and Afghanistan. ("Commission on Wartime Contracting In Iraq and Afghanistan, Transforming Wartime Contracting: Controlling Costs, Reducing Risk, Final Report to Congress", August 2011, 1.)" Quoted in Moshe Schwartz and Jennifer Church, *Department of Defense's Use of Contractors to Support Military Operations: Background, Analysis, and Issues for Congress*, Congressional Research Service, May 17, 2013, http://fas.org/sgp/crs/natsec/R43074.pdf (accessed October 15, 2014).
[41] In 2007, the Government Accountability Office found that Operation and Management and service contract costs increased from $133.4 billion (U.S. billion) to $209.5 billion – by 57 percent – in relation to global war on terrorism and contingency operations. U.S. Government Accountability Office, *Trends in Operation and Maintenance Costs and Support Services Contracting*, May 2007, http://www.gao.gov/assets/270/261042.pdf (accessed October 15, 2014).
[42] David Isenberg, "A Government in Search of Cover: Private Military Contractors in Iraq," in *From Mercenaries to Market: The Rise and Regulation of Private Military Companies*, ed. Simon Chesterman and Chia Lenhardt (New York: Oxford University Press, 2007), 82, 87.

relationship with the security firm.[43] This is an extreme case of a military use of civilians – often ex-military or ex-intelligence officials in a kinetic and highly sensitive environment. Their recent government affiliations further confuse the issue of appropriate roles. Accountability remains a problem. Yet the issue of accountability is preceded by the question of whether some quasi-military functions should ever be performed by contractors. The intertwining of civil and military roles is complex enough in gray area warfare without the intervening government losing control of its monopoly of force by outsourcing military tasks to contractors over whom it lacks full control.

In other less sensitive areas, contractors may perform adequately, but the lack of supervision and means for swift punishment of wrongdoing have led to criticism even in non-kinetic situations. The incentives for these contractors and the degree of their commitment necessarily differ from those of government personnel. And in many cases, their actions have proven inconsistent with, or even destructive to policy goals.[44] Delayed work and shoddy results point to inadequate oversight, undermining the public support that counterinsurgency is designed to generate. Different U.S. departments, especially those of State and Defense, employ contractors

---

[43] James Risen, "Before Shooting in Iraq, a Warning on Blackwater," *The New York Times*, June 29, 2014, http://www.nytimes.com/2014/06/30/us/before-shooting-in-iraq-warning-on-blackwater.html (accessed October 12, 2014). Conviction of most of the perpetrators was obtained. See Matt Apuzzo, "Ex-Blackwater Guards Given Long Terms for Killing Iraqis," *The New York Times*, April 13, 2015, http://www.nytimes.com/2015/04/14/us/ex-blackwater-guards-sentenced-to-prison-in-2007-killings-of-iraqi-civilians.html (accessed April 17, 2015).
   In the Nisour Square shooting, Blackwater contractors provided security for the U.S. Embassy and other needed operations. However, the military dependence on such contractors should also be noted: "The use of contractors to perform noncombat duties is advantageous to commanders in terms of freeing up uniformed military personnel to project combat power. However, while working to build a cohesive total force, commanders must remember that, while contractors provide many functions formerly performed by military members and commanders often become comfortable with their support contractors (almost to the point of referring to them as my people), contractors are not military members." Lieutenant Colonel Stephen M. Blizzard, "Increasing Reliance on Contractors on the Battlefield: How Do We Keep from Crossing the Line?," *Air Force Journal of Logistics* 28, no. 1 (Spring 2004): 8.
[44] Minow, "Outsourcing Power," 110–127.

from some of the same firms with little coordination between departments.[45] Criticism is particularly pointed in assistance and reconstruction work where no formal chain of command exists.[46] The sheer number of contractors (approximately equal to the number of uniformed service members in both Iraq and Afghanistan) performing a wide range of tasks requires extensive, effective, and costly government supervision. Shrinking budgets means resources for adequate supervision are lacking.

Another issue is legal recourse against contractors and legal protection for them. There have been some developments to improve the situation: the 2000 Military Extraterritorial Jurisdiction Act provides for criminal accountability for "persons employed by or accompanying the Armed Forces outside the United States." It addresses civilians contracted by the Department of Defense.[47] The Act was later supplemented with the FY-2005 National Defense Authorization Act, which expanded the original Act's jurisdiction to contractors supporting defense operations – a jurisdictional gap identified when the contractors allegedly responsible for the Abu Ghraib detainee abuse turned out to have been hired by the CIA and Department of the Interior, not the Department of Defense.[48]

---

[45] Over the past decade, firms such as DynCorp, Triple Canopy, Blackwater, and Blackbird Technologies have held contracts with both the Departments of Defense and State concurrently.

[46] See Office of the Inspector General, USAID, *Audit of USAID/Afghanistan's Oversight of Private Security Contractors in Afghanistan*, May 21, 2010. Moreover, in May 2014, *The Washington Post* reported that International Relief and Development, the greatest recipient of USAID grants and cooperative agreements, required employees to sign confidentiality agreements to not speak disparagingly about the organization to funders – which would include reporting to the federal government instances of project waste or mismanagement. Scott Higham and Steven Rich, "Auditors Examining Nonprofit Organization's Confidentiality Agreements, 'Revolving Door,'" *The Washington Post*, May 6, 2014, http://www.washingtonpost.com/investigations/auditors-examining-nonprofits-confidentiality-agreements-and-revolving-door/2014/05/06/92c2723a-d539-11e3-95d3-3bcd77cd4e11_story.html (accessed October 10, 2014).

[47] 18 U.S. Code § 3261: Criminal offenses committed by certain members of the Armed Forces and by persons employed by or accompanying the Armed Forces outside the United States.

[48] Major Aimee M. Batemen, "A Military Practitioner's Guide to the Military Extraterritorial Jurisdiction Act in Contingency Operations," *The Army Lawyer*, December 2012.

Between 2007 and 2012, the law was used to prosecute twenty-five contractors[49] for a range of crimes.[50] A parallel Civilian Extraterritorial Jurisdiction Act was proposed in 2011 to address extraterritorial felonies by civilian contractors employed by U.S. agencies other than the Department of Defense.[51]

Given the present security environment, dependence on civilian contracting will likely continue both to bolster military capacity and to assist in reconstruction, despite indications that budgets for contractors are shrinking.[52] If dependence on contractors is not

[49] Ibid, 4.

[50] For example, in his testimony to the Senate Judiciary Committee in May 2011, Assistant Attorney General Lanny A. Breuer noted: "In United States v. Christopher Drotleff, et al.... we obtained jury convictions in Norfolk, Virginia of two Department of Defense contractors for involuntary manslaughter of a civilian in Afghanistan. In United States v. Sean T. Brehm, we secured a conviction from a Department of Defense contractor on charges of assault with a deadly weapon in Afghanistan. And in United States v. Jorge Thornton, we secured a conviction from a Department of Defense contractor for abusive sexual contact while working at a U.S. military Forward Operating Base in Iraq. We have also investigated and prosecuted non–Department of Defense contractors whose work related to 'supporting the mission of the Department of Defense overseas.'" Assistant Attorney General Lanny A. Breuer (statement to the Senate Judiciary Committee, Civilian Extraterritorial Jurisdiction Act, May 25, 2011), http://www.justice.gov/criminal/pr/testimony/2011/crm-testimony-110525.html (accessed October 15, 2014).

[51] See Rachel M. Kelly, "Ensuring Contractor Accountability Overseas: A Civilian Extraterritorial Jurisdiction Act Would Be Preferable to Expansion of the False Claims Act," *William and Mary Business Law Review* 5, no. 2 (2014): 591–619, The Civilian Extraterritorial Jurisdiction Act died in committee during the 111th and 112th Congresses but was reintroduced for consideration by Senator Patrick Leahy in July 2014. http://scholarship.law.wm.edu/cgi/viewcontent.cgi?article=1077&context=wmblr (accessed October 24, 2014); Lauren Carasik, "Blackwater Guilty Verdict Long Overdue," *Al-Jazeera America*, October 22, 2014, http://america.aljazeera.com/opinions/2014/10/blackwater-guiltyverdictforiraqsnisoursquareshootings.html (accessed October 24, 2015).

[52] According to a Department of Defense budget briefing at the time of writing, reducing the contractor budget in FY 2015 appears to be part of a move to "improve efficiency": "To free up funds for defense mission needs, the FY 2015 budget continues the recent emphasis on improved efficiency across DoD. Institutional reforms in the budget will save $18.2 billion in FY 2015 and an estimated $94 billion through FY 2019. *Efficiency actions include a 20 percent cut in headquarters operating budgets, reduced contractor funding*, targeted reductions in civilian personnel, reductions in funding for defense support agencies, savings in military health care, and savings from deferred military construction projects

accompanied by more oversight, the potential for abuses such as Nisour Square will continue. The greater likelihood of abuses or mistakes in turn means the greater potential for undermining the trust-building goodwill that counterinsurgency requires. Moreover, the failure to clarify appropriate contractor roles further undermines efforts to create smooth civilian-military cooperation in general.[53] Therefore, greater accountability and role definition for private civilian contractors is crucial in the continued gray area security environment counterinsurgency seeks to affect.

Interveners' Civilian Agency Capacity and Ability of Civilians and Military to Collaborate Effectively

Most discussions of civilians' inability to rise to the demands placed on them by counterinsurgency operations focus on operational shortcomings. But the problem is equally acute at the highest levels of the U.S. government. It appears that the most senior civilian leadership has not fully confronted either the political dimensions of these conflicts or the implications of reconstructing the toppled government. Participants in discussions about the ongoing deterioration in Iraq and Afghanistan maintain that senior civilian policy makers failed to take on the major tough issues emerging from the interventions – such as the violent sectarianism in Iraq, the Pakistani military intelligence service's collusion with insurgents,

---

and family housing" (emphasis added). Department of Defense, "DoD Releases Fiscal 2015 Budget Proposal and 2014 QDR," news release, March 4, 2014, http://www.defense.gov/releases/release.aspx?releaseid=16567 (accessed October 12, 2014).

53 The RAND Corporation produced a study in 2010 that surveyed the military and Department of State personnel on the roles, costs, and benefits of private security contractors. The survey found that although the working relationship between the security contractors and both the military and the Department of State was relatively smooth, the pay disparity between contractors and the military had a negative impact on the military's recruitment and morale, and Department of State personnel generally believed that private security contractors were not respectful of local or international laws. Sarah K. Cotton, Ulrich Petersohn, Molly Dunigan, Q Burkhart, Megan Zander-Cotungo, Edward O'Connell, and Michael Webber, *Hired Guns: Views about Armed Contractors in Operation Iraqi*, (RAND Corporation, 2010).

and the regrowth of Taliban dominance in Afghanistan's eastern provinces.[54] Although top military officials often sought to change the conversation to focus attention on underlying political issues, cabinet-level discussions remained stubbornly fixated on matters of military tactics. No one seemed to be manning the overarching policy helm.

The absence of systematic, full discussions within leadership circles is notable. The lack of an open dialogue between Secretary of Defense Robert Gates and President Obama emerges significantly from the pages of Gates's memoir.[55] For example, Gates thought Obama's Cairo speech raised expectations in the Arab world that would be followed by disillusionment, which indeed turned out to be the case. But he did not offer the president his views in advance or after the speech.[56] He also had strong ideas about U.S. goals in Afghanistan but seemed to let the debate dwell endlessly on the number of troops to be deployed in the surge.[57] He did not make the effort to ensure that an open and frank civil-military dialogue – over the civilian as well as the military implications of the conflicts – take place. Nor did three successive national security advisors push discussions in that direction, even though doing so is one of the functions of that position. This kind of discursive dialogue has not been institutionalized. [58] It still seems to depend on the right personality mix. Secretary Gates seemed more forthcoming in his relationship with President George W. Bush. While personality mesh is always important, it is too rare and evanescent to be a foundation for policy.

Eliot Cohen's analysis of civilian leadership intervention into the details of military campaigns is historically enlightening, but civilian abdication on issues that arguably fall into the civilian "lane" can also create an "unequal dialogue" in the opposite

---

[54] Senior U.S. official, in confidential discussion with the author, June 12, 2011.
[55] Robert Gates, *Duty: Memoirs of a Secretary at War* (New York: Alfred A. Knopf, 2014).
[56] Ibid., 331.
[57] Ibid., 338–349.
[58] Marina Travayiakis, "Discourse Matters: Impact of Civil-Military Relations on the Post-Conflict Planning Process" (PhD dissertation, Fletcher School of Law and Diplomacy, Tufts University, 2014).

direction. The roles of civilian and military in warfare are necessarily intertwined. And because separation is neither possible nor wise, a more systematic approach is needed to ensure that free, full, and ongoing dialogue take place. Both the civilian and the military dimensions of the conflict must be fully explored and probed in tandem. Collaboration is necessary at every stage and every level of operations in order to make wise decisions and allow for adjustments, from the moment of intervention until the last withdrawal. Moreover, there is no shortage of civilian strength at the highest policy levels, where close civil-military collaboration on policy formation sometimes does take place, at least in times of crisis. In the United States, the National Security Council was developed in 1947[59] for just that purpose, but its effectiveness has varied with personalities and administrations. At the theatre level, no structure has been devised to assure deep collaboration, and the variation in effectiveness is stunning.[60]

Interveners' Military and Civilian Willingness to Accept High Danger

"The more successful the counterinsurgency is, the less force can be used and the more risk must be accepted."[61] By their nature, counterinsurgency operations imply increased danger for all those involved. Counterinsurgency is labor intensive and takes place in potentially hostile environments. Troops are expected to live in relatively unprotected small bases scattered among host nation's villages. This is an understandably hard sell to the men and women of the military who must accept the risks laid plain in the *Counterinsurgency Field Manual*. The discontent was palpable among some troops and their families when General McChrystal revised the rules of engagement in Afghanistan to reduce civilian

---

[59] National Security Act of 1947: 50 U.S. Code § 3001, July 26, 1947.
[60] Andrea Strimling Yodsampa, "No One in Charge: A New Theory of Coordination and an Analysis of US Civil-Military Coordination in Afghanistan 2001–2009" (PhD dissertation, Fletcher School of Law and Diplomacy, Tufts University, 2011), http://media.proquest.com/media/pq/classic/doc/2425089111/fmt/ai/rep/NPDF?_s=Xjm4UMKS4I21nasGEIAm4ETcP9E%3D (accessed October 14, 2014).
[61] *Counterinsurgency Field Manual*, § I–151.

casualties, so that ISAF would limit pursuit of insurgents and reduce air strikes in populated areas.[62] Under these rules, protection of the forces must give way to a certain extent to the protection of the host country civilians. The imperative that civilians – both diplomats and development workers – engage as directly as possible with host country nationals also increases their risk. And civilians are not as well trained or equipped for even occasional combat conditions as their counterparts in uniform.

Not only do diplomats and civilians working for donor agencies and international organizations face increased risk, employees of nongovernmental organizations working at field level express concern that the militarization of much aid provision in an effort to "win hearts and minds" away from insurgents distorts their mission. The increasing militarization of aid, in their opinion, also makes them and those who accept their aid potential targets for insurgents.[63] Whether or not this is true, close interaction with military personnel remains unattractive to civilians in government-funded international development programs and NGOs. Frustration is felt on the military side as well, given the culturally different modes of operation that often seem ad hoc and lacking adequate planning, risk assessment, or crisis-response processes.

The Afghanistan and Iraq wars provided the opportunity to engage in imaginative experiments to provide civilian expertise, despite the low ratio of government civilians to military. Designed to deal with risk, Provincial Reconstruction Teams (PRTs) extended the reach of reconstruction activities into the provinces, provided a forum for developing closer relations with the communities they

---

[62] Dexter Filkins "US Tightens Airstrike Policy in Afghanistan," *New York Times*, June 21, 2009, http://www.nytimes.com/2009/06/22/world/asia/22airstrikes.html?_r=0 (accessed March 30, 2015).

International Security Assistance Force, *ISAF Commander's Counterinsurgency Guidance*, 2–6; David Sharp, "Fallen Marine's Father Rips Gen. Stanley McChrystal's New Rules of Engagement in Afghanistan," *Associated Press*, October 13, 2009, http://www.cleveland.com/world/index.ssf/2009/10/fallen_marines_father_rips_gen.html (Last accessed October 14, 2014). See also Sebastian Junger, *War* (New York: Twelve, 2010).

[63] Edward Burke, "Leaving the Civilians Behind: The 'Soldier-Diplomat' in Afghanistan and Iraq," *Prism* 1, no. 2 (2009): 27–46, http://cco.dodlive.mil/files/2014/02/3_Prism_27-46_Burke.pdf (accessed April 18, 2015).

served, and offered an opportunity for civilian and military actors to work together cooperatively to help avoid any tension about their respective roles.

However, because Afghanistan PRTs were sponsored and run by many different national governments, sharply differing activities and approaches prevailed, with no effective mechanism for harmonization across the Afghan national territory. In the beginning, a "thousand flowers bloomed." Each nation had its own goals, its own concepts of operations, and even different ratios of civilians to military, although most had a predominance of military. Military officials led some PRTs, but other patterns also emerged, including joint civil-military leadership and even a few civilian directors. Some had close relations with governors; others were distant and cool.[64] Some were multipurpose; others focused on one functional area, like the South Korean PRT on police training. In sum, PRT accomplishments were diverse and uneven, and many lacked adequate oversight from their parent nations.[65] Much was learned in the process, and many efforts to standardize and use "lessons learned" to improve and unify a concept of operations were made. But before harmonization could be fully implemented, these efforts were overtaken by the 2011 withdrawal from Iraq and the 2014–2015 partial withdrawal from Afghanistan. Nevertheless, the use of PRTs has been an important experiment in civil-military cooperation under counterinsurgency and an attempt to develop useful relationships at the field level that might help extend civilian work in the host country population in situations heretofore considered too dangerous for civilians.

Commitment to Counterinsurgency Means a Commitment to the Long Term

After more than a decade in Iraq and even longer in Afghanistan, it is clear that the commitment to all of the tasks of rebuilding a

---

[64] Robert Perito, Nima Abbaszadeh, Mark Crow, Marianne El-Khoury, Jonathan Gandomi, David Kuwayama, Christopher MacPherson, Meghan Nutting, Nealin Parker, and Taya Weiss, "Provincial Reconstruction Teams: Lessons and Recommendations" Woodrow Wilson Graduate Workshop on Provincial Reconstruction Teams, January 2008), http://wws.princeton.edu/sites/default/files/content/docs/news/wws591b.pdf (accessed October 12, 2014).

[65] Ibid.

war-torn society capable of creating a government responsive to its people and resilient to terrorism is a long-term effort with no guarantee of success.

But even patience and endurance, were they plentiful, are of little value if campaign objectives are not thought through in advance. "If you don't know where you're going," as the old adage says, "you will never get there." And, in the Afghanistan conflict, for example, it was not until 2011 that the U.S. government began articulating what its final objectives were. In both the Iran and Afghanistan conflicts, the objectives seem to have changed over time. As the goals of democratization, or even a government with popular support, in both Iraq and Afghanistan seemed too difficult to attain, the more modest objective of eliminating terrorism took their place. Yet, events seem to demonstrate that it may not be possible to achieve the latter without the former. The unraveling of rebuilding efforts in both of those countries has been stunning.

Once some clarity of objectives is articulated, interveners need a lucid appreciation of the conditions required to achieve those objectives. Then and only then can policies be designed to generate those conditions. In such fluid situations as Iraq and Afghanistan presented, policies must be subject to scrutiny and reevaluation along the way. Constant and systematic policy review is needed, enabled by a widely inclusive discursive dialogue and a willingness to discard approaches that are counterproductive, even when doing so is embarrassing or violates bureaucratic equities. Because of the complexity of most war-torn societies, policies that seemed promising may well prove to be counterproductive.[66] The involved bureaucracies have differing perceptions of the situation and different operating procedures, particularly when

---

[66] Of the conflicts or insurgencies themselves, Jeremiah Pam notes: "[T]he factors that start, sustain and stop people from taking up arms and joining an organized resistance, often against great odds, on their own soil, are sufficiently special and interactively complex to be thought of as a distinct complex problem in itself – even though it obviously never can or should be analytically isolated from other social, political and international factors." Jeremiah S. Pam, "The Paradox of Complexity," in *Complex Operations: NATO at War and on the Margins of War*, ed. Christer M. Schnaubelt (Rome: NATO Defense College, July 2010), 24, 26, 34.

working with international allies. Jeremiah Pam argues that there is a "paradox of complexity." His central thesis in a 2010 paper is that:

> On the one hand, seeing the ways in which these kinds of security and foreign policy operations are complex provides benefits to situational understanding in all sorts of critical ways. Yet we should at the same time be constantly on our guard not to respond to that complexity with strategies and plans that are so complex that they are in practice incapacitating.[67]

Theories about civilian-military relations fail to express the dysfunction and lack of collaboration that have been observed in the late twentieth and first part of the twenty-first centuries. As discussed in Chapter 2, Samuel Huntington's 1957 description of and prescriptions for an insulated professional military were unachievable, if not unwise. Peter Feaver's concept of agency does not fully express the intertwining of political and operational military issues, particularly in the gray areas of warfare and its aftermath. A comment from Michele Flournoy, Department of Defense Under Secretary for Policy in 2009, expressed the dysfunction in Afghanistan clearly. She told Secretary Gates:

> I saw little to convince me that we have a comprehensive interagency plan or concept of operations. I still believe that many competing – and often conflicting – campaigns are ongoing in Afghanistan: counterinsurgency, counterterrorism, counternarcotics, and efforts at nation building. Interagency planning, coordination and resourcing are, by far, the weakest link.... Commanders believe that the substantial planned increase of U.S. forces and capabilities, combined with growth in the ANSF [Afghan National Security Forces], will improve their ability to "clear" and "hold" some key areas. These forces alone will remain insufficient to "build" enough to reduce the insurgency and promote Afghan self-reliance.[68]

Finally, as David Galula points out, the host population cannot be fundamentally hostile to the intervention. Ideally it should support the intervention's aims. But the people must at least be convinced that the counterinsurgency is making progress and will prevail: "The myth of Sisyphus is a recurrent nightmare for the counterinsurgent."[69]

---

[67] Ibid., 27.
[68] Gates, *Duty*, 341.
[69] David Galula, *Counterinsurgency Warfare: Theory and Practice* (New York: Frederick A. Praeger, Inc., 1964), 58, 60. In the final chapter of Albert Camus'

Summing Up

In the end, it is possible, as many observers have argued, that the stated goals of counterinsurgency and the related rebuilding and nation-building tasks undertaken are simply unachievable, particularly given all of the obstacles to a fruitful civil-military relationship. But it is hard to relinquish this robust goal, given the perceived vulnerability that caused the intervention in the first place. Commentators suggest that the objectives need merely to be pruned back. They warn against attempts to recreate every necessary institution at once, or even to construct western-type democracies at all. "Maximalism," one commentator argues, "is doomed to failure because the host nation lacks a near-term political basis for success, while national donors lack the funds and patience to persist."[70] But it is not clear what "minimalism" would look like in a situation where the knotted net of physical and institutional reconstruction tasks is so tangled. And more limited objectives may be unconvincing to local populations while failing to ward off crucial missteps – such as taking too little stock of the needs and aspirations of that very population. "Donors decide what to fund in terms of their own national or organizational interests, without local consultation."[71] Thus, interveners' insensitivity and delay – even while pursuing scaled-back goals – fuel local hostility and resistance. Meanwhile, the interveners' public constituency becomes war-weary and other priorities demand attention and resources. Indefinite commitment

The Myth of Sisyphus, Camus uses the plight of Sisyphus – a Greek mythological figure who is fated to spend eternity rolling a boulder up a mountain, only to have it roll back down the mountain once it reaches the top, forcing Sisyphus to start over again – as a metaphor for the futility and absurdity of modern life.

[70] Marina Ottaway, "Promoting Democracy after Conflict: The Difficult Choices," *International Studies Perspectives* 4, no. 3 (July 3, 2003): 314–322, http://onlinelibrary.wiley.com/doi/10.1111/1528-3577.403007/full (accessed April 18, 2015).

[71] Susan Woodward has commented that the attempt to rebuild state machinery after conflict too often lacks "local legitimacy." She argues that peacebuilding and state-building efforts tend to be secondary to the primary goal of building an internationally acceptable state. Susan L. Woodward, "National Versus International Legitimacy in State Building Operations," *Critique Internationale* 3, no. 28 (July–September 2005): 4. See also Astri Suhrke, *When Less Is More: The International Project in Afghanistan* (New York: Columbia University Press; London: Hurst Publishers, 2011).

without dramatic results is beyond the stamina of most nations' domestic politics.

One explanation for the lack of success with counterinsurgency has been simply "bureaucratic inertia." Komer, commenting on the reluctance of both military and civilian bureaucracies to change their repertoires, quoted John Paul Vann: "[W]e don't have twelve years' experience in Vietnam. We have one year's experience twelve times over."[72] The comment could apply equally to Afghanistan and Iraq, especially given the typically short deployments of key interveners in those cases. He also contended that "adaptive response requires much more than well-conceived policy; it requires adequate machinery at all levels for effective follow-through."[73]

Observations about American bureaucratic inertia are also applicable to UN peace operations and their many less-than-successful attempts to create unified, coherent missions. The Brahimi Report of 2000 decried the fact that "[t]here is currently no integrated planning or support cell in the Secretariat that brings together those responsible for political analysis, military operations, civilian police, electoral assistance, human rights, [or] development."[74] This is exactly Komer's lament from his experience in Vietnam, using similar language.[75] Even with subsequent improvements, it is generally agreed that efforts to reduce "stovepipes," or bureaucratic hoarding and failure to collaborate, remain a problem. Exhortations, agency reorganizations, study commission results, and government and international agency directives have not succeeded in creating the effective integrated effort required to cope with the ambiguities to which counterinsurgency is a response.[76]

---

[72] Komer, *Bureaucracy Does Its Thing*, 65, 71.

[73] Ibid., 154, 151–161.

[74] General Assembly Security Council, *Comprehensive Review of the Whole Question of Peacekeeping Operations in All Their Aspects*, Report A/55/305-S/2000/809, § IV(B), 2000, 198, http://www.refworld.org/docid/524e97e84.html (accessed October 12, 2014).

[75] Komer, *Bureaucracy Does Its Thing*, 114, 148–149.

[76] See Norwegian Ministry of Foreign Affairs, *Implementing United Nations Multidimensional and Integrated Peace Operations*, May 31, 2008, http://www.regjeringen.no/en/dep/ud/documents/Reports-programmes-of-action-and-plans/Reports/2008/synthesis_report.html?id=534042 (accessed October 12, 2014).

The implacability of bureaucracy is hurdle enough. But Professor Michael Glennon has an explanation beyond bureaucratic inertia for the frequent failure of counterinsurgency campaigns. Reaching back to the nineteenth-century English scholar Walter Bagehot and his theory of "double government," Glennon argues that American national security decision making is dominated by two separate sets of institutions: the "dignified" constitutional or Madisonian accountable institutions on the one hand, and "efficient" unaccountable institutions on the other. He calls these institutions "Trumanites" after the president who created this bureaucratic substratum.

Glennon argues:

US national security policy is defined by the network of executive officials who manage the departments and agencies responsible for protecting U.S. national security and ... operate largely removed from public view and from constitutional constraints. The public believes that the constitutionally established institutions control national security policy, but that view is mistaken. Judicial review is negligible; congressional oversight is dysfunctional; and presidential control is nominal.[77]

He argues that policy is not made by the senior elected officials, nor even by Congress with the checks and balances provided by the Constitution. Rather, it is made and executed by a consistent substratum of permanent staff invisible to the public and answerable neither to elected officials nor to the public. As Glennon puts it, "Together these institutions comprise a 'disguised republic' that obscures the massive shift in power that has occurred, which if widely understood would create a crisis of public confidence." He continues: "This crisis has been averted because the efficient institutions have been careful to hide where they begin and where the dignified institutions end."[78] His examples are both startling and persuasive, particularly in analyzing the surprising consistency in national security policy from the George W. Bush to the Barack Obama administrations, despite the deep ideological differences

[77] Michael J. Glennon, "National Security and Double Government," *Harvard National Security Law Journal* 5, no. 1 (2014): 1–114, http://harvardnsj.org/wp-content/uploads/2014/01/Glennon-Final.pdf (accessed October 14, 2014).
[78] Ibid., 11.

expressed in their presidential speeches and in both of Obama's
presidential campaigns.

Most relevant to the observations in this book, Glennon suggests that "the Trumanite network is as little inclined to stake out
new policies as it is to abandon old ones. The Trumanites' grund-
norm is stability, and their ultimate objective is preservation of the
status quo."[79] If this analysis is correct, improving responsiveness
in international security strategy and implementation may seem a
wan hope.

We cannot know now whether the United States, its allies, or
other nations will once again pursue a counterinsurgency policy
with all the hopes that the *Counterinsurgency Field Manual* offered
after time has passed and the present failures have been forgotten.
But if civilian and military policy makers decide to do so, it would
be desirable to review the conditions for success along the lines
discussed here. Hopefully, that will prompt the leadership to engage
civilians and military in deliberative discourse – not only about when
or whether to intervene but also about what the ultimate objectives
are if intervention is decided to be necessary. Further deliberation
is needed to understand the conditions required in order to reach
agreed-upon objectives, and equally important, how and when to
withdraw. However, it is not only the pursuit of a successful counterinsurgency strategy that requires such deep civil-military cooperation. Any security strategy in the current environment requires it.

[79] Michael J. Glennon, *National Security and Double Government* (Oxford: Oxford
University Press, 2014), 25.

5

Legal Implications of Counterinsurgency

Opportunities Missed but Not Lost

The legal issues surrounding counterinsurgency highlight missed opportunities for adequate legal guidance. They do not raise concerns about the legality of the actions of counterinsurgency, as is the case with targeted killings. Counterinsurgency, as such, does not transgress international law, so long as its actions comply with the laws of occupation and the laws of armed conflict.[1]

As for mandating intensified civil-military relations in a counterinsurgency environment, legal means exist, or can be developed, to do so. The question remains whether any legal framework that mandated civil-military processes would be sufficient to overcome the problems of bureaucratic inertia, turf hoarding, personal chemistry, or even "double government" discussed in Chapter 4. Thus far, expressions of concern and intent in widely respected commission reports – and even the significant reorganization of cabinet departments and intelligence structures – have not materially altered bureaucratic "stovepipes." Executive orders and (rather weak) requirements written into the Department of Defense authorization and appropriations legislation have not effected dramatic changes in standard operating procedures.

The Clinton-era Presidential Decision Directive 56 (PDD 56) mandated civil-military planning and training, and created a structure within the National Security Council (NSC) to help assure

---

[1] Antonia Chayes, "Chapter VII1/2: Is Jus Post Bellum Possible," *European Journal of International Law*, 24 no. 1 (2013); 291–296, http://www.ejil.org/pdfs/24/1/2382 .pdf (accessed April 18, 2015).

civil-military collaboration in cases of military intervention and complex peace operations. It was distilled from the interventions and peace operations experience of the early 1990s particularly "Operation Provide Comfort", the allied efforts to protect the population in northern Iraq after the first Iraq war, and the American debacle in Somalia.[2] PDD 56 required that the Deputies Committee of the NSC create an Executive Committee to develop a "political-military" plan to integrate all elements of a U.S. response to a crisis. The process was elaborate, and the training and "rehearsals" of the planning process were designed to provide an integrated outcome in which all the necessary actors had a role. An early draft of the concept was previewed in Haiti in 1994, when the capitulation of the government made a peacebuilding operation possible.[3] It took until 1997 for the concept, conceived as a corrective to the Somalia disaster of 1993, to be approved government-wide. But it was never fully implemented. It did not govern the Dayton peace talks that ended the Bosnian war.[4] While elements of the PDD process continue in training procedures, the process was not sufficiently institutionalized to survive the changes of administration. The winding down of PDD 56 complex contingency planning is a cautionary tale for all efforts at interagency cooperation. The Interagency Transformation and Analysis Program created by PDD 56 continued into the George W. Bush administration. But without a robust

---

[2] White House, "Managing Complex Contingency Operations," Presidential Decision Directive 56 (May 1997), http://www.fas.org/irp/offdocs/pdd56.htm (accessed October 12, 2014); see also John L. Hirsch and and Robert B. Oakley, *Somalia and Operation Restore Hope: Reflections on Peacemaking and Peacekeeping* (Washington, DC: United States Institute of Peace Press, 1995).

[3] Antonia Handler Chayes and Abram Chayes, *Planning for Intervention: International Cooperation in Conflict Management* (The Hague: Kluwer Law International, 1999), 160–163.

[4] Richard Holbrooke, *To End a War* (New York: Random House, 1998), 336–337. Presidential Decision Directive-56 calls for the National Security Council, in conjunction with the Departments of State and Defense, to work with the appropriate U.S. government educational institutions – including the National Defense University, the National Foreign Affairs Training Center, the Army War College, and the Naval War College – to develop and conduct an interagency research, training and education program. See William P. Hamblet and Jerry G. Kline, "PDD 56 and Complex Contingency Operations," *Joint Forces Quarterly*, Spring 2000; David W. Bowker, "The New Management of Peace Operations Under PDD-56," *The Fletcher Forum* 22 no. 2 (Summer/Fall 1998): 63.

legal mandate, institutional and cultural differences between the Department of Defense and the State Department, as well as other civilian departments began to surface. The precise, detailed planning process that DoD tried to institute in a training annex was rejected by nonmilitary departments. Comprehensive planning is not part of the fabric of civilian agencies, and the differences in approach began to erode the process. While simulations and exercises continued, and the Department of Homeland Security recognized their value, the impetus was lost, along with the needed funding. Efforts were continued in the military, at Fort Leavenworth, the Army War College at Carlisle, PA, and the Joint Staff College, Norfolk, VA. But without strong backing from the President, the process fizzled out in 2008 and has not been revived.[5]

The Bush administration's National Security Presidential Directive (NSPD) 44 mandated a less elaborate process, but it fared no better.[6] President Obama clarified the functions of the NSC early in his first term with Presidential Policy Directive (PPD) 1,[7] but thus far no process similar to PDD 56 has been recreated.[8] In further

[5] Interview, April 23, 2015, with Erik Kjonnerod, formerly Director of Applied Strategic Learning at the National Defense University, and in 2011 its Associate Provost.

[6] Under President Bush, National Security Presidential Directive 44 (NSPD 44) designated the secretary of state to coordinate the U.S. response to international stabilization and reconstruction interventions on behalf of all agencies. A lack of funding for the effort meant that NSPD 44 did not bring significant changes. National Security Presidential Directive 44, "Management of Interagency Efforts Concerning Stabilization and Reconstruction," December 7, 2005, http://www.fas.org/irp/offdocs/nspd/nspd-44.html (accessed October 12, 2014).

[7] Under President Obama, Presidential Policy Directive 1 (PPD 1) expanded the National Security Council by adding the secretaries of homeland security and the treasury, the attorney general, the U.S. ambassador to the United Nations, and the president's chief of staff. Likewise, PDD 1 created interagency policy committees to encourage holistic dialogue on specific issues. These structural changes have not provided notable examples of their success, however. White House, Presidential Policy Directive 1, "Organization of the National Security Council System," February 13, 2009, https://www.hsdl.org/?view&did=34560 (accessed October 11, 2014).

[8] Some collaboration is specifically encouraged by Executive Order 13636, encouraging collaboration between the Department of Defense and Department of Homeland Security regarding cybersecurity in 2013. Executive Order 13636, "Improving Critical Infrastructure Cybersecurity," February 12, 2013) http://www.whitehouse.gov/the-press-office/2013/02/12/executive-order-improving-critical-infrastructure-cybersecurity (accessed October 12, 2014).

steps to integrate civil-military effectiveness, the National Security Strategy of 2010 demands a "whole-of-government" approach, but that exhortation has not been followed by significant action yet.[9]

In the United States, presidential directives and executive orders have the force of law within an administration and may be powerful or weak.[10] However, facing bureaucratic resistance, they have not yet been sufficient to mandate civilian-military dialogue in planning and execution. They are less robust than legislation and may not be enthusiastically implemented. Moreover, they may be reversed by congressional action and are often changed by a new administration. Even successful revolutionary executive acts may be slow to bear fruit. For example, President Franklin D. Roosevelt's famous Executive Order 8802[11] prohibiting racial discrimination in the defense industry, followed by President Truman's order to counter discrimination in the armed forces, started a long-term revolutionary process in the armed forces and in employment practices, but the process took almost twenty years and even so, had to be reinforced by later legislation.[12]

In fact, language was inserted into the Defense Authorization Act of 2012 to accomplish a whole-of-government approach to national security policy. It was built on the 2010 National Defense Strategy calling for greater interagency cooperation.[13] In broad language, it required the president to produce a plan to "implement

[9] The 2010 National Security Strategy states: "We are improving the integration of skills and capabilities within our military and civilian institutions, so they complement each other and operate seamlessly. We are also improving coordinated planning and policymaking and must build our capacity in key areas where we fall short. This requires close cooperation with Congress and a deliberate and inclusive interagency process, so that we achieve integration of our efforts to implement and monitor operations, policies, and strategies." The White House, *National Security Strategy* (Washington, DC, 2010), 14, https://www.whitehouse.gov/sites/default/files/rss_viewer/national_security_strategy.pdf (accessed April 18, 2015).
[10] For example, Executive Order 9981, 3 C.F.R. 722, July 26, 1948. As Cass Sunstein points out, some executive orders are easily followed, while others are mired in complexity. Cass R. Sunstein, *Simpler: The Future of Government* (New York: Simon & Schuster, 2013).
[11] Executive Order No. 8802, 3 C.F.R. 957, 1938–1943.
[12] Civil Rights Act of 1964, Pub. L. No. 88–352, 78 Stat. 241, July 2, 1964.
[13] The White House, *National Security Strategy*, 14.

organizational changes, programs, and any other efforts to achieve each component of the whole-of-government integration vision prescribed by the National Security Strategy." It even imposed a timeline for the actions to be taken toward achieving this goal.[14] The Defense Authorization Act of 2013 also refers to the whole-of-government approach creating a committee formed with representatives from designees from departments and agencies to address interagency opportunities. The Government Accountability Office was tasked with reporting on the progress of this approach within two fiscal years.[15] Yet, despite legislative exhortations in 2012 and 2013, there was no reference to the 2012 implementation plan in the Defense Authorization Act of 2014. Even though the broad approach received congressional approval over several years, a robust effort was not made to make it come alive. While such a collaborative approach is important to all national security operations, it is the lifeblood of counterinsurgency. Ironically, examples of outstanding cooperation among specific leaders show that the goal of civil-military collaboration is attainable, if episodic.

A Saturation Approach for Deepening Civil-Military Cooperation

The proposal here applies especially to potential future counterinsurgency efforts, but equally to any contemplated military action. The prevalence of a persistent gray area between peace and war has made security efforts by the United States and its allies more consistently intertwined with diplomacy than traditional state-on-state wars. Therefore, civilians will be involved even more than before at most levels of decision making and action. The nature of that involvement cries for improvement.

---

[14] National Defense Authorization Act for Fiscal Year 2012, Pub. L. No. 112–81 (December 31, 2011), § 1072, "Implementation Plan for Whole-of-Government Vision Prescribed in the National Security Strategy," http://www.gpo.gov/fdsys/pkg/PLAW-112publ81/html/PLAW-112publ81.htm (accessed April 17, 2015).

[15] National Defense Authorization Act for Fiscal Year 2013, Pub. L. No. 112–239 (January 2, 2013), § 1107, "Interagency Personnel Rotations," http://www.gpo.gov/fdsys/pkg/PLAW-112publ239/pdf/PLAW-112publ239.pdf (accessed April 17, 2015).

Given the discouraging experience with executive orders and weak legislation, it may be that the best way to overcome the obstacles that have plagued a more integrated foreign and security policy since the Vietnam War is through multiple, combined efforts rather than through a single approach such as legislation. A saturation approach would entail more than one step at a time. It involves several initiatives taken simultaneously to demonstrate real intent to operate the type of full normative change needed to ensure that civilians and the military are communicating at all levels, especially at the fundamental planning stage.

First, within the United States, it would begin with an executive order. The approaches and experience of PDD 56 and NSPD 44, as well as recent work in the State Department and US AID in conflict analysis,[16] would all be building blocks for such a directive. A detailed executive order would be a first step in implementing the "whole- of- government" approach, which otherwise still waits to be developed in detail. The exceptions permitted to PDD 56 in the final years of the Clinton administration meant that it did not stand much of a chance of enduring. However, both the executive order and the intensive training could be revitalized and made a requirement for high-level officials in the relevant bureaucracies. To be successful, *all* of the educational institutions that train future military and diplomatic leaders should focus on the need to engage in cooperative civil-military dialogue and planning, but that training will come to little if military and civilian institutions are unsupportive of such efforts.

A second measure that the President and Department of Defense could take without legislation would be to mandate the Southern Command (SOUTHCOM)/Africa Command (AFRICOM) model for all combatant commands, starting with the geographic commands. Admiral James Stavridis, then Commander of SOUTHCOM, wrote:

In its reorganization, U.S. Southern Command adopted an integrated multiparty approach to security in its area of focus. While fully respecting the prerogatives of the State Department to execute development, our

---

[16] See, for example, the Interagency Conflict Assessment Framework, piloted in 2008, to bring together U.S. agency representatives to jointly analyze a conflict. Department of State, *Interagency Conflict Assessment Framework (ICAF)*, July 2008, http://www.state.gov/documents/organization/187786.pdf (accessed October 8, 2014).

reorganization efforts included multinational, nongovernmental and even private sector collaboration to enhance understanding of regional dynamics and amplify the benefits of cooperation activities.[17]

SOUTHCOM, covering Central and Latin America and the Caribbean, poses a set of issues that call for an integrated approach, including civil strife, democratization, trafficking in drugs and humans, and illegal entry. The Joint Interagency Task Force (JIATF) South, working with international partners, covered a six-million-mile area of smuggling, interdicted cocaine, and other illegal drugs.[18] The Command additionally dealt with issues of democratization and rule of law. Admiral Stavridis developed and implemented a whole-of-government approach by integrating nonmilitary staff into the command. Most important was appointing a former ambassador as one of two deputy commanders.[19] This model represents a departure from the more conventional structure, which has a U.S. State Department "political adviser" (POLAD). What is most compelling, however, was the institution of an ongoing civil-military strategic planning process based on military experience, but including all the civilian elements of SOUTHCOM – whose experience and inclinations would not have encouraged such a process. "[T]he U.S. government requires a truly interagency strategic planning process for national security and foreign policy," Stavridis wrote. "This capability is a critical requirement for effectiveness in an emerging regional and global operating environment in which challenges and opportunities will proliferate, issues will become increasingly interdisciplinary, and the resources available to the U.S. government may be significantly constrained."[20]

At its creation in 2008, AFRICOM was given a mandate for a similarly integrated approach. In the words of its former commander, General Carter Ham, in his March 2013 address to the Senate, this mandate permitted AFRICOM to "address the greatest near term

[17] James G. Stavridis, *Partnership for the Americas: Western Hemisphere Strategy and US Southern Command* (Washington, DC: National Defense University Press, 2010), 54.
[18] Ibid., 83–84.
[19] Ibid., 116.
[20] Ibid., 87.

threats to our national security while simultaneously building long term relationships and fostering regional cooperation."[21] It has been critical from its creation that AFRICOM also had a State Department deputy, and that the relevant State Department bureaus approved of the concept. As General Ham related in an interview, an initial nervousness in the State Department about the militarization of foreign policy had to be overcome, but a partnership and openness regarding Command priorities developed.[22] Central to this collegiality has been the co-location of a group of civilian officials, including a deputy for civil-military activities and an interagency team representing ten government departments, at Command Headquarters.

The variety of AFRICOM's portfolio is stunning, ranging from efforts to prevent terrorist acts at the hands of al-Qaeda affiliates, to dealing with local extremist insurgencies, such as those in Libya and Mali, to taking action against piracy and trafficking in people and illicit substances. In September 2014, it organized an effort to combat the spread of Ebola by constructing hospitals and communication centers. On the "opportunity" side of the ledger, AFRICOM conducts military-to-military capacity building in a wide range of countries, and even makes efforts to strengthen democracy and "rule of law" in Botswana. Training efforts have been intensive, with varying results, as might be expected. One of the most promising efforts has been AFRICOM's work with the African Union.

General Ham displays impressive, detailed country-by-country knowledge and knowledge of both concerns and opportunities. Judging from public speeches, his successor, General David Rodriguez, promises the same commitment and strength based on the depth of local knowledge he developed in Afghanistan. AFRICOM has multiplied the effectiveness of its relatively small staff and budget. The Command has been able to draw on a number

[21] General Carter Ham (statement to the Senate Arms Services Committee, U.S. Africa Command and U.S. Transportation Command in Review of the Defense Authorization Request for FY 2014 and the Future Years Defense Program, March 7, 2013), http://www.africom.mil/Newsroom/Transcript/10566/transcript-africom-transcom-commanders-testify-before-senate-armed-services-committee (accessed October 11, 2014).

[22] General Carter Ham, in discussion with the author, October 5, 2013. This was also noted in an address made by General Ham at the Fletcher School of Law and Diplomacy, April 2013.

of different intelligence sources and to get country experts to come to the Command.[23]

However, not all interagency dialogue was initially a success. Some US AID personnel showed the same reluctance to work closely with the military, and to align priorities, as described in the discussion about NGOs.[24] But this reluctance has varied by country and is evolving constantly. General Ham, when traveling, found it difficult to get out of the gilded "cocoon" that accompanies official travel, especially of high-ranking military officials. Yet there were times, he recounted, when he could get out among families and students and "cobble together a pretty good picture of the issues" in a country.[25]

The model employed in both SOUTHCOM and AFRICOM is a promising one. In some cases, it has been followed by other Commands, but in other cases it has been resisted. Admiral Stavridis, later Commander of European Command (EUCOM) and the NATO Supreme Allied Commander, appointed a State Department official as deputy and was again in close touch with civilian and international agencies given the complex diplomatic and political problems that EUCOM faces.[26] The success of such emulation depends, to some extent, on leadership, personality fit, and adequacy of the budget. But these efforts show that whole-of-government approaches can work. While Dana Priest was concerned about civilian leadership's abdication to the military in the regional commands, it may be that the inequality of resources between military and civilian agencies has created an opportunity for integration at the COCOM level that on a national level has thus far proven "too hard" to achieve.

The third step in a saturation strategy would be an effort to secure legislation to strengthen an approach mandated by executive action. The Goldwater-Nichols Department of Defense Reorganization

---

[23] Ibid.

[24] Ibid.

[25] Ibid.

[26] For more information on both SOUTHCOM and AFRICOM's interagency collaboration efforts, see "Interagency Collaboration Practices and Challenges at DoD's Southern and Africa Commands" (testimony of the Government Accountability Office Director of Defense Capabilities and Management John H. Pendleton, July 28, 2010), http://www.gao.gov/assets/130/125158.html (accessed December 12, 2014).

Act of 1986 is a useful model.[27] It fundamentally altered standard operating procedures within the U.S. military by forcing officers from separate, competing, and often non-interoperable services to train and deploy together. Combatant commands were integrated. Goldwater-Nichols provided joint training and planning that has now become routine. Joint assignments became a requirement for coveted promotions. Over time, the law has helped change a culture of destructive rivalry. Yet initially, the changes encountered stiff resistance, both within and outside the Department of Defense bureaucracy.[28] The impact of the legislation proved essential to military efforts in both Iraq and Afghanistan.[29] Analogous legislation could mandate a collaborative process, cooperative planning efforts, and an intensive ongoing training experience that includes military and relevant civilians who will be working together in-theatre, regionally, and centrally. It should provide means to change the incentive structures (i.e., linking promotions to designing and participating in civ-mil exercises and deployments) in all the involved departments to counteract bureaucratic separatist tendencies.

Admittedly, such legislation cannot ensure wise decision making. Bad policy can also be made jointly. But a strong legal mandate can at least create the environment that fosters civil-military

---

[27] Goldwater-Nichols Department of Defense Reorganization Act of 1986, 10 U.S. Code 111, http://www.govtrack.us/congress/bills/99/hr3622 (accessed October 15, 2014). Others have made this suggestion as well. See James Dobbins, Seth G Jones, Keith Crane, and Beth Cole DeGrasse, *The Beginner's Guide to Nation-Building* (Santa Monica: RAND, Corporation, 2007), http://www.rand.org/pubs/monographs/MG557.html (accessed December 12, 2014), vi; Tonya L. Jankunis, "Military Strategists Are from Mars, Rule of Law Theorists Are from Venus: Why Imposition of the Rule of Law Requires a Goldwater-Nichols Modeled Interagency Reform," *Military Law Review* 197 (2008): 16–101, http://oai.dtic.mil/oai/oai?verb=getRecord&metadataPrefix=html&identifier=ADA519182 (accessed December 12, 2014).

[28] James R. Lochner III, "Has It Worked?: The Goldwater-Nichols Reorganization Act," *Naval War College Review* LIV no. 4 (Autumn 2001): 95–115, https://www.usnwc.edu/getattachment/744b0f7d-4a3f-4473-8a27-c5b444c2ea27/Has-It-Worked--The-Goldwater-Nichols-Reorganizatio (accessed April 18, 2015).

[29] James R. Lochner III, *Victory on the Potomac: The Goldwater Nichols Act Unifies the Pentagon* (College Station: Texas A&M University Press, 2002). For a description of the initial limited success of the Goldwater-Nichols Act, see Bernard E. Trainor, "Jointness, Service Culture, and the Gulf War," *Joint Forces Quarterly* (Winter 1993–1994): 71–74.

planning and discourse to generate more and better policy options. In fact, a provision could be inserted into the Defense Authorization or Appropriations acts, after hearings and discussion. But it would need to be more forceful than the previous efforts were.

Such a strategy of saturation cannot be U.S.-centric because military action is almost never unilateral. It should also include directives by regional organizations, especially NATO, and tangible support from the UN Security Council. NATO has maintained a Civil-Military Cooperation (CIMIC) doctrine that has been intensified since the conflict in the Balkans. The doctrine is not very ambitious in defining the purpose of CIMIC: "the facilitation of interaction between military and civilian actors in support of the goals of NATO commanders", while ensuring that the conflicting goals of civilian actors are "harmonized as far as possible."[30] But there seem to be encouraging developments in NATO training processes that move toward a truly integrated approach, with civilians helping to design the training, which might lead to more effective training and practice in civil-military planning.[31]

A saturation strategy must also include the United Nations when it authorizes military action or even robust peacekeeping under chapter 7 of the UN Charter. Earlier efforts were made at integration in the Brahimi Report of 2000,[32] and current integrative efforts

[30] Allied Joint Doctrine for Civil-Military Cooperation, ed. A, ver. 1 (AJP-3.4.9), February 2013, 2.1, https://www.gov.uk/government/uploads/system/uploads/attachment_data/file/142538/20130306_ajp3_4_9_jdp3_90_cimic.pdf (accessed April 4, 2015).

[31] NATO's "Comprehensive Approach" was introduced as a strategic concept in 2010 and updated in 2012 in order to improve its crisis-management capabilities. The "Comprehensive Approach Action Plan" has a list of tasks that were meant to be "implemented by a dedicated civilian-military task force that involves all relevant bodies and commands." The civilian-military cooperation that was pursued included "[forming] an appropriate but modest civilian capability to interface more effectively with other actors" and setting up "a Comprehensive Approach Specialist Support (COMPASS) programme … in 2009 to build up a database of national civil experts in three main fields – political, stabilisation and reconstruction, and media – to be drawn upon for advice at the strategic, operational and theatre levels." NATO, *A Comprehensive Approach to Crisis Management*, http://www.nato.int/cps/en/natolive/topics_51633.htm (accessed December 12, 2014).

[32] United Nations, *Report of the Panel on United Nations Peace Operations*, August 21, 2000, http://www.un.org/en/ga/search/view_doc.asp?symbol=A/55/305 (accessed December 12, 2014).

are now being made through the reorganization of relevant UN
agencies, and the UN Peacebuilding Commission,[33] both of which
are now under further review after the appointment of a High Level
Independent Panel on UN Peacekeeping Operations.[34] But real legal
impact would come from the inclusion of civil-military mandates in
every Security Council resolution that demands action, along with
funding that permits a substantial civil-military effort. Together, all
of these efforts, combined with impetus from the European Union
and other regional organizations, might begin to offer a legal framework that would support more effective counterinsurgency when
policy makers decide it is an essential strategy. But more important, it may help create a whole-of-government approach so sorely
needed more generally.

[33] The UN Peace Commission was created in 2005 by resolutions of the General
Assembly (resolution 60/180) and the Security Council (resolutions 1645 and
1646). DPKO has undergone several reorganizations. For example, see the 2005
report entitled "Peace Operations 2010" and the later reorganization of DPKO to
create a Department of Field Support (United Nations General Assembly report
A/64/633, January 26, 2010).
[34] United Nations, "Reform of Peacekeeping," http://www.un.org/en/peacekeeping/
operations/reform.shtml (accessed December 12, 2014).

6

Counterterrorism

The Unquiet Warfare of Targeted Killings

Inter arma silent leges

Within less than a decade of U.S. presence in Afghanistan, it became clear that the counterinsurgency strategy was not succeeding. The strategy was not initiated when the intervention began. Even after a strategic reassessment in 2009, and the efforts of General Stanley McChrystal, its stringent conditions for success were not met. The Taliban and its bloody insurgency had revived.[1] In Iraq, where it seemed for a time as if some form of counterinsurgency had turned the tide, increasingly hopes were dashed that the country might become a sustainable democracy. The United States and the world economy were in recession and had contracted dramatically. Attention was turning inward – away from these countries. The United States had withdrawn from Iraq in 2011, and had announced plans to substantially withdraw from Afghanistan in 2014.

However, the violent militant insurgency group ISIS, (or the Islamic State), changed both the situation and the boundaries in

[1] According to Sarah Chayes, the strategy in Afghanistan was developed for Iraq in 2007 and then imported back to Afghanistan in 2009. It was too late. General McKiernan, who was in charge of the International Security Assistance Force (ISAF) in 2008–2009 had been begging for more troops in Afghanistan, but President Bush did not supply them then. Admiral Mike Mullen expressed shock at the relative "poverty" of the force in Afghanistan when he first attended to the situation there. By the time President Obama made the decision to try counterinsurgency in late 2009, the mood and resources were already very different. Sarah Chayes, in discussion with the author, November 15, 2014.

Iraq and Syria with mass recruitment and successful cross-border assaults. Despite war fatigue and donor disillusionment, the United States managed to cobble together a coalition to counteract the onslaught. The fragile coalition included several Arab nations with varying contributions, as well as the United Kingdom, Australia, France; and an opening to Turkish assistance.[2]

The threat of terrorism – not solely in Iraq and Afghanistan – has demanded many different strategies depending on the circumstances and the country. In Iraq and Syria, counterterrorism was only part of a "hot" war fought with ground troops and conventional bombing. In Yemen and Somalia, it remained essentially a covert operation, until early 2015 when the Yemen government was routed. In Afghanistan, the alternative strategy to counterinsurgency, counterterrorism, came to play a larger part beginning in late 2010, changing the make-up of the intervention.

One central component of a counterterrorism campaign – targeted killing, particularly the use of lethal unmanned aerial vehicles (UAVs or drones) – has led to a division of civilian and military roles, and the appropriateness of this division raises difficult questions. This is not a case of the military seeping into traditionally civilian domains; rather, it is one that raises the question of whether civilians – CIA personnel – are performing a military function. If so, what are the implications for appropriate "management of violence," and has there been a merger of roles? Moreover, the legal basis for such activity remains clouded and secretive, raising further doubts about who does what and about the operations generally.[3] Aspects of counterterrorism other than targeted killing may also raise important questions about civil-military relations and the

---

[2] Dexter Filkins, "What We Left Behind," *The New Yorker*, April 21, 2014, http://www .newyorker.com/magazine/2014/04/28/what-we-left-behind (accessed December 12, 2014).

[3] For an overview of eight legal arguments asserted since 2002 to justify U.S. counterterrorism drone attacks, see Mary Ellen O'Connell, "International Law and Drone Attacks Beyond Armed Conflict Zones," in *Drones and the Future of Armed Conflict, Ethical, Legal, and Strategic Implications* (D. Cortright et al., eds., 2015). See also Christine Gray, "Targeted Killings: Recent US Attempts to Create a Legal Framework," *Current Legal* Problems 66 no. 75 (2013): 75–106, http://clp.oxfordjournals.org/content/66/1/75.full.pdf+html (accessed April 18, 2015).

boundaries of legality. Although worth pursuing, many of these operations are screened even further behind the wall of secrecy than targeted killing. But at least, certain counterterrorism practices, such as extreme rendition and aggressive interrogation amounting to torture, have been terminated.[4]

"We've been taking a lot of kinetic activities against them, actually," said General Petraeus, sent to Afghanistan by President Obama in June 2010 to work his Iraq-turnaround magic. "I don't know if there's an incident a day, but certainly close to it, where our intelligence, surveillance and reconnaissance assets are detecting a group planting [improvised explosive devices], and U.S. forces go after that group."[5] In the same interview, General Petraeus sought to explain how both approaches, counterinsurgency and counter-terrorism, could be combined. But *The Washington Post* columnist David Ignatius, watching Petraeus at work, suggested the balance between the two might be shifting. He wrote:

[T]he real action has been "enemy-centric" – in stepped-up operations to capture or kill Taliban leaders, along with support for Karzai's attempt to cut a political deal with them. President Obama, having signed off in December on the counterinsurgency approach, is now watching his commander execute a strategy whose biggest successes have come from hard-nosed counterterrorist tactics – the midnight raid, kick-down-the-door ferocity of the Joint Special Operations Command.[6]

Counterterrorism: Everyone's Job?

That the finely honed and multiple techniques of counterterrorism would be employed in the gray area that has characterized terrorism

[4] Executive Order 13491, "Ensuring Lawful Interrogations," http://www .whitehouse.gov/the_press_office/EnsuringLawfulInterrogations (accessed December 12, 2014). See also Senate Select Committee on Intelligence, *Committee Study on the Central Intelligence Agency's Detention and Interrogation Program*, December 3, 2014, http://www.intelligence.senate.gov/study2014/sscistudy1.pdf (accessed December 12, 2014).

[5] Spencer Ackerman, "Drones Surge, Special Ops Strike in Petraeus Campaign Plan," *Wired*, August 18, 2010, http://www.wired.com/dangerroom/2010/08/ petraeus-campaign-plan/ (accessed November 10, 2014).

[6] David Ignatius, "Petraeus Rewrites the Playbook in Afghanistan," *The Washington Post*, October 19, 2010, http://www.washingtonpost.com/wp-dyn/content/article/ 2010/10/18/AR2010101803596.html (accessed April 18, 2015).

and insurgencies worldwide should be no surprise.[7] But this rapid expansion of a new war-fighting capability raises different questions about civil-military relations and about how the legal underpinning for counterterrorism activities might affect role definition for and cooperation between civilian and military actors. Within the United States, responsibility for preventing would-be terrorists from carrying out attacks encompasses most major departments and agencies of government.[8] Apart from the obvious mandates of the Defense Department, CIA, and Department of State, the Departments of Justice, Homeland Security, Treasury, Agriculture, and Commerce are also deeply involved.[9] Even the federal judiciary has played an important part in managing American responses to terrorism in a series of Supreme Court and lower court opinions that altered the landscape of legally acceptable practices governing

---

[7] The term "terrorism" does not lend itself to a precise definition in either scholarship or policy. To illustrate its complexity, a 2002 study by Leonard Weinberg, Ami Pedahzur, and Sivan Hirsch-Hoefler yielded seventy-three different definitions of terrorism from a survey of only fifty-five scholarly journal articles. The authors of the study compared their findings to an earlier study by Alex Schmid that arrived at twenty-two "definitional elements" of the term "terrorism," which had been distilled from 109 different definitions that Schmid had received when he surveyed scholars in 1988. See Leonard Weinberg, Ami Pedahzur, and Sivan Hirsch-Hoefler, "The Challenges of Conceptualizing Terrorism," *Terrorism and Political Violence* 16, no. 4 (Winter 2004): 777–794.

[8] As with counterinsurgency, a holistic approach to counterterrorism should entail not only capturing the individuals actively participating in violence but also working to delegitimize their organizations, de-radicalize their associates, and promote civil society and good governance in their communities. See Daniel Byman, "U.S. Counterterrorism Options: A Taxonomy," *Survival* 49, no. 3 (Autumn 2007): 121–150.

[9] In fact, there are many U.S. domestic-focused agencies that have counterterrorism responsibilities. Among them are the U.S. Justice Department Counterterrorism Section, advising on law enforcement and legislation. See The United States Department of Justice, National Security Division, Counterterrorism Section, http://www.justice.gov/nsd/counter_terrorism.htm (accessed April 18, 2015); the U.S. Treasury Department's Office of Terrorism and Illicit Finance, drafting economic sanctions, http://www.treasury.gov/resource-center/terrorist-illicit-finance/Pages/default.aspx (accessed April 18, 2015); and even the obscure U.S. Food and Drug Administration's Center for Veterinary Medicine's Counterterrorism Coordinator, addressing potential bioterrorism through livestock (see U.S. Food and Drug Administration, "Emergency Preparedness and Response: CVM and Counterterrorism," http://www.fda.gov/EmergencyPreparedness/Counterterrorism/ucm122296.htm) (accessed April 18, 2015).

counterterrorism.[10] And states and cities have operations of their own, often well financed.

The military defined counterterrorism in the 2009 Joint Doctrine on Counterterrorism as "actions taken directly against terrorist networks and indirectly to influence and render global and regional environments inhospitable to terrorist networks."[11] Counterterrorism is considered, as is counterinsurgency, a necessary response to "irregular warfare."[12] Responsibility for counterterrorism within the military lies squarely with Special Operations Forces (SOF) under U.S. Special Operations Command (SOCOM).[13]

Established in 1987 following the passage of the Goldwater-Nichols Act and the Nunn-Cohen Amendment of 1986, SOCOM represented a consensus on the need to consolidate and modernize U.S. Special Operations Forces.[14] SOCOM's stated mission is to "provide fully capable Special Operations Forces to defend the United States and its interests" and to "synchronize planning of global operations against terrorist networks," under the auspices of its three priorities: one of which was to "deter, disrupt, and defeat terrorist threats."[15] As of March 2012, SOCOM had for all its missions, approximately 66,000 active duty, reserve,

[10] See Hamdan v. Rumsfeld, 548 U. S. 557 (2006); Hamdi v. Rumsfeld, 542 U. S. 507 (2004); and Boumediene v. Bush, 553 U. S. 723 (2008).

[11] *Counterterrorism*, Joint Publication 3–26, November 13, 2009, vi.

[12] Ibid., viii.

[13] Of JSOC, Commander Admiral William H. McRaven stated: "We are the lead Combatant Command tasked with synchronizing the planning of global operations against terrorist networks." See Senate Armed Services Committee, 112th Congress (March 6, 2012) (posture statement of Admiral William H. McRaven), http://www.fas.org/irp/congress/2012_hr/030612mcraven.pdf (accessed December 12, 2014).

[14] The evolution of SOCOM can be traced from the failed Desert One Iranian hostage rescue attempt in 1980. For a complete history of SOCOM from its inception through its involvement in Somalia, Haiti, the Balkans, and the Global War on Terror, see *United States Special Operations Command History, USSOCOM*, 6th ed. (March 2008), http://www.socom.mil/Documents/history6thedition .pdf (accessed April 4, 2015). For a specific history on SOCOM operations from 1987 to 1995, see Wayne A. Downing, "Joint Special Operations," *Joint Forces Quarterly* (Summer 1995): 22–27.

[15] USSOCOM Public Affairs, *Fact Book: United States Special Operations Command 2014*, 41, http://www.socom.mil/News/Documents/USSOCOM_Fact_ Book_2014.pdf (accessed April 18, 2015).

and civilians assigned within its four components,[16] plus the
Joint Special Operations Command, and operated in more than
seventy-five countries.[17]

Although now under SOCOM's umbrella, Joint Special
Operations Command (JSOC) predates the establishment of the
Command by seven years.[18] Considered the most clandestine special
operations organization, JSOC is reported to command the military's
most elite and highly skilled special mission units (SMU), including
the Navy's SEAL Developmental Group, popularly known as SEAL
Team 6 or DEVGRU, which carried out the raid that killed Osama
bin Laden,[19] as well as the Army's First Special Forces Operational
Detachent-Delta. According to the government-sanctioned website,
JSOC's purpose is "to study special operations requirements and
techniques, ensure interoperability and equipment standardiza-
tion, plan and conduct special operations exercises and training,
and develop joint special operations tactics."[20] Special Operations
forces, and JSOC's nimble and exacting force in particular, have
constituted a key component of U.S. operations in both Iraq and
Afghanistan. JSOC was a one-stop military shop that could begin

[16] These four components include the military branch's special operations: the
U.S. Army Special Operations Command, the Naval Special Warfare Command,
the Air Force Special Operations Command, and the Marine Corps Special
Operations Command.

[17] See the comprehensive Posture Statement of Admiral William H. McRaven before
the Senate Armed Services Committee in which he stated "Since 9/11, our operations, ranging from peacetime engagement and building partner capacity, to direct
action raids and irregular warfare, have contributed significantly to not only our
own National Security, but global stability at large." http://www.armed-services
.senate.gov/imo/media/doc/McRaven_03-11-14.pdf (accessed April 24 2015)

[18] Linda Robinson, *The Future of U.S. Special Operations Forces* (New York: Council on
Foreign Relations, 2013); Susan L. Marquis, *Unconventional Warfare: Rebuilding
U.S. Special Operations Forces* (Washington, DC: Brookings Institution Press,
1997); Dana Priest and William M. Arkin, "Top Secret America: A Look at the
Military's Joint Special Operations Command," *The Washington Post*, September 2,
2011, http://articles.washingtonpost.com/2011-09-02/world/35273073_1_navy-
seal-joint-special-operations-command-drones (accessed December 12, 2014).

[19] Dana Priest and William M. Arkin, "Top Secret America: A Look at the Military's
Joint Special Operations Command," *The Washington Post*, September 2, 2011,
http://articles.washingtonpost.com/2011-09-02/world/35273073_1_navy-seal-
joint-special-operations-command-drones (accessed December 12, 2014).

[20] See USSOCOM, Joint Special Operations Command, http://www.socom.mil/
Pages/JointSpecialOperationsCommand.aspx (accessed April 18, 2015).

to deal with al-Qaeda, which by 2003 had become a decentralized network of organizations.

In 2003, Osama bin Laden remained at large and al-Qaeda in Iraq (AQI) had become rampant. In an effort to make progress in the "war on terror" JSOC created Joint Task Force 714 to bolster its operations and permit it to respond with greater speed and efficiency than the enemy. This was expanded into Afghanistan in 2004 with the Joint Interagency Task Force under the U.S. forces mission (Operation Enduring Freedom or OEF). The Task Force sought ways for U.S. forces to "become a network" just like the enemy with whom they were dealing.[21] General Stanley McChrystal pointed out that this network brought the "CIA's human intelligence ... the National Security Agency's intercepted signals; the FBI's forensic and investigative expertise; the Defense Intelligence Agency's military reach; and the National Geospatial-Intelligence Agency's 'dazzling mapping ability' together in the Afghanistan theatre."[22] It also included CIA's Special Activities Division. As the military and the CIA were thus brought closer together in the fight against al-Qaeda, the lines between their missions and responsibilities became blurred.

The CIA's role in counterterrorism, as described by its Counterterrorism Center, is "[to work] with other U.S. government agencies and with foreign liaison partners [to] target terrorist leaders and cells, disrupt their plots, sever their financial and logistical links, and roil their safe havens."[23] This work encompasses far more than either the CIA's classic intelligence or traditional covert action functions, verging more and more into direct military action. One manifestation of this increasing paramilitary role has been strikes by CIA-controlled UAVs. Although the concept of striking the

---

[21] Gideon Rose, "Generation Kill: A Conversation with Stanley McChrystal," *Foreign Affairs* 92, no. 2 (2013): 2–8, http://www.foreignaffairs.com/discussions/interviews/generation-kill (accessed November 3, 2014).

[22] In 2011, General Stanley McChrystal noted: "In bitter, bloody fights in both Afghanistan and Iraq, it became clear to me and to many others that to defeat a networked enemy we had to become a network ourselves." General Stanley McChrystal, "It Takes a Network: The New Front Line of Modern Warfare," *Foreign Policy*, February 22, 2011, http://www.foreignpolicy.com/articles/2011/02/22/it_takes_a_network (accessed December 12, 2014).

[23] Central Intelligence Agency, *The Work of a Nation*, https://www.cia.gov/library/publications/resources/the-work-of-a-nation (accessed April 18, 2015).

enemy with unmanned aerial vehicles was first developed in World War II, its widespread use was early in the twenty-first century, by OEF in its first combat year, and by the CIA in Yemen in 2002.[24] The CIA increased its UAV operations from 2006 to 2008 in order to strike at al-Qaeda and its sympathizers "at a pace they could not absorb."[25]

Targeted Killing

The Alston Report on Extrajudicial, Summary, or Arbitrary Executions, presented to the UN General Assembly Human Rights Council in 2010, defines targeted killing as "the intentional, premeditated and deliberate use of lethal force by States or their agents under color of law or by an organized armed group in armed conflict against a specific individual who is not in the custody of the perpetrator."[26] That report also notes that such killings have been justified as a legitimate response to "terrorist threats" and as a necessary response to asymmetric warfare.[27] Although targeted assassinations are probably as old as humankind's history, technological

---

[24] Andrew Callum "Drone Wars: Armed Unmanned Aerial Vehicles," *International Affairs Review*, XVIII no. 3 (Winter 2010), http://www.iar-gwu.org/node/144 (accessed April 2, 2015); see also Doyle McManus, "A U.S. License to Kill, a New Policy Permits the C.I.A. to Assassinate Terrorists, and Officials Say a Yemen Hit Went Perfectly. Others Worry About Next Time," *The Los Angeles Times*, January 11, 2003, http://articles.latimes.com/2003/jan/11/world/fg-predator11 (accessed April 2, 2015). Mark Mazzetti, "A Secret Deal on Drones, Sealed in Blood," *The New York Times*, April 6, 2013, http://www.nytimes.com/2013/04/07/world/asia/origins-of-cias-not-so-secret-drone-war-in-pakistan.html?_r=0 (accessed December 12, 2014).

[25] Greg Miller, "At CIA, a Convert to Islam Leads the Terrorism Hunt," *The Washington Post*, March 24, 2012, http://www.washingtonpost.com/world/national-security/at-cia-a-convert-to-islam-leads-the-terrorism-hunt/2012/03/23/gIQA2mSqYS_print.html (accessed December 12, 2014).

[26] United Nations, *Report of the Special Rapporteur on Extrajudicial, Summary or Arbitrary Executions Philip Alston*, UN Human Rights Council Report, UN Doc. A/HRC/14/24/Add. 6, May 28, 2010, 3, http://www2.ohchr.org/english/bodies/hrcouncil/docs/14session/A.HRC.14.24.Add6.pdf (accessed December 12, 2014). After a detailed analysis of applicable law, the report also states: "The greater concern is because they make it easier to kill without risk to a State's forces, policymakers and commanders will be tempted to interpret the legal limitations on who can be killed and under what circumstances too expansively."

[27] Ibid., 6.

advances provide an immediate opportunity to kill individuals or small groups by using remotely launched UAVs: armed Predators, the first generation of armed UAVs, Reapers, and Avengers, commonly called drones. They can strike "efficiently" without invasion or risk to targeting personnel, and arguably with less collateral damage than manned air strikes. U.S. drone attacks reportedly constitute 95 percent of targeted killings,[28] and have killed between 3,200 and 4,600 people in total as of early 2014.[29] They occur in areas, such as Somalia or Yemen, where there may be little or no other kinetic action by outside powers.

Since the terrorist threat to the homeland seems to be persistent and now worldwide, UAV strikes have seemed to be an effective response to widespread and mobile terrorism. The president's May 23, 2013 speech at the National Defense University first acknowledged what was already publicly known – that the United States was engaged in the wide use of drone strikes to target individuals and groups.[30] The lack of risk to the user makes their widespread use attractive.[31] Yet despite their efficiency, obviating the need for significant forces in country, widespread concern accompanies their increased use. The United States and its closest allies no longer have a monopoly on UAVs and therefore may soon become targets themselves. Many countries now possess surveillance drones, and a vastly increased number will soon have the capacity to strike.[32]

---

[28] Micah Zenko, *Reforming U.S. Drone Strike Policies: Council on Foreign Relations Report*, January 2013, 8, http://www.cfr.org/wars-and-warfare/reforming-us-drone-strike-policies/p29736 (accessed November 11, 2014).

[29] New America Foundation, Drone Wars Dataset, http://securitydata.newamerica.net/world-drones.html (accessed April 18, 2015); see also Bureau of Investigative Journalism, Covert Drone War Datasets, http://www.thebureauinvestigates.com/2012/09/06/covert-drone-war-the-complete-datasets/ (accessed December 15, 2014).

[30] President Barack Obama (speech, National Defense University, Washington, DC, May 23, 2013), http://www.whitehouse.gov/the-press-office/2013/05/23/remarks-president-national-defense-university (accessed December 12, 2014).

[31] John Kaag and Sarah Kreps raise ethical questions about the use of such warfare when there is "the ability to conduct military operations at ever lower costs and this presents a moral hazard – a situation where an actor takes on risky behavior while not shouldering the consequences or risks of said behavior." John Kaag and Sarah Kreps, *Drone Warfare* (Cambridge: Polity Press, 2014), 135.

[32] Guy Taylor, "U.S. Intelligence Warily Watches for Threats to U.S. Now that 87 Nations Possess Drones," *The Washington Times*, November 10, 2013,

Additionally, the very secrecy of the program has heightened inherent ambiguities about which agencies of government – civilian or military – are, or should be, responsible for UAV operations and therefore which legal provisions might apply. From the inception of lethal UAV operations, both military officers and CIA operatives have conducted them. Publicly available information suggests that their roles have been intertwined; the distribution of activities seems to defy any conventional role division. The allocation seems to fit no logical model of civil-military relations – past or present.

Although targeted killing presents a different set of civil-military and legal issues from those of counterinsurgency, both fit into the same strategic environment of combating terrorism in gray area warfare. Greater civil-military role clarity, with public explanation, may ease some of the discomfort that secrecy generates. A number of legal issues also need further development. Strikes that have killed American citizens have required special justification under domestic law, and have caused intense debate. Both domestic and international legal issues have become intertwined with issues of sovereignty morality and accountability. International cooperation may be necessary to establish a sturdier, more widely acceptable legal framework if the use of targeted killing is continued.[33]

http://www.washingtontimes.com/news/2013/nov/10/skys-the-limit-for-wide-wild-world-of-drones/?page=all (accessed November 12, 2014). There are varying numbers given for armed drone proliferation, but all accounts agree that the numbers are substantial and growing enough to pose a threat to the United States and its allies. Thus far, only the United States, the United Kingdom, and Israel have actually used lethal drones to strike an enemy.

[33] Allen Buchanan and Robert O. Keohane, "International Institutional Regulation of Lethal Drones" (Unpublished Paper, Princeton University, October 5, 2014). A later version appears as "Toward a Drone Accountability Regime," in *Ethics and International Affairs* 29, No. 1 (2015), 15–27.

7

Civil-Military Issues in Targeted Killing by UAVs

Far off, like a dull rumour of some other war
What are we doing here?

Wilfred Owen, "Exposure"

The fact that both the military and the CIA have carried out UAV operations[1] created problems of role definition that are almost the opposite of those in the counterinsurgency situation. There, reconstruction functions had traditionally been considered civilian, but persistent violence, shortages of civilian personnel and resources made it difficult to avoid military participation. In the case of targeted killing, the function seems more clearly a military one, but is also carried out by civilians in the CIA. While it is true that parts of the CIA have had a covert, quasi-military role since the passage of the National Security Act of 1947,[2] routine conduct of bombing operations, even remotely, seems closer to a traditional military function.

The reasons for public discomfort about widespread use of UAVs to strike terrorists are complex. Apart from legal issues, some of this concern amounts to more than just a feeling that it is more appropriate for the military to be responsible for conducting violence than the civilian CIA. Discomfort seems also to revolve around the institutional reputation of the CIA – its secrecy and history of

---

[1] Henceforth, all references to UAV operations should be considered those operations using UAVs with lethal strike capabilities and not those used solely for intelligence, surveillance, and reconnaissance (ISR) missions.

[2] National Security Act of 1947: 50 U.S. Code § 3001, July 26, 1947.

acts of questionable legality. First, although the CIA has long been involved in covert operations, its reputation has been increasingly tarnished since 9/11, even as it recovered somewhat from the Bay of Pigs disaster more than a half century ago, and even from the Church Committee findings in the 1970s.[3] Widespread abuses of enhanced interrogations, practices such as waterboarding, extraordinary renditions of suspects, maintenance of secret "black" sites, and even indications that CIA leadership has hidden some agency activities from high government officials have all heightened internal and international public impressions of the agency's rogue behavior.[4]

[3] David M. Barrett. "The Two Stories about Bay of Pigs You Never Heard," *History News Network*, September 5, 2005, http://historynewsnetwork.org/article/14951 (accessed December 3, 2014). In fact, questionable CIA practices continued well into the 1970s, when the Church Committee, chaired by Senator Frank Church, uncovered a number of attempted assassinations of foreign government leaders as well as wide mail "eavesdropping." The concern about assassinations led President Ford to issue Executive Order 11905, replaced by President Reagan's Executive Order 12333 (still in existence today), and later raised questions about the legality of targeted killing. It was publicly announced in 2007 that two years earlier, the CIA had destroyed videotapes documenting severe interrogation methods used on terrorism suspects. See Mark Mazzetti, "C.I.A. Destroyed 2 Tapes Showing Interrogations," *The New York Times*, December 7, 2007, http://www.nytimes.com/2007/12/07/washington/07intel.html?pagewanted=all&_r=0 (accessed November 16, 2014). This concern with the CIA was compounded in March 2014 with the accusation by Senator Dianne Feinstein that not only had the CIA blocked the declassification of a 6,000-page Senate Intelligence Committee's report on CIA interrogation methods since September 11, 2001, but that it monitored the computers of the Senate staffers drafting the report. See Patricia Zengerle and Richard Cowan, "U.S. Senate Leader Orders Probe of Alleged CIA Computer Hacking," *Reuters*, March 20, 2014 http://www.reuters.com/article/2014/03/20/us-usa-cia-interrogations-idUSBREA2J16F20140320 (accessed October 28, 2014). For an account of the 2014 torture report, see Jeremy Ashkenas, Hannah Fairfield, Josh Keller, and Paul Volpe, "7 Key Points from C.I.A. Torture Report," *The New York Times*, December 9, 2014, http://www.nytimes.com/interactive/2014/12/09/world/cia-torture-report-key-points.html (accessed April 18, 2015).

[4] Mark Mazzetti, *The Way of the Knife: The CIA, a Secret Army and a War at the Ends of the Earth*, (New York: Penguin Press, 2014), 118–121. See also Greg Miller, Adam Goldman, and Ellen Nakashima, "CIA Misled Interrogation Program, Senate Report Says," *The Washington Post*, March 31, 2014, http://www.washingtonpost.com/world/national-security/cia-misled-on-interrogation-program-senate-report-says/2014/03/31/eb75a82a-b8dd-11e3-96ae-f2c36d2b1245_story.html?wpisrc=al_national (accessed October 28, 2014); Jane Mayer "A Reporter at Large: The Black Sites," *The New Yorker*,

Second, lack of public discourse about the legality of targeted killing has further heightened impressions of a lack of accountability.[5] This is discussed in Chapter 8.

Third, the respective roles of the President, national security staff, the Director of National Intelligence (DNI), the Director of the CIA, the Secretary of Defense, the Chairman of the Joint Chiefs of Staff, and the Secretary of State in developing the policy and defining targeting criteria remain opaque – as do decisions about when not to strike. And the lack of transparency continues to leave questions about the rationale for the current division of responsibility among the involved actors and whether the current role allocation

August 13, 2007, http://www.newyorker.com/reporting/2007/08/13/070813fa_fact_mayer?currentPage=all (accessed October 17, 2014); and Jane Mayer, *The Dark Side* (New York: Doubleday, 2008), 126–136. There was discontent with the administration that permitted the CIA action: "'Enhanced interrogation techniques are an example where people within the Administration, senior people, were fully briefed and oversight committees were briefed,' the former senior intelligence official says." Massimo Calabresi, "CIA Tapes Furor: A Legacy of Mistrust," *Time*, December 7, 2007, http://content.time.com/time/nation/article/0,8599,1692571,00.html (accessed December 12, 2014). Linda Greenhouse, referring to the Torture report, states: "What caught my eye, thanks to *The Blog of Legal Times*, was an episode recounted on pages 140 to 142 of the report's 499-page executive summary. On those few pages, the report recounts that in January 2004, shortly after the Supreme Court had shocked the administration of President George W. Bush by agreeing to decide whether the Navy base at Guantánamo Bay lay without the jurisdiction of the federal courts, the C.I.A. decided it might need to take pre-emptive action. Its general counsel raised with Bush administration lawyers the question of whether five high-value detainees being held there (including Abu Zubaydah and Ramzi bin al-Shibh) should be sent back to black sites in other countries to make sure they would remain out of the judiciary's reach. The answer was yes. In the publicly released report, the locations to which they were sent are blacked out." Linda Greenhouse, "Guantanamo Dreams," *The New York Times*, December 24, 2014, http://www.nytimes.com/2014/12/25/opinion/guantnamo-dreams.html?ref=opinion (accessed December 25, 2014).

[5] There was a running public battle between Senator Diane Feinstein, supported by Senator Jay Rockefeller, and the CIA about the publication of a report on the CIA's interrogation program. The report was held up for more than two years. See Miller, Goldman, and Nakashima, "CIA Misled Interrogation Program." Dianne Feinstein and Jay Rockefeller, "Why the Senate Report on the CIA's Interrogation Program Should Be Made Public," *The Washington Post*, April 10, 2014, http://www.washingtonpost.com/opinions/the-senate-report-on-the-cias-interrogation-program-should-be-made-public/2014/04/10/eeeb237a-c0c3-11e3-bcec-b71ee10e9bc3_story.html (accessed November 15, 2014); see also Mazzetti, *The Way of the Knife*, 235.

makes sense and contributes to a careful and restrained policy.[6] The Edward Snowden revelations, though not specifically relevant to the use of UAVs, have heightened general concerns about secrecy and lack of accountability in all counterterrorism activities.[7]

The continuing silence about all of these issues and how they are intertwined has further magnified unease and lack of trust in government.[8] Some conclude that the only reason the CIA has taken over the lion's share of UAV strikes is that CIA covert action is less subject to legal scrutiny and legal accountability – and therefore the CIA is more able to obfuscate legal violations. But is it really true that the U.S. military operates under tighter legal constraints and is subject to more supervision than the CIA?[9]

---

[6] As Peter Singer writes: "What troubles me – is how a new technology is short-circuiting the decision-making process for what used to be the most important choice a democracy could make. Something that would have previously been viewed as a war is simply not being treated like a war." Peter Singer, "Do Drones Undermine Democracy?," *The New York Times*, January 21, 2012, http://www.nytimes.com/2012/01/22/opinion/sunday/do-drones-undermine-democracy.html?pagewanted=all (accessed December 12, 2014).

[7] Katherine Jacobsen and Elizabeth Barber, "NSA Revelations: A Timeline of What's Come out Since Snowden Leaks Began," *Christian Science Monitor*, October 16, 2013, http://www.csmonitor.com/USA/2013/1016/NSA-revelations-A-timeline-of-what-s-come-out-since-Snowden-leaks-began/June-5-8-2013 (accessed December 12, 2014).

[8] According to the Pew Research Center and their ongoing polling of American trust of the U.S. government, the results of an October 2013 survey listed public trust at an all-time low of 19 percent. Pew Research Center for the People and the Press, "Public Trust in Government: 1958–2013," October 18, 2013, http://www.people-press.org/2013/10/18/trust-in-government-interactive/ (accessed June 18, 2014). This is in line with a Gallup survey conducted in September 2013 that indicated that Americans have dramatically lost trust in the U.S. government not only to address domestic issues but also to address international issues. Joy Wilke and Frank Newport, "Fewer Americans than Ever Trust Government to Handle Problems," *Gallup Politics*, September 13, 2013, http://www.gallup.com/poll/164393/fewer-americans-ever-trust-gov-handle-problems.aspx (accessed June 18, 2014). Finally, a December 2013 Associated Press/University of Chicago poll indicated that when asked "How confident are you in the ability of the FEDERAL government to make progress on the important problems and issues facing the country in 2014?," 70 percent of respondents answered "Not at all/Not very." The Associated Press-NORC Center for Public Affairs Research, "The People's Agenda: America's Priorities and Outlook for 2014," http://www.apnorc.org/projects/Pages/the-peoples-agenda-americas-priorities-and-outlook.aspx (accessed April 24, 2015).

[9] See Greg Miller, Julie Tate, and Barton Gellman, "Documents Reveal NSA's Extensive Involvement in Targeted Killing Program," *The Washington Post*, October 16, 2013,

The Alston Report of 2010 argued so, noting that "unlike a state's armed forces, its intelligence agents do not generally operate within a framework which places appropriate emphasis on ensuring compliance with international humanitarian law, rendering violations more likely."[10] When I asked a high-ranking Pentagon official at a lecture to explain the division of responsibility, he said he "could not go there" but did state that the military operates under defined legal restraints and that its members are made cognizant of legal rules at every level.[11] Another military officer who operates drones explained to me that CIA decisions could be made faster, and time was often critical.[12]

The perception thus exists that the CIA is less accountable than the military, and reactions to CIA-conducted drone strikes have thus been both outspoken and acted upon. In May 2012, the U.S. Ambassador to Pakistan Cameron Munter resigned because he felt undermined in critical diplomatic moments by CIA-conducted drone strikes of which he had no knowledge and over which he had no control.[13]

The shorthand around military and intelligence circles in Washington is the "Title 10 v. Title 50" debate, referring to title numbers in the U.S. statutes that govern the military and intelligence

---

http://www.washingtonpost.com/world/national-security/documents-reveal-nsas-extensive-involvement-in-targeted-killing-program/2013/10/16/29775278-3674-11e3-8a0e-4e2cf80831fc_story.html (accessed December 12, 2014); Micah Zenko, *Crumbling Wall between the Pentagon and CIA*, Council on Foreign Relations, April 28, 2011, http://www.cfr.org/united-states/crumbling-wall-between-pentagon-cia/p24812 (accessed December 12, 2014).

[10] United Nations, *Report of the Special Rapporteur on Extrajudicial, Summary or Arbitrary Executions Philip Alston*, UN Human Rights Council Report, UN Doc. A/HRC/14/24/Add. 6, May 28, 2010, 73. http://www2.ohchr.org/english/bodies/hrcouncil/docs/14session/A.HRC.14.24.Add6.pdf (accessed December 12, 2014).

[11] Senior military officer, in confidential discussion with the author, April 2014.

[12] Operational-level Air Force officer, in confidential discussion with the author, November 5, 2014.

[13] "Munter wanted the ability to sign off on drone strikes – and, when necessary, block them. Then CIA director Leon Panetta saw things differently. Munter remembers one particular meeting where they clashed. He said, 'I don't work for you,' and I said, 'I don't work for you,' the former ambassador recalls." Tara McKelvey, "A Former Ambassador to Pakistan Speaks Out," *The Daily Beast*, November 20, 2012, http://www.thedailybeast.com/articles/2012/11/20/a-former-ambassador-to-pakistan-speaks-out.html (accessed December 12, 2014).

services, respectively. What is implied, without a great deal of analysis, is that there are specified and separate roles and missions for the military and the intelligence agencies under U.S. law, and the statutory allocation should not be breached. The debate runs both ways: not only are involved Americans concerned about the increasing use of military force by intelligence agencies but the intelligence community also complains that the military is encroaching on its functions.

In a 2011 article, Andru Wall, a former legal adviser to the U.S. Joint Special Operations Command (JSOC), effectively debunks the idea of such encroachment: "Often unacknowledged, the essence of this concern is the belief that intelligence operatives live in a dark and shadowy world, while military forces are the proverbial knights on white horses."[14] Yet Wall also points out that the Secretary of Defense has significant authority over intelligence and covert activities, including joint supervision of the National Security Agency (NSA) and supervision over Cyber Command. The Defense Intelligence Agency is an intelligence-gathering agency within the Department of Defense (DoD), and JSOC is deeply involved in covert activities, including the raid that killed Osama bin Laden. Covert military operations under JSOC operate in secrecy and are less subject to scrutiny than overt military operations. In that respect, they share many characteristics of CIA covert action. The statutory distinction is illusory, even as perceptions remain palpable.

The argument that congressional oversight of intelligence operations is less intense than that of military matters also becomes less persuasive upon closer scrutiny. Since military and intelligence agencies operate under different legal authorities, they are subject to different congressional committee supervision. If a strike were a military operation, for example, directed by Central Command (CENTCOM), it would be taking place under a Title 10 authorization, accountable to the armed services committees of Congress.[15] These committees exercise detailed fiscal control over DoD expenditures and transfers of appropriated funds, and scrutinize the use

---

[14] Andru Wall, "Demystifying the Title 10 v. Title 50 Debate: Distinguishing Military Operations, Intelligence Activities and Covert Action," *Harvard National Security Law Journal* 3 (2011): 88.

[15] 10 U. S. Code sub. A, pt. I, ch. 3, §127 (2003).

of personnel.[16] A CIA action would come under Title 50, which requires presidential findings and notice to Congress.[17] The CIA reports to the Senate Select Committee on Intelligence (SSCI) as well as the Joint Intelligence Oversight Committee of Congress. Intelligence operations involving sensitive covert action require presidential approval and immediate notification of both the House Permanent Select Committee on Intelligence (HPSCI) and SSCI.[18] One could argue that such divided responsibility for one type of action weakens supervision, but perhaps the reverse is true: more committees mean more questions.[19] It is not clear which set of congressional committees, if any, exercises closer supervision. The preference for military control is probably based more on a military tradition of law-abidingness than on active congressional supervision, particularly after the intelligence agency abuses during the first decade of the twenty-first century. If anything, the rigor of congressional oversight in both areas may be open to question – again a problem heightened by the Snowden revelations.[20] I discuss alternative ways for providing objective accountability in the concluding sections.

Secrecy in role definition has led also to the suspicion of a policy vacuum, as well as lack of effective oversight. It is unclear to the public, both in the United States and abroad, who decides which strikes are undertaken and by which agency, and which actions are eschewed. It is not apparent that the CIA and military possess different enough operational skills to explain the division of responsibility. There have been a variety of assumptions about role allocation.

---

[16] David Nather, "Drones: Tough Talk, Little Scrutiny," *Politico*, February 9, 2013, http://www.politico.com/story/2013/02/drones-tough-talk-little-scrutiny-87405 .html (accessed December 12, 2014).

[17] Wall, "Demystifying the Title 10 v. Title 50 Debate," 102.

[18] Marshall Curtis Erwin, "Sensitive Covert Action Notifications: Oversight Options for Congress," Congressional Research Service, April 10, 2013, http://fas.org/sgp/ crs/intel/R40691.pdf (accessed April 17, 2015).

[19] Nather, "Drones."

[20] Michael V. Hayden, "Beyond Snowden: An NSA Reality Check," *World Affairs Journal*, January/February 2014, http://www.worldaffairsjournal.org/ article/beyond-snowden-nsa-reality-check (accessed December 12, 2014); Darren Samuelsohn, "Hill Draws Criticism over NSA Oversight," *Politico*, March 2, 2014, http://www.politico.com/story/2014/03/hill-draws-criticism-over-nsa-oversight-104151.html (accessed December 12, 2014).

In one version, the CIA has responsibility for Pakistan, the DoD
for Yemen, and both operate in Somalia. But it has been reported
that the drone strike that hit Anwar al-Awlaki, a terrorist on the
"kill list," was conducted by the CIA, while a military strike killed
his son – though both were killed in Yemen.[21] One commentator
thought all the assets belonged to the military but were leased to the
CIA, which has command and control of an undefined number of
missions and its own UAVs but has been asking for more.[22] Another
said assets were traded back and forth. Some observers suggest
that the allocation is a product of bureaucratic happenstance, like
crooked streets in a town that has grown from cow paths. "But,"
as Mark Mazzetti observed, "for all the secrecy, drone warfare has
been institutionalized, ensuring that the missions of the CIA and
the Pentagon continue to bleed together as the two organizations
fight for more resources to wage secret war."[23] In the area of targeted killing, as in counterinsurgency, contractors are widely used,
and although the facts are classified, investigative reporters indicate
that these contractors have been used in a military operational role.
Such accidents as a contracted civilian drone operator's participation in a 2010 U.S. strike that killed fifteen innocent Afghans only
underscores the degree of care required for targeted killing.[24] The
commitment to high standards of certainty and accountability are
hard to replicate outside of government personnel.[25] Even with government targeting, tragic mistakes occur, such as the killing of two

[21] Mazzetti, *The Way of the Knife*, 310.
[22] Greg Miller, "CIA Seeks to Expand Drone Fleet, Officials Say," *The Washington Post*, October 18, 2012, http://articles.washingtonpost.com/2012-10-18/world/35502344_1_qaeda-drone-fleet-cia-drones (accessed December 12, 2014).
[23] Mazzetti, *The Way of the Knife*, 313. Mazzetti goes on to say: "Sometimes, as in Yemen, the two agencies run parallel and competing drone operations. Other times they carve up the world and each take part of the remote controlled war – the CIA in Pakistan and the Pentagon running the drone war in Libya." See also Micah Zenko, "Clip the Agency's Wings," *Foreign Policy*, April 16, 2013, http://www.foreignpolicy.com/articles/2013/04/16/clip_the_agencys_wings_cia_drones (accessed December 12, 2014).
[24] David S. Cloud, "Civilian Contractors Playing Key Roles in U.S. Drone Operations," *Los Angeles Times*, December 29, 2011, http://articles.latimes.com/2011/dec/29/world/la-fg-drones-civilians-20111230 (accessed December 12, 2014).
[25] Ibid. See also Mazzetti, *The Way of the Knife*, 53.

western hostages, one of them a U.S. citizen, together with the ter-rorists that were holding them.[26]

Would there be fewer mistakes – like striking an innocent wed-ding party – if only the military were in charge? Would repercus-sions for those mistakes be more forthcoming? Does competition to strike the most enticing targets add friction to the relation-ship between actors? Does it lead to wasteful one-ups-manship? Unfortunately, there is no way to determine whether the current division results in smooth operations or confused overlap. It is equally plausible that there is considerable civil-military tension as it is that the relationship runs smoothly.

The White House is said to have announced a move toward greater military control over drones in a classified policy paper issued the day after the president's address to the National Defense University on May 23, 2013. The president's intent was under-scored by a direct statement a year later at West Point.[27] Although the move inspired press comments at the time, doubts remain as to whether the change actually took hold. Even several years "after President Obama signaled his desire to shift the campaign to the Defense Department, the Central Intelligence Agency's drone

---

[26] Scott Shane, "Drone Strikes Reveal Uncomfortable Truth: U.S. is Often Unsure About Who Will Die" *New York Times*, April 23, 2015, http://www.nytimes .com/2015/04/24/world/asia/drone-strikes-reveal-uncomfortable-truth-us-is-often-unsure-about-who-will-die.html?rref=world/asia&module=Ribbon& version=context&region=Header&action=click&contentCollection=Asia%20 Pacific&pgtype=article&_r=0 (accessed April 24, 2015). See also "Report of the Special Rapporteur on the Promotion and Protection of Human Rights and Fundamental Freedoms While Countering Terrorism, Ben Emmerson," February 28, 2014, A/HRC/20/5.

[27] Tabassum Zakaria and Mark Hosenball, "Pentagon to Take Over Some CIA Drone Operations: Sources," *Reuters*, May 20, 2013, http://www .reuters.com/article/2013/05/21/us-usa-drones-idUSBRE94K03720130521 (accessed December 12, 2014); President Barack H. Obama (speech, United States Military Academy, West Point, NY, May 28, 2014), White House official website, http://www.whitehouse.gov/the-press-office/2014/05/28/remarks-president-united-states-military-academy-commencement-ceremony (accessed October 2, 2014); New York City Bar Association, *The Legality under International Law of Targeted Killings by Drone Launched by the United States*, June 2014, 58, http://www2.nycbar.org/pdf/report/uploads/20072625-TheLegalityofTargetedInternationalKillingsbyUS-LaunchedDrones.pdf (accessed October 2, 2014).

operations center in Langley[, Virginia,] is still behind the vast majority of strikes."[28]

Unfortunately, secrecy about roles even clouds whatever developments in cooperation may have occurred. For example, it was reported in June 2014 that Special Operations Forces and the FBI working together captured Ahmed Abu Khattala, the alleged mastermind of the Benghazi attack on the U.S. consulate that killed Ambassador J. Christopher Stevens in 2012.[29] This implies a degree of cooperation, in stark contrast to the successive drone strikes – the first by the CIA that killed al-Awlaki and the second by the military that killed his son a few weeks later. But, given the ongoing secrecy shrouding these activities, the public has not been informed whether such cooperation resulted from an improved process, and, if so, how, or whether it was simply more fortuitous ad hoc-ery. The past several years have undoubtedly witnessed more discussion about the use of drones – a slight lifting of the curtain of secrecy. Still, this budding conversation has only served to highlight questions about the relationship between civilian and military roles and the legal undergirding that supports that allocation in a democracy.

Isolated revelations do not portend open public discourse and debate, and issues remain about the program's compliance with law. As new facts are revealed, it remains a question whether the President of the United States controls or can control clandestine military or quasi-military operations in important detail.[30] Yet such control is a bedrock principle of the civilian control that is essential to democracy. Michael Glennon may be correct that the national

[28] Greg Miller, "CIA Remains behind Most Drone Strikes, Despite Effort to Shift Campaign to Defense," *The New York Times*, November 25, 2013, http://www.washingtonpost.com/world/national-security/cia-remains-behind-most-drone-strikes-despite-effort-to-shift-campaign-to-defense/2013/11/25/c0c07a86-5386-11e3-a7f0-b79092923 2e1_story.html (accessed December 12, 2014).

[29] Karen DeYoung, Adam Goldman, and Julie Tate, "US Captures Benghazi Suspect in Secret Raid," *The Washington Post*, June 17, 2014, http://www.washingtonpost.com/world/national-security/us-captured-benghazi-suspect-in-secret-raid/2014/06/17/7ef8746e-f5cf-11e3-a3a5-42be35962a52_story.html (accessed December 12, 2014).

[30] See Benjamin McKelvey, note in "Due Process Rights and the Targeted Killing of Suspected Terrorists: The Unconstitutional Scope of the Executive Killing Power," *Vanderbilt Journal of Transnational Law* 44 (2011): 1358.

security establishment is an unaccountable bureaucratic substratum.[31] Such a dual structure might explain the current situation, but it does not help resolve it. Or what has been occurring may be better summarized by more of Komer's phrase "bureaucracy does its thing," which at least allows for the possibility that senior civilian leaders could reassert control if they so chose to do so, and could then change direction. Since President Obama was said to be reportedly taking steps to transfer control of drone warfare to the military, but it might be somewhat reassuring to the public to know that whether such a shift actually has taken place, and if traditional military legal oversight is firmly in place. Regardless of whether CIA drone operators are more skilled, more dedicated, and still needed, if they were to report to military supervisors and be subject to the same legal constraints as the military, this shift would be reassuring once made transparent. Any necessary legal adjustments should not prove insuperable.

[31] Michael J. Glennon, "National Security and Double Government," *Harvard National Security Journal* 5 (2014): 12. See also the discussion in Chapter 3.

8

The Legal Underpinnings for Targeted Killing by UAV

Framing the Issues

This book began with a quotation from the federal judge hearing the civil suit brought by the family of Anwar al-Awlaki in order to emphasize the fact that the variety of civilians involved in these shadowy conflicts even includes the judiciary, and to underscore the salience of legal issues to debates about how the United States should conduct operations in today's gray area of war. Those killings awakened the American public to the problems of UAV use and caused widespread international concern – even alarm – and an unusual amount of comment.[1] Questions about drone attacks

[1] "[T]he Awlaki case adds another wound to the body of human-rights protections that had hitherto been sacred. This action carves out the legal pathway for a state to silence not only external but internal dissent, by defining the citizen as an 'enemy of the state.' Legally it matters little that in this case Awlaki was indeed an enemy of the state. With the evidence being kept secret, the precedent has been set." Maajid Nawaz, "U.S. Drone Killing of Anwar al-Awlaki Reinforces Terrorists," *The Guardian*, October 1, 2011, http://www.theguardian.com/world/2011/oct/01/drone-killing-anwar-al-awlaki (accessed December 12, 2014). See also John J. Gibbons, "War on Terror: Life, Death, and Drones," *Los Angeles Times*, July 19, 2013, http://articles.latimes.com/2013/jul/19/opinion/la-oe-gibbons-targeted-killings-drones-20130719 (accessed December 12, 2014); Laura Raim, "The Legality of al-Awlaki's Death is in Question," trans., *Le Figaro*, October 10, 2011, http://www.lefigaro.fr/international/2011/10/01/01003-20111001ARTFIG00365-la-legalite-du-meurtre-d-al-awlaki-mise-en-question.php (accessed December 12, 2014); Harvey Silverglate, "Obama Crosses the Rubicon: The Killing of Anwar al-Awlaki," *Forbes*, October 6, 2011, http://www.forbes.com/sites/harveysilverglate/2011/10/06/obama-crosses-the-rubicon-the-killing-of-anwar-al-awlaki/ (accessed December 12, 2014); and Ken Anderson, "Anwar Al-Aulaqi Killed in Drone Strike in Yemen," *Opinio Juris*, September 30, 2011, http://opiniojuris.org/2011/09/30/anwar-al-aulaqi-killed-in-drone-strike-in-yemen/ (accessed December 12, 2014).

reached the federal courts before the executive branch officially acknowledged their existence.[2] The leaked February 2013 Department of Justice White Paper that developed legal justification for targeted killings of Americans was a complex, intricately detailed memorandum that addressed both U.S. domestic law and international law. But it raised as many questions as it answered.[3] An even more detailed classified legal memorandum was supplied to select members of Congress, and a redacted version made public in mid-2014, when it first seemed that its author, David Barron, would not receive the necessary votes for confirmation as a U.S. appellate judge.[4] Although officials have outlined the legal rationale for such actions to specialized audiences,[5] it took a U.S. Court of Appeals decision to compel the government to reveal a more detailed legal basis for targeted killings by UAVs.[6] The question of whether

[2] Nasser al-Awlaki filed an initial suit against the Obama administration for the deaths of his son and grandson in 2010. The case was dismissed for lack of standing and for raising "non-justiciable political questions." See al-Aulaqi v. Obama, 727 F. Supp. 2d 1 (D.D.C. 2010). A second complaint (al-Aulaqi v. Panetta) was filed in July 2012. For updated information, see al-Aulaqi v. Panetta, Legal Documents, American Civil Liberties Union, https://www.aclu.org/national-security/al-aulaqi-v-panetta-complaint (accessed December 12, 2014).

[3] Department of Justice White Paper, *Lawfulness of a Lethal Operation Directed against a U.S. Citizen Who Is a Senior Operational Leader of Al-Qa'ida or An Associated Force*, draft, November 8, 2011, http://www.fas.org/irp/eprint/doj-lethal.pdf (accessed December 12, 2014).

[4] Michael D. Shear and Scott Shane, "Congress to See Memo Backing Drone Attacks on Americans," *The New York Times*, February 6, 2013, http://www.nytimes.com/2013/02/07/us/politics/obama-orders-release-of-drone-memos-to-lawmakers.html?pagewanted=all&_r=0 (accessed December 12, 2014).

[5] Although earlier speeches, such as that of Harold Koh to the American Society of International Law in 2010, acknowledged targeted killing, they did not purport to explain its legal rationale; instead, they simply stated that such actions were legal. Attorney General Eric Holder did outline the legal basis for U.S. lethal action broadly in a speech at Northwestern University Law School, but this was to a specialized and somewhat narrow audience.

[6] The appointment of Professor David Barron to the U.S. Court of Appeals was held up until a Department of Justice memorandum on the legality of drones that had been written by him was released. NY Times v. US, Ct. of Appeals, 2d Cir, slip op, June 23, 2014. See Noah Bierman, "Barron Likely to Be Confirmed to Appeals Court," *Boston Globe*, May 20, 2014, http://www.bostonglobe.com/news/politics/2014/05/20/david-barron-author-controversial-drone-memo-looks-likely-for-confirmation-appeals-court-democrats-say/sCoPW4fmoaN9qgaWWxHUTL/story.html (accessed December 12, 2014); Rand

and when such operations are lawful – especially the targeting of U.S. citizens under American constitutional law – has only been grudgingly and partly addressed. The U.S. government has not fully and persuasively presented either the international nor the domestic legal basis for such operations.

Legal issues surrounding targeted killing differ from those of counterinsurgency, whose operations pose no major issues about legality, except perhaps in terms of the rationale for intervention in the first place. By contrast, targeted killing raises troubling questions of legality. These issues may only affect the definition of civil-military roles tangentially. But doubts about both U.S. domestic and international legality create problems for international allies, for American national leadership, for the public whose support is necessary, and for the men and women in the chain of command who both mandate and perform operations.

President Obama did address some of these mounting legal concerns in his 2013 National Defense University speech. He outlined the legal justification for targeted killing by stating:

America's actions are legal. We were attacked on 9/11. Within a week, Congress overwhelmingly authorized the use of force. Under domestic law, and international law, the United States is at war with al Qaeda, the Taliban, and their associated forces. We are at war with an organization that right now would kill as many Americans as they could if we did not stop them first. So this is a just war – a war waged proportionally, in last resort, and in self-defense.[7]

Legally, that statement would establish that the laws of armed conflict provide the justification for actions taken. Under international law, as under American domestic law, a set of rules governs when resort to force is permitted and permissible behavior on the battlefield. However, President Obama made another comment in the same address. He stated that "we must define our effort not as a

Paul, "Show Us the Drone Memos," *The New York Times*, May 11, 2014, http://www.nytimes.com/2014/05/12/opinion/show-us-the-drone-memos.html?_r=0 (accessed December 12, 2014).

[7] President Barack Obama (address, National Defense University, Washington, DC, May 23, 2013), http://www.whitehouse.gov/the-press-office/2013/05/23/remarks-president-national-defense-university (accessed December 12, 2014).

boundless 'global war on terror,' but rather as a series of persistent, targeted efforts to dismantle specific networks of violent extremists that threaten America."[8] That characterization contradicts the notion that there is a war on terror. Moreover, on other occasions, the Obama administration made clear that it was abandoning the concept of a "Global War on Terror."

Kinetic action in a situation that is less than war calls forth a different set of international legal rules. By downplaying the notion that by conducting these strikes the United States was engaging in "war" outside of Afghanistan and Iraq, the administration may have eased some diplomatic and domestic political concerns, but it may have made the legal issues more difficult. And, issues of domestic legality in such situations also might differ from those in wartime situations.

The Justice Department, in its Office of Legal Counsel memorandum (the Barron memorandum), whose redacted release was mandated by the Federal Court of Appeals for the Second Circuit on April 21, 2014,[9] took the position that the United States is in a global, noninternational armed conflict with non–state actors.[10] As I explain later in this chapter, that opinion maintains that such a situation permits the United States to strike the enemy wherever it might present a threat. Over time, and in a different administration, further doctrinal analysis may change or refine the American position. Nor does the American legal position seem to be shared even by some of our close allies. European allies are currently developing their own interpretations. Scholarly legal commentary, possible U.S. legislation, EU decisions or directives, U.S. Supreme Court opinions, and opinions by the International Court of Justice are likely to refine or alter the legal positions taken by the Barron memorandum. Although doctrinal refinements tend to remain the business of the legal and scholarly community, if an issue arises

---

[8] Ibid.

[9] Anwar Al-Aulaqi: FOIA Request – OLC Memo, https://www.aclu.org/national-security/anwar-al-aulaqi-foia-request-olc-memo (accessed December 12, 2014).

[10] But see the argument in Mary Ellen O'Connell, "The Choice of Law against Terrorism," *Journal of National Security Law and Policy* 4 (2010): 343–368.

that triggers moral outrage, the government is obliged to provide enough legal clarity to be comprehensible to a wider community.

President Obama couched further justification in moral and practical terms, arguing:

> Where foreign governments cannot or will not effectively stop terrorism in their territory, the primary alternative to targeted lethal action would be the use of conventional military options. As I've already said, even small special operations carry enormous risks. Conventional airpower or missiles are far less precise than drones, and are likely to cause more civilian casualties and more local outrage.[11]

Would a clearer legal framework make a difference to allies, to publics in the United States and around the world, and to those who perform operations? A democratic society demands reasonable legal justification – certainly in the long run.

A flowing legal scholarship has burgeoned on the legality of targeted killing, and it is not the purpose of this chapter to either repeat or argue with that body of discourse. It is sufficient for my purposes to demonstrate that the relevant legal commentary reveals serious issues of ambiguity and interpretation. In the area of targeted killing, it is not clear whether either new international agreements or, for the United States, changes in legislative authorization or further oversight could resolve some of the dilemmas that targeted killing poses. It is complex and difficult to be able to characterize the widespread threat of terrorism and insurgencies persuasively under international law. The plausibility of legal justification remains a problem. But it should not be necessary for the public to have access to legal memoranda only when they are leaked or produced by court order. The U.S. failure to even offer a plausible legal position to a broad domestic and international audience in terms that can be widely understood has diminished domestic and international confidence. Even worse, presidential insistence since 2001 that another large-scale terrorist attack must be avoided at all costs – a "not on my watch" mentality – has distorted both policy actions and legal justification.

---

[11] President Barack Obama (address, National Defense University).

Justification under International Law: When is a Strike Permissible?

Apart from permissible military action in a war zone, the basic justification for drone attacks when a nation is not at war is self-defense, based on Article 51 of the UN Charter, its historic antecedents in customary international law, and principles of necessity, proportionality and state responsibility. Article 51 reads: "Nothing in the present Charter shall impair the inherent right of individual or collective self defense if an armed attack occurs."[12] If that requirement were to be taken literally, it would require a physical attack before a response could be made. Therefore, some interpretations of customary law also permit acts of self-defense if there is imminence of an attack.[13] Daniel Bethlehem, former Legal Adviser of the United Kingdom Foreign & Commonwealth Office, explains the British view, paralleling at least part of the American government's position, which has not been fully and publicly articulated. He quotes Lord Peter Goldsmith:

It is argued by some that the language of Article 51 provides for a right of self-defence only in response to an actual armed attack. However, it has

---

[12] United Nations, Charter of the United Nations, 1 UNTS XVI (October 24, 1945), ch. 7, art. 51, http://www.refworld.org/docid/3ae6b3930.html (accessed December 12, 2014).

[13] See Oscar Schachter, "The Right of States to Use Armed Force," *Michigan Law Review* 82 (1984): 1634–1635; Jeh Johnson, "A Drone Court: Some Pros and Cons" (keynote address, Center on National Security, Fordham Law School, March 18, 2013), http://www.lawfareblog.com/2013/03/jeh-johnson-speech-on-a-drone-court-some-pros-and-cons/ (accessed December 12, 2014); Eric Holder (speech, Northwestern University School of Law, March 5, 2012), http://www.justice.gov/iso/opa/ag/speeches/2012/ag-speech-120305l.html (accessed December 12, 2014); United Nations, *Report of the Special Rapporteur on Extrajudicial, Summary or Arbitrary Executions Philip Alston*, UN Human Rights Council Report, UN Doc. A/HRC/14/24/Add. 6, May 28, 2010, 45 n. 92, 73, http://www2.ohchr.org/english/bodies/hrcouncil/docs/14session/A.HRC.14.24.Add6.pdf (accessed December 12, 2014): "Under a more permissive view that more accurately reflects State practice and the weight of scholarship, self-defense also includes the right to use force against a real and imminent threat when 'the necessity of that self-defense is instant, overwhelming, and leaving no choice of means, and no moment of deliberation.'" Harold Hongju Koh, "The Obama Administration and International Law" (speech, Annual Meeting of the American Society of International Law, Washington, DC, March 25, 2010), http://www.state.gov/s/l/releases/remarks/139119.htm (accessed December 12, 2014).

been the consistent position of successive United Kingdom Governments over many years that the right of self-defence under international law includes the right to use force where an armed attack is imminent. It is clear that the language of Article 51 was not intended to create a new right of self-defense. Article 51 recognizes the inherent right of self-defence that states enjoy under international law. That can be traced back to the "Caroline" incident in 1837 ... It is not a new invention. The Charter did not therefore affect the scope of the right of self-defence existing at that time in customary international law, which included the right to use force in anticipation of an imminent armed attack.

The Government's position is supported by the records of the international conference at which the UN charter was drawn up and by state practice since 1945. It is therefore the Government's view that international law permits the use of force in self-defense against an imminent attack *but does not authorize the use of force to mount a pre-emptive strike against a threat that is more remote.* (emphasis added). [14]

The United States has relied heavily on the justification of imminence in attempting to justify drone strikes against individuals and small groups far from actual armed conflict hostilities. [15] That justification seems to be in accordance with the president's statements that we

[14] Lord Peter Goldsmith, quoted in Daniel Bethlehem, "Self-Defense against an Imminent or Actual Armed Attack by Nonstate Actors," *American Journal of International Law* 106 (2012): 771. A complete and careful analysis of the U.S. position was developed in June 2014 by the Committee on International Law of the New York City Bar Association in *The Legality under International Law of Targeted Killings by Drones Launched by The United States*, especially 64–69, 84–100, http://www2.nycbar.org/pdf/report/uploads/20072625-TheLegalityofTargetedInternationalKillingsbyUS-LaunchedDrones.pdf (accessed April 25, 2015). Some legal scholars specializing in the law on resort to force, however, do not share the view that the plain terms of Article 51 may be ignored. In addition, they point out that complying with the principles of necessity, proportionality, and state responsibility in self-defense depends on evidence of the actual armed attack that is occurring. See, e.g., Mary Ellen O'Connell, "Dangerous Departures from the Law of Self-Defense," *American Journal of International Law* 107 (2013): 380–386 (response to Daniel Bethlehem, citing Olivier Corten, Yoram Dinstein, and Christine Gray).

[15] John Brennan, "Strengthening Our Security by Adhering to Our Values and Laws" (speech, Harvard Law School, Cambridge, MA, September 16, 2011), http://www.whitehouse.gov/the-press-office/2011/09/16/remarks-john-o-brennan-strengthening-our-security-adhering-our-values-an (accessed December 12, 2014); John Brennan, "The Ethics and Efficacy of the President's Counterterrorism Strategy" (speech, Woodrow Wilson International Center for Scholars, Washington, DC, April 30, 2012), http://www.wilsoncenter.org/event/the-efficacy-and-ethics-us-counterterrorism-strategy (accessed December 12, 2014).

are engaged in specific targeted efforts to dismantle networks of threatening terrorists, and underscores the ambiguity of the gray area.[16] But whether a particular threat is imminent or remote must be justified on a factual basis. And whether the targeted killing of an individual or small group, disassociated with the state where they are present, can be justified under UN Charter Article 51 is an argument that has caused ongoing controversy.[17] The American military response to 9/11 – "Operation Enduring Freedom" in October 2001, attacking the Taliban in Afghanistan – complied with Article 51 and its clause of that "measures taken by Members in exercising this right of self-defense shall be immediately reported to the Security Council…."[18] But the United States has not complied with that requirement in most of its UAV strikes thereafter. And although mostly discussed among scholars, some argue that a threat need only be imminent at the time force is initiated and that once the Article 51 right to self-defense has been triggered, continued use of force does not require a regular re-assessment of imminence.[19]

However, the U.S. Justice Department, in the Barron memorandum, based its argument primarily on the position that the United States was on a wartime footing, stating:

[W]e conclude that DoD would carry out its operation [the one that killed al-Awlaki] as part of the non-international armed conflict between the

---

[16] Another issue is whether small attacks linked together can amount to the status of an "armed attack" ("accumulation doctrine"). See a discussion contending the persuasiveness of this argument in New York City Bar Association, *Legality under International Law of Targeted Killings*, 78–79.

[17] See the extended discussion about the principles suggested by Daniel Bethlehem, "Self-Defense against an Imminent or Actual Armed Attack by Nonstate Actors," *American Journal of International Law* 106 (2012): 769–777, and Mary Ellen O'Connell, "Dangerous Departures from the Law of Self-Defense," *American Journal of International Law* 107 (2013): 380–386, including Daniel Bethlehem's response to comments and criticisms about his principles.

[18] United Nations, Charter of the United Nations, ch. VII, art. 51, "Action with Respect to Threats to the Peace, Breaches, and Acts of Aggression," http://www .un.org/en/documents/charter/chapter7.shtml (accessed December 12, 2014).

[19] Kenneth Anderson, "The U.S. Government Position on Imminence and Active Self-Defense," *Lawfare* (blog), February 7, 2013, http://www.lawfareblog .com/2013/02/the-us-government-position-on-imminence-and-active-self-defense/ (accessed December 12, 2014). See also Department of Justice White Paper, 7–8 and Robert Chesney, "Postwar," *Harvard National Security Law Journal* 5 (2014): 305–333.

United States and al-Qaida, and thus, on those facts, the operation would comply with international law so long as DoD would conduct it in accord with the applicable laws of war that govern targeting in such a conflict.[20]

In so doing, under international law, the memorandum had to over-come the interpretation of the Geneva Convention Common Article 3 that such noninternational armed conflicts only meant civil wars. To do so, the memorandum then relied on the Supreme Court case of *Hamdan v. Rumsfeld*[21] to justify the position that Common Article 3 covered the conflict between a state and a non-state actor such as al-Qaeda. The facts and issues in *Hamdan* were entirely different from those in the al-Awlaki case. The Hamdan Court used the determination that the United States was in a non-international armed conflict with al-Qaeda as a building block to reach the major issue in the case – the legality of the Military Commissions Act for detention in Guantanamo. Still addressing international law, the "Barron memorandum" then had to justify the fact that the conflict could legally be extended beyond the immediate battle-field of Afghanistan in order for the rule to cover a drone strike in Yemen. The same argument was made as that in the leaked Justice Department White Paper of 2013, arguing that the unconventionally fluid nature of terrorist organizations that operate beyond national borders require broad geographic reach to protect and defend the homeland. Both memoranda also rely on the negative: no authority restricts such an interpretation. The issue of invading sovereignty is addressed here separately, as is targeting an American citizen.

Who May Be Targeted

Under international rules, it is far from clear that a legally justifi-able response to the 2001 al-Qaeda armed attack can be stretched

---

[20] David J. Barron to Eric H. Holder, July 16, 2010, "Applicability of Federal Criminal Laws and the Constitution to Contemplated Lethal Operations against Shaykh Anwar al-Aulaqi," U.S. Department of Justice, Office of Legal Counsel, Office of the Assistant Attorney General, 23–24, https://www.aclu.org/sites/default/files/field_document/2014-06-23_barron-memorandum.pdf (accessed April 14, 2015).

[21] Hamdan v. Rumsfeld, 548 U. S. 557 (2006); Hamdi v. Rumsfeld, 542 U. S. 507 (2004); and Boumediene v. Bush, 553 U. S. 723 (2008).

to include indefinite use of force not only against al-Qaeda but also against the Afghan Taliban, the Pakistani Taliban, other Pakistani terrorist organizations such as Lashkar-e-Taiba; al-Qaeda in the Arabian Peninsula (AQAP), al-Shaba'ab in Somalia, and other terrorist groups. Authorization for use of force against ISIS, formed after 2001 and repudiated by Al Q'aeda, is especially problematic.[22] Far greater public disclosure of the underlying facts would be required to provide the necessary confidence that the requisite linkages exist in place and time.

Under both the interpretation that states have a right of self-defense against attacks by non-state actors and the interpretation that the United States and its allies are in an ongoing armed conflict with non–state actors,[23] issues remain about *which* non–state actors may be legitimately targeted. The decision in each case requires an interpretation of whether such a strike meets the standards of imminence of attack by those persons, whether a strike meets the requirements of state responsibility, and whether the killing is proportionate to the threat. Even more rigid standards are imposed by international human rights law than by the laws of armed conflict.[24] But serious questions of both fact and law remain regarding whether international law plausibly permits the United States to meld a collection of Islamic terrorist organizations into one single, worldwide actor that can be attacked in many different and seemingly unrelated sovereign states indefinitely.[25]

Such connections may indeed exist, as is the case in Yemen and generally for AQAP. But these connections may be merely verbal assertions by domestically oriented terrorist groups. Such incidents

---

[22] Department of Justice White Paper, I, 3; see also Craig Martin, "Going Medieval: Targeted Killing, Self Defense, and the Jus ad Bellum Regime," in *Targeted Killings: Law and Morality in an Asymmetrical World*, ed. Claire Finkelstein et al., (Oxford: Oxford University Press, 2012), 223.

[23] See, for example, United Nations Security Council resolution 1368, UN Doc. S/RES/1368, September 12, 2001, http://www.un.org/News/Press/docs/2001/SC7143.doc.htm (accessed December 12, 2014); United Nations Security Council resolution 1373, UN Doc. S/RES/1373, September 28, 2001; Hamdan v. Rumsfeld, 548 U. S. 557 (2006); Hamdi v. Rumsfeld, 542 U. S. 507 (2004); and Boumediene v. Bush, 553 U. S. 723 (2008).

[24] New York City Bar Association, *Legality under International Law of Targeted Killings*.

[25] Ibid.

as the al-Shaba'ab attack on the Westgate Mall in Nairobi in
September 2013 and its massacre of nearly 150 university students in Kenya in April 2015 do suggest more than an in-country
intent.[26] Even so, the evidence officially provided to the public that
the myriad terrorist groups now in the crosshairs of U.S. drones in
fact all stem from an original (legally sanctioned) al-Qaeda source
has not been factually developed, at least not publicly, convincing
though it may be in classified accounts.[27] To be persuasive, the
argument for the legality of targeting such entities must be based
on a continuing specific threat posed by terrorist organizations
that have a relationship to the original al-Qaeda – and it must be
made public. Professor Jack Goldsmith, who is otherwise supportive of targeted killings, states: "If the organizations are 'inflated'
enough to be targeted with military force, why cannot they be
mentioned publicly? [There is] a countervailing very important
interest in the public knowing whom the government is fighting
against in its name."[28]

Another requirement of the laws of armed conflict is that no
alternative to the use of force is available for targeting a particular
individual or group. This case of "necessity" was effectively made
to the UN Security Council after 9/11 when the Taliban government

[26] Jeffrey Gettleman, Isma'il Kushkush, and Rukmini Callimachi, "Somali Militants
Kill 147 at Kenyan University," *The New York Times*, April 2, 2015, http://www
.nytimes.com/2015/04/03/world/africa/garissa-university-college-shooting-in-
kenya.html?_r=0 (accessed April 14, 2015).

[27] Rachel Briggs, "The Changing Face of al Qaeda" (discussion paper, Institute
for Strategic Dialogue, 2012); "Who Runs al-Qaeda?," *The Economist*,
August 8, 2013, http://www.economist.com/blogs/economist-explains/2013/08/
economist-explains-5 (accessed December 12, 2014); Ben Hubbard, "The
Franchising of Al Qaeda," *The New York Times*, January 25, 2014, http://www
.nytimes.com/2014/01/26/sunday-review/the-franchising-of-al-qaeda.html?_r=0
(accessed December 12, 2014). The connections between al-Qaeda and al-Qaeda
in the Arabian Peninsula (AQAP) seem well established. See New York City Bar
Association, *Legality under International Law of Targeted Killings*, 30–47 and
associated footnotes.

[28] Cora Currier, "Who Are We at War With? That's Classified," *ProPublica*, July 26,
2013, http://www.propublica.org/article/who-are-we-at-war-with-thats-classified
(accessed December 12, 2014). See also Jennifer Daskal and Stephen I. Vladeck,
"After the AUMF," *Harvard National Security Journal* 5 (2014): 122–123,
http://harvardnsj.org/wp-content/uploads/2014/01/Daskal-Vladeck-Final1.pdf
(accessed April 14, 2015).

was harboring al-Qaeda. UN Security Council resolutions in 2001 were supportive and strong in their demand for state efforts to evict such terrorist groups.[29]

In later strikes in other nations, including the raid that killed Osama bin Laden in Abbotobad, the justification of "necessity" has been bolstered by the argument that a host nation is "unwilling or unable" to deal with terrorists within its borders – a complex doctrine that is developed later in this chapter.[30]

Although the criteria for specific targeting decisions must remain classified, it is questionable whether such cases as a group of unidentified young men gathering in a suspicious location represents "imminence" sufficient to justify a targeted attack known as a "signature strike." Thus both *jus ad bellum*, which means in the parlance of the laws of war "the justification for attack," and *jus in bello*, or "acceptable conduct in war," discussed later in this chapter, demand standards of necessity and proportionality, although the meaning may differ in these two different contexts.[31]

Where Are Attacks Permissible: Sovereignty Issues in Defining the War Zone

To the extent that the drone strikes may be a legally permissible form of kinetic action to eliminate an imminent threat or to prevent a spreading amorphous terrorist campaign, the question remains whether such strikes are permissible anywhere, any time.[32] Any attacks on the sovereign soil of another country with which we are

---

[29] See United Nations Security Council resolutions 1368 and 1373. Together, these resolutions express both acknowledgment of appropriate reliance on chapter VII of the Charter and the gravity of the terrorist attack by the requirements imposed on all member states, inter alia, to prevent the movement of terrorists across borders, to evict terrorists from their borders, and to cooperate to prevent financing of terrorist activities; http://www.un.org/press/en/2001/SC7143.doc.htm (accessed April 18, 2015) and http://www.un.org/en/sc/ctc/specialmeetings/2012/docs/United%20Nations%20Security%20Council%20Resolution%201373%20%282001%29.pdf (accessed April 18, 2015).

[30] Barron memorandum, 24–26.

[31] Gabor Rona and Raha Wala, "No Thank You to a Radical Rewrite of the Jus ad Bellum," *American Journal of International Law* 107, no. 2 (April 2013): 386.

[32] U.S. domestic law prohibits assassinations by any "person employed by or acting on behalf of the United States Government." Executive Order 123333, 87 Stat.

not at war ordinarily require the consent of its government. The
United States received such permission from Yemen before its govern-
ment collapsed, as well as from the tenuous government in Somalia.[33]
The United States previously inferred Pakistan's "tacit consent," but
Pakistan's vocal disapproval of drone strikes following the 2011
Osama bin Laden raid makes it harder to assume that consent was
not revoked, unless, of course, secret arrangements have been made
and the outrage was for domestic Pakistani public consumption.[34]
While justification for violating sovereignty might turn on a factual
demonstration of imminence of attack on the U.S. homeland, its
embassies, or bases, it is hard to argue that any and all suspected terrorists may be freely targeted throughout the world.[35]

555, pt. 2, para. 11. See also Michael N. Schmitt, "State Sponsored Assassination
in International and Domestic Law," *Yale Journal of International Law* 17
(1992): 609–686. Schmitt notes that the prohibition would not apply to a wartime situation. Finally, Harold Koh, in his address to the American Society of
International Law, brushed the use of the assassination prohibition to prevent
targeted killing by stating that "under domestic law, the use of lawful weapons
systems – consistent with the applicable laws of war – for precision targeting
of specific high-level belligerent leaders when acting in self-defense or during an
armed conflict is not unlawful, and hence does not constitute 'assassination.'"
Koh therefore lays out effectively four reasons why the Executive Order does
not apply: the targeting program uses: (1) lawful weapons (2) to precisely target (3) a high-level belligerent (4) in a situation where the United States is acting *either* in self-defense or in war. See Koh, "The Obama Administration and
International Law."

[33] Karen DeYoung, "U.S. Recognizes Somalia, Citing Success of a Campaign
against Militants," *The Washington Post*, January 17, 2013, http://articles
.washingtonpost.com/2013-01-17/world/36410076_1_somalia-somali-clan-
leader-mohamud (accessed December 12, 2014).

[34] Adam Entous, Siobham Gorman, and Evan Perez, "U.S. Unease over Drone
Strikes," *The Wall Street Journal*, December 26, 2012, http://www.wsj.com/
articles/SB10000872396390444100404577641520858011452 (accessed April
18, 2015). See also Karen DeYoung. "Pakistani Ambassador to U.S. Calls CIA
Drone Strikes a 'Clear Violation,'" *The Washington Post*, February 5, 2013, http://
articles.washingtonpost.com/2013-02-05/world/36756792_1_afghan-taliban-
cia-drone-strikes-afghan-militants (accessed December 12, 2014).

[35] Jordan Paust, "Self-Defense Targetings of Non-State Actors and Permissibility of
U.S. Use of Drones in Pakistan," *Journal of Transnational Law and Policy* 19,
no. 2 (2009): 237–280; See" Mary Ellen O'Connell, "The Questions Brennan
Can't Dodge," *The New York Times*, February 6, 2013, http://www.nytimes
.com/2013/02/07/opinion/the-questions-brennan-cant-dodge.html (accessed April
14, 2015). "[D]rone attacks have been carried out in Yemen, Somalia and Pakistan

The United States contends it may strike in a sovereign state's territory without consent if it is determined that "the host nation is unwilling or unable to suppress the threat posed by the individual target."[36] While the international community recognized and supported the American invasion of Afghanistan, an analysis of UN Security Council resolutions on Afghanistan, the Taliban, and al-Qaeda from before and during the war reveals that the UN Security Council did not address the issue that the military campaign against al-Qaeda might extend beyond the borders of Afghanistan.[37] As mentioned, both the "Barron memorandum" and the earlier Department of Justice White Paper point to the unconventionally fluid nature of terrorist organizations as grounds for acting to protect the United States, without geographic constraints:

Particularly in a non-international armed conflict, where terrorist organizations may move their operations from one country to another, the determination of whether a particular operation would be part of an ongoing armed conflict would require consideration of the particular facts and circumstances in each case, including the fact that transnational non-state organizations such as al Qaeda may have no single site serving as their base of operations.[38]

The White Paper admits, but is not deterred by, the lack of legal authority.[39] This "unwilling or unable" standard also seems to argue the negative. It makes the case that if no international agreement nor any judicial precedent delineates geographic limits to reach transnational non-state actors, no sovereignty limits are

and may soon begin in Libya, Mali and Nigeria. None of these countries have attacked America, so no right of self-defense can be invoked under the United Nations Charter."

[36] Department of Justice White Paper, 1–2.

[37] Mumtaz Baloch, a Pakistani diplomat, explores these issues in an unpublished paper: "Implications of the Use of Drones on State Sovereignty" (thesis, Fletcher School of Law and Diplomacy, Tufts University, 2013), 19.

[38] Department of Justice White Paper, 4.

[39] "The Department has not found any authority for the proposition that when one of the parties to an armed conflict plans and executes operations from a base in a new nation, an operation to engage the enemy in that location cannot be part of the original armed conflict, and thus subject to the laws of war governing that conflict, unless the hostilities become sufficiently intense and protracted in the new location. That does not appear to be the rule of the historical practice." Department of Justice White Paper, 4.

imposed – so long as the host country's own efforts to curb the non-state enemy are judged insufficient.[40] That standard does seem to fill a gap in the law of self-defense. Ashley Deeks and others find support in the laws of neutrality, and prior use of the concept.[41] The doctrine was developed to permit one belligerent to respond to a co-belligerent's use of a neutral country when that neutral fails to meet its obligation to repel such use of its territory.[42] Professor Jack Goldsmith concurs:

> This standard is not settled in international law, but it is sufficiently grounded in law and practice that no American president charged with keeping the country safe could refuse to exercise international self-defense rights when presented with a concrete security threat in this situation. The "unwilling or unable" standard was almost certainly the one the United States relied on in the Osama bin Laden raid inside Pakistan.[43]

Yet as Deeks points out, "unwilling or unable" still lacks clear legal content or a well-balanced test to provide it with legitimacy. It is "incompletely theorized."[44] She therefore offers some common-sense tests that might help create greater legitimacy. In summary, they include: (1) consent or cooperation from the territorial state to an intervention; (2) the seriousness of the threat to the victim state; (3) a request that the territorial state act in a timely manner; (4) an articulate, reasonable assessment of the territorial state's capability; (5) proportionate means used by the victim state; and (6) prior inter-actions between the victim state and the territorial state.

However, nations have not attempted to develop such exten-sive factual justification for the doctrine in situations where it has been relied on. Moreover, other scholars argue that the current U.S. approach does not represent state practice.[45] Even in Deeks' case study of a raid by Colombia into Peru to prevent lethal attacks

---

[40] Sikander Ahmed Shah, *International Law and Drone Strikes in Pakistan: The Legal and Socio-Political Aspects* (London: Routledge, 2014), 73–95.

[41] Ashley Deeks, "Unwilling or Unable: Towards a Normative Framework for Extra-Terrritorial Self Defense," *Virginia Law Review* 52 (2012): 483.

[42] Ibid., 499–500.

[43] Jack Goldsmith, "Fire When Ready," *Foreign Policy*, March 19, 2012, (accessed December 12, 2014).

[44] Deeks, "Unwilling or Unable," 505.

[45] Michael J. Glennon, "Law, Power, and Principles," *American Journal of International Law* 107, no. 2 (April 2013): 378; Mary Ellen O'Connell,

in its homeland, the Organization of American States (OAS) found the cross-border attack unjustified.[46] To the extent that the "unwilling or unable" doctrine is needed and relied on, wider acceptance can only be gained with some public acknowledgment that a careful factual analysis of the sort proposed by Deeks has been made.

The legal and policy issues of drone strikes in the Northwest Federally Administered Tribal Areas (FATA) and the Northwest Frontier Province of Pakistan, on the Haqqani leadership, and even the killing of Osama bin Laden so close to the Pakistani military academy are not simple. Pakistan is not, strictly speaking, a war zone, yet it appears that it has allowed its territory to be available to terrorists and insurgents to plan and carry out attacks against Afghan and ISAF troops, or failed to take adequate preventive measures. There was a strong, if unspoken, perception in parts of the U.S. government that Pakistan was colluding with the Taliban and even al-Qaeda. That sentiment was made explicit by Admiral Mike Mullen in his testimony before the Senate Armed Services committee on September 22, 2011, when he said: "In choosing to use violent extremism as an instrument of policy, the government of Pakistan and most especially the Pakistani army and ISI jeopardizes not only the prospect of our strategic partnership, but Pakistan's opportunity to be a respected nation with legitimate regional influence."[47]

The legal justification may be on somewhat firmer footing in Pakistan than in other nations. ISAF troops have been engaged in legitimate military action in neighboring Afghanistan, where they have been under constant attack emanating from Pakistan. But the issue of "hot pursuit" is a maritime legal concept that is not often relied on in this context, even though respect for sovereignty has been breached with as thin a rationale.[48] After troop withdrawal,

---

"Dangerous Departures," *American Journal of International Law* 107, no. 2 (April 2013): 380.

[46] Deeks, "Unwilling or Unable," 539–540, especially n. 198.

[47] Michael Mullen (statement on Afghanistan and Iraq to the Senate Armed Services Committee, September 22, 2011), http://www.cfr.org/afghanistan/mullens-testimony-afghanistan-iraq-before-senate-armed-services-committee-september-2011/p26021 (accessed December 12, 2014).

[48] See Lionel Beehner, *Can States Invoke Hot Pursuit to Hunt Rebels?*, Council on Foreign Relations Backgrounder, June 7, 2007, http://www.cfr.org/iraq/can-states-invoke-hot-pursuit-hunt-rebels/p13440 (accessed December 12, 2014).

the only justification may be imminence of attack on the few troops remaining, or by request of the government of Pakistan.

Pakistan may be a "frenemy," but it is a sovereign nation and a declared ally to which the United States continues to provide liberal amounts of financial and military assistance.[49] The politics of the relationship have been as wicked as the legal issues. America has been dependent on Pakistan for supply routes for troop support in Afghanistan, and Pakistan's displeasure has been expressed by choking off those routes. After ISAF departs, the future of Afghanistan's government will be deeply affected by its neighbor's behavior and its potential for disruption.[50]

The 2014 bombing of ISIS-held territory in Syria, another country whose consent was not secured, was tersely justified by Samantha Power as a response to a request from Iraq to deal with the "serious threats of continuing attacks from ISIL coming out of safe havens in Syria." Power's letter to Secretary General of the United Nations Ban Ki-Moon relied on two legal doctrines. First, she argued that Syria is "unwilling and unable" to "prevent the use of its territory for those attacks."[51] Second, the Article 51 inherent right includes both collective as well as individual self-defense.[52]

The doctrine is used mostly in maritime cases, enshrined in Article 111 of the 1982 UN Convention on the Law of the Sea. It is questionable as a matter of international law for the pursuit of insurgents into Pakistan.

[49] Hassan Abbas, "Pakistan 2020: A Vision for Building a Better Future" (report, Pakistan 2020 Study Group, Asia Society, May 2011), 51, http://asiasociety .org/files/pdf/as_pakistan%202020_study_group_rpt.pdf (accessed December 12, 2014).

[50] Justified concerns about nuclear proliferation and inadequate stewardship of its nuclear arsenal also require a healthier ongoing relationship than now exists. It is hard to say whether a policy of restraint or military boldness will prevail. Dexter Filkins, "We Don't Know Which Side the Pakistanis Are On," *Frontline*, May 2011, http://www.pbs.org/wgbh/pages/frontline/ afghanistan-pakistan/secret-war/dexter-filkins-we-dont-know-what-side-the- pakistanis-are-on/ (accessed December 12, 2014).

[51] It is ironic that Assad offered to cooperate with the United States and thus was presumably "willing," but the United States did not want any Syrian government control over targeting, given Assad's grim agenda of targeting all opposition.

[52] Samantha Power to Ban Ki-Moon, September 23, 2014, http://www.cbsnews.com/ htdocs/pdf/00_2014/09-2014/USlettertoSecretaryGeneral092314.pdf (accessed October 31, 2014).

Unfortunately, no full public legal analysis was given at the time to support that claim. In *Nicaragua v. the United States of America*, the International Court of Justice (ICJ) rejected the argument of collective self-defense when the United States applied it on behalf of El Salvador to justify the U.S. attacks on Nicaragua.[53] The argument of collective self-defense for Iraq may be somewhat more plausible on the facts, but such an argument was not developed at the time.[54]

President Obama, in his National Defense University (NDU) address, stated: "To do nothing in the face of terrorist networks would invite far more civilian casualties – not just in our cities at home and our facilities abroad, but also in the very places like Sana'a and Kabul and Mogadishu where terrorists seek a foothold." He continued:

[I]t is false to assert that putting more boots on the ground is less likely to result in civilian deaths or less likely to create enemies in the Muslim world. The results would be more U.S. deaths, more Black Hawks down, more confrontations with local populations, and an inevitable mission creep in support of such raids that could easily escalate into new wars.[55]

Thus, on the basis of total resulting harm to civilians, Obama justified military action, but especially action of a specific type – targeted killings. This policy argument may have merit – it is a cautious case made for immediate self-protection, but it provides no further legal justification. Moreover, this exercise of the President's obligation to keep a nation safe may only achieve a short-term benefit. Assuring near-term safety – "not on my watch" – may only be purchased at the price of long-term safety – at significant opportunity cost. Two significant risks exist. First, as mentioned, there is a risk of "blowback." It can be argued that widespread targeted killing in nations that pose no immediate threat outside their own

---

[53] *Case Concerning Military and Paramilitary Activities in and Against Nicaragua* (Judgement) [1986] International Court of Justice Report 14. See Kathleen Hennessey and Christie Parsons, "Obama Faces Hurdles at UN Security Council," *The Los Angeles Times*, September 22, 2014, http://www.latimes.com/world/middleeast/la-fg-obama-isis-20140923-story.html (accessed December 12, 2014).

[54] Ibid. The fact that ISIS attacks have largely originated in Syria, even though supported by Iraqi Sunnis, and the Iraqi government plea for cross-border action seem to present a stronger case than the meager support that Nicaragua was giving the Salvadorean rebels. A strong U.S. argument developing that factual distinction would have been useful.

[55] President Barack Obama (address, National Defense University).

immediate territories, such as Yemen, may produce new generations of terrorists who are more dangerous than those killed, and who may, as ISIS has, widen their threats and actions. Second, the risk of armed drone proliferation presents a future risk to American and its allies. Unarmed drones are already a safety hazard.[56] Technology will not remain in one corner of the globe.

Terrorism may indeed be ubiquitous and pose ongoing threats to the United States, but if there were unaddressed terrorist activities in NATO countries, such as Germany or Turkey, a U.S. drone strike without authorization would not occur, nor any act other than an attempt to extradite and thereafter to prosecute, even when responses are slow to materialize.

Furthermore, even America's staunchest allies have rejected the U.S. position on the ability to strike foreign sovereign territory without consent. The European Union passed a resolution on February 27, 2014, stating that "drone strikes outside a declared war by a State on the territory of another State without the consent of the latter or of the UN Security Council constitute a violation of international law and of the territorial integrity and sovereignty of that country."[57] The resolution contained an even broader condemnation of extra-judicial killings. Concerned about the findings in the Emmerson Report, a further resolution condemning extrajudicial killings and calling for transparency and accountability by the EU nations that cooperated in such programs was tabled in December 2014.

Jus in Bello: What Is Permissible in War

U.S. officials also insist that drone strikes are consistent with principles of legal use of force under international law once the hurdle of entering into conflict has been passed. No adequate definition or

---

[56] Nick Wingfield, "Now, Anyone Can Buy a Drone. Heaven Help Us," *The New York Times*, November 26, 2014, http://www.nytimes.com/2014/11/27/technology/personaltech/as-drones-swoop-above-skies-thrill-seeking-stunts-elicit-safety-concerns.html (accessed April 17, 2015). See also Benjamin Wittes and Gabriella Blum, *The Future of Violence: Robots and Germs, Hackers and Drones – Confronting a New Age of Threat* (New York: Basic Books, 2015).

[57] European Parliament resolution on the use of armed drones, 2014/2567, RSP, February 25, 2014, RC\1021121EN.doc.

criteria have been fully developed for the same principles of necessity, distinction, and proportionality that are demanded for actions once in war.[58] Nor has American policy that distinguishes combatants from noncombatants – or "distinction" – been made clear by government lawyers although direct participants may certainly be targeted. The international legal principle of distinction, as enshrined in Article 48 of Additional Protocol I of 1977 to the Geneva Convention, requires that parties to a conflict distinguish between combatants and civilians and target only military objectives.[59] Civilians who are directly participating in hostilities may be targeted when engaged directly in hostilities. The term "unlawful combatant" has been used in domestic law in the United States, but the concept is not enshrined in the Geneva Conventions.[60] Nor is there plausible justification for "signature strikes" that target groups of unidentified young men. The practice of signature strikes reflects a questionable interpretation of the principle of distinction.[61] Micah Zenko states:

President Obama extended and expanded this practice into Yemen which "in effect counts all military age males in a strike zone as combatants

---

[58] Department of Justice White Paper, 8. See also the Barron memorandum.

[59] "Protocol Additional to the Geneva Conventions of 12 August 1949, and relating to the Protection of Victims of International Armed Conflicts (Protocol I), 8 June 1977," International Committee of the Red Cross, https://www.icrc.org/applic/ihl/ihl.nsf/7c4d08d9b287a42141256739003e636b/f6c8b9fee14a77fdc125641e0052b079 (accessed April 17, 2015). See Also Additional Protocol II, Article 13.

[60] Because there is there is no definition of a "combatant" in non-international armed conflict (NIAC), the ICRC has proposed a "continuous combatant function" to serve as a proxy for defining a combatant in a NIAC to fill this gap in international law. Nils Melzer, "Interpretive Guidance on the Notion of Direct Participation in Hostilities Under International Humanitarian Law," International Committee of the Red Cross, May 2009, https://www.icrc.org/eng/assets/files/other/icrc-002-0990.pdf (accessed April 18, 2015). See also Jakob Kellenberger, "Current Challenges Faced by the International Committee of the Red Cross and International Humanitarian Law" (speech, New York City, March 5, 2008), International Committee on the Red Cross, https://www.icrc.org/eng/resources/documents/misc/ihl-challenges-050308.htm (accessed April 18, 2015); "Direct Participation in Hostilities: Questions and Answers," International Committee of the Red Cross, June 2, 2009, https://www.icrc.org/eng/resources/documents/faq/direct-participation-ihl-faq-020609.htm (accessed April 18, 2015).

[61] Jo Becker and Scott Shane, "Secret 'Kill List' Proves a Test of Obama's Principles and Will," *The New York Times*, May 29, 2012, http://www.nytimes.com/2012/05/29/world/obamas-leadership-in-war-on-al-qaeda.html?pagewanted=all&_r=0 (accessed December 12, 2014).

unless there is explicit intelligence posthumously proving them innocent." Human rights advocates, international law experts and current and former U.S. officials dispute whether this methodology meets the principle of distinction for the use of force.[62]

As Micah Zenko also observed, public statements defining who is a legitimate target have varied with the authorized speaker – from (1) high-level al-Qaeda leaders who are planning attacks, to (2) high-level individuals, to (3) individuals who are part of al-Qaeda or its associated forces, to (4) simply anyone threatening the United States.[63] Even though the Additional Protocol permits the targeting of civilians who are direct participants in a conflict, such variance in definition also suggests a laxity in the standards of proportionality.[64]

Of the 3,200–4,600 deaths by UAVs in 2013,[65] most have occurred in Pakistan, but a fair number were executed in Yemen, with a smaller number in Somalia. Syria and Iraq are now added to the list, although bombing by conventional aircraft has dominated in the fight against ISIS.[66] The Emmerson Report to the

---

[62] Micah Zenko, *Reforming U.S. Drone Policies* (New York: Council on Foreign Relations Special Report no. 65 (2013): 12, http://www.cfr.org/wars-and-warfare/reforming-us-drone-strike-policies/p29736 (accessed April 20, 2015). The International Committee of the Red Cross (ICRC) standards require a "continuous combat function" in order to justify targeting those who are not members of the armed forces. ICRC Guidance 1007. Sudarsan Raghavan, "When U.S. Drones Kill Civilians, Yemen's Government Tries to Conceal It," *The Washington Post*, December 24, 2012, http://www.washingtonpost.com/world/middle_east/when-us-drones-kill-civilians-yemens-government-tries-to-conceal-it/2012/12/24/bd4d7ac2-486d-11e2-8af9-9b50cb4605a7_story.html (accessed December 12, 2014); "Tracking America's Drone War," *The Washington Post*, http://apps.washingtonpost.com/foreign/drones/ (accessed December 12, 2014).

[63] Micah Zenko, discussion, Council on Foreign Relations Meeting, Cambridge, MA, October 22, 2012

[64] Nils Melzer, "Interpretive Guidance on the Notion of Direct Participation in Hostilities Under International Humanitarian Law," International Committee of the Red Cross, May 2009, https://www.icrc.org/eng/assets/files/other/icrc-002-0990.pdf (accessed April 18, 2015).

[65] Ibid.; See also "Get the Data: Drone Wars," The Bureau of Investigative Journalism, http://www.thebureauinvestigates.com/category/projects/drones/drones-graphs/ (accessed April 18, 2015); "International Security Data Site," New America Foundation, http://securitydata.newamerica.net/ (accessed April 18, 2015).

[66] Jack Serle, "Why Drones are not Enough in Iraq and Syria," The Bureau of Investigative Journalism, September 11, 2014, http://www.thebureauinvestigates.com/2014/09/11/why-drones-are-not-enough-in-iraq-and-syria/ (accessed April 18, 2015).

Human Rights Council investigated a number of specific strikes, many by UAVs. It documented the many civilian casualties, some in cases where alleged terrorists have also been killed, but also cases of wrong identification.[67] Accounts alleging that civilian rescuers and funeral attendees have been targeted in second-round strikes[68] might be less puzzling if the United States would reveal how it establishes strike targets. Greater transparency in its efforts to avoid collateral damage to civilians and their property would clarify whether the United States is meeting the requirement of proportionality in its conduct of UAV strikes.[69] We would expect a "kill list" to be classified, but why should the criteria for targeting not be made public? It is hardly plausible that all of the signature strikes removed terrorists who were actually poised to strike at America or Europe. These unanswered questions remain troubling and give rise to the view expressed by opponents of targeted killing that it is easier to kill than to capture, much less prosecute, an alleged terrorist.

Domestic American Legal Issues

As a matter of U.S. law, targeted killings have been specifically justified under the Authorization for Use of Military Force (AUMF), a joint resolution passed immediately after 9/11 that authorizes the President to use "all necessary and appropriate force" against those "nations, organizations, or persons he determines planned, authorized, committed, or aided the terrorist attacks that occurred

---

[67] Ben Emmerson, "Report of the Special Rapporteur on the Promotion and Protection of Human Rights and Fundamental Freedoms While Countering Terrorism," Office of the High Commissioner for Human Rights, http://daccess-dds-ny.un.org/doc/UNDOC/GEN/G14/119/49/PDF/G1411949.pdf?OpenElement (accessed April 18, 2015).

[68] Chris Woods and Christina Lamb, "CIA Tactics in Pakistan Include Targeting Rescuers and Funerals," The Bureau of Investigative Journalism, February 4, 2012, http://www.thebureauinvestigates.com/2012/02/04/obama-terror-drones-cia-tactics-in-pakistan-include-targeting-rescuers-and-funerals/ (accessed December 12, 2014).

[69] Additional Protocol to the Geneva Conventions of 1949, June 8 1977, Article 48, 51(b) (5), https://www.icrc.org/applic/ihl/ihl.nsf/Article.xsp?action=openDocument&documentId=8A9E7E14C63C7F30C12563CD0051DC5C (accessed April 18, 2015).

on September 11, 2001, or harbored such organizations or persons."[70] Underlying that joint resolution is the constitutional Commander-in-Chief powers of the President under Article II, Section 2 of the U.S. Constitution. The War Powers Resolution of 1973 was the Congressional effort to assert its joint constitutional authority by requiring presidential notification of entry into conflict, with a sixty-day period after which Congress must justify the use of force, or the administration would be required to withdraw.[71] That act has often been ignored by successive administrations, and attempts to increase its effectiveness have failed.[72] It is notable that President Obama did notify Congress of the initiation of bombing ISIS in Iraq on August 17, 2014, under both his constitutional authority and that of the War Powers Resolution. Congress, interestingly, did not respond after the sixty-day period expired. U.S. attacks continued.

Although the AUMF has been considered sufficient to justify the Osama bin Laden raid, its authorization to include terrorist cells in Somalia, terrorists with little relationship to the original al-Qaeda organization beyond their name, and those created long after 9/11, has been questioned.[73] If indeed the facts support a linkage among these disparate groups, then as a matter of domestic law, the AUMF might arguably be sufficient. But reliance becomes increasingly attenuated over time, especially when Iraq has flared up with terrorists whom al-Qaeda disavows. So long as the underlying factual and legal cases remain classified, it can be argued, as Professor Jack Goldsmith does, that "executive-branch decisions since 2001 have led the nation to a new type of war against new enemies on a new battlefield without focused national debate, deliberate

[70] Authorization for Use of Military Force, Pub. L. No. 107–40, § 2(a), 115 Stat. 224, 224 (2001), http://www.gpo.gov/fdsys/pkg/PLAW-107publ40/pdf/PLAW-107publ40.pdf (accessed December 12, 2014).

[71] War Powers Resolution, 50 U. S. Code 1548–1553.

[72] Glennon, Michael J., The War Powers Resolution, Once Again (February, 10 2009), *American Journal of International Law*, January 2009. Available at SSRN: http://ssrn.com/abstract=1340622.

[73] Robert Chesney, "A New Drone Strike in Somalia: Is the 2001 AUMF Needed?," *Lawfare* (blog), September 2, 2014, http://www.lawfareblog.com/2014/09/a-new-drone-strike-in-somalia-is-the-2001-aumf-needed/ (accessed October 3, 2014).

congressional approval or real judicial review."[74] The President recognized the legal shortcomings of relying on the AUMF in his May 23, 2013, address, when he urged Congress to "refine and ultimately repeal, the AUMF's mandate."[75] In the hands of a fractious Congress, however, "refining" may not turn out to be the narrowing, careful authorization process the President envisioned.

Apart from the question of whether the president has the right to conduct these strikes at all, under the Constitution and the AUMF, one of the most contentious legal issues domestically has been whether there is a denial of due process in targeting American citizens such as al-Awlaki. The Justice Department's White Paper, the President's May 2013 speech, and the Barron memorandum all developed the justification for that case and for several other strikes by describing them as actual imminent threats that had a basis in past incitement of violence, including a plot to explode an airliner over American soil. The legal opinions tried to demonstrate that there was no feasible alternative.

With respect to constitutional rights, then Attorney General Eric Holder argued that "due process does not necessarily mean judicial process" in a wartime situation. The wartime analogies relied on by the Justice Department may fit the situation in Afghanistan and Iraq, where American troops have been under attack daily. The Justice Department memoranda relied on Supreme Court balancing tests, weighing private rights against governmental interests[76] to explain why it was infeasible to capture and provide constitutional due process rights to an American citizen who was serving as an enemy combatant.

The Department of Justice relied in part on *Ex Parte Quirin*, in which German soldiers, including an American citizen, were tried by military commission as unlawful combatants in the midst of a

---

[74] Jack Goldsmith, "U.S. Needs a Rulebook for Secret Warfare," *The Washington Post*, February 5, 2013, http://articles.washingtonpost.com/2013-02-05/opinions/36757699_1_government-lawyers-secret-warfare-al-qaeda (accessed December 12, 2014).

[75] President Barack Obama (speech, National Defense University).

[76] Hamdi; Mathews v. Eldridge 424 U.S. 319 (1976). The facts and rationale in applying the balancing test to a case involving a claim for denial of due process in hearing about disability benefits under Social Security seem quite unrelated to the circumstances of killing al-Awlaki.

declared war. Those Nazi soldiers had surreptitiously landed on American beaches, abandoned their uniforms, and were captured carrying explosive devices. It is a stretch for the government to rely on that case and other similar cases to justify presidential power to target an American citizen in a location that was not directly related to the Iraq or Afghan wars. Yet although the facts in these cases are so different from al-Awlaki's situation, a legal rationale has been constructed from them. The argument is made that, first, the capture and trial of al-Awlaki was not possible, and second, the action taken to kill him was proportionate to the imminence of the threat to the United States.

The evidence against al-Awlaki was not without basis. He was an international voice threatening the United States; he allegedly recruited and helped train Umar Farouk Abdulmutallab, the "underwear bomber" who attempted to down a U.S. plane on Christmas 2009. He helped oversee the plot to detonate explosive devices on two U.S.-bound cargo planes in 2010. Alberto Gonzales, former Attorney General to President George W. Bush, concluded in his carefully analyzed article: "[C]onsidering the totality of the circumstances, the President's actions with respect to Al-Aulaqi were lawful." [77] Yet even so, he was not comfortable with the arguments that the government had made. He recommended something closer to due process than an unconstrained presidential determination to protect future American citizens who might be placed on the kill list. He had several suggestions. They included a congressional definition of what constitutes an enemy combatant; a requirement that the president inform Congress of each citizen designated as an enemy combatant; and even a requirement that a neutral body pass on the President's deliberation to target such individuals. [78] These recommendations suggest that if many more citizens are to be targeted, some changes in procedures should be instituted to afford greater protection to them.

In relying on war cases, the legal analogy assumes that a wartime situation existed such that normal judicial processes are not

---

[77] Alberto Gonzales, "Drones: The Power to Kill," *George Washington University Law Review* 82, no. 1 (2014): 28.
[78] Ibid., 49–58.

feasible. The case might be more persuasive under the *Quirin* rationale if the argument that America is in a war with al-Qaeda and its networks, including AQAP, is also persuasive. That argument depends on carefully developed facts that there is a real war against related groups of terrorists in areas beyond Afghanistan and Iraq to justify targeting a U.S. citizen.[79] The demonstration of factual linkages to al-Qaeda must be sufficiently persuasive to the relevant publics to gain national and international support. These linkages have become progressively attenuated with time. The Barron memorandum states:

> Moreover, DoD would conduct the operation in Yemen, where, according to the facts related to us, AQAP has a significant and organized presence, and from which AQAP is conducting terrorist training in an organized manner and has executed and is planning to execute attacks against the United States. Finally, the targeted individual himself, on behalf of that force, is continuously planning attacks from that Yemeni base of operations against the United States, as the conflict with al-Qaida continues.[80]

This statement does not clear up the confusion created by alternative and contradictory presidential statements in 2013, which has

---

79 See Cass Sunstein and Jack Goldsmith, "Military Tribunals and Legal Culture: What a Difference Sixty Years Makes" (working paper, University of Chicago Public Law and Political Theory, 2002) http://www.law.uchcago.edu/Lawecon/index.html (accessed December 12, 2014). See also Harvey Silverglate, "Obama Crosses the Rubicon: The Killing of Anwar al-Awlaki," *Forbes*, October 6, 2011, http://www.forbes.com/sites/harveysilverglate/2011/10/06/obama-crosses-the-rubicon-the-killing-of-anwar-al-awlaki/ (accessed December 12, 2014). Other issues were raised by the Department of Justice memorandum, such as whether the targeting killing of al-Awlaki violated the law against the murder of an American citizen abroad and whether the public authority exemption applies under that statute (18 U. S. Code 1119). Although they are important, as is the issue of whether the law applies to the CIA as well as the military, those issues are not within the scope of the more limited discussion in this book.

80 The White Paper unsurprisingly uses very similar language to that in the Barron memorandum: "The United States retains its authority to use force against al Qaeda and associated forces outside the area of active hostilities when it targets a senior operational leader of the enemy force who is actively engaged in planning operations to kill Americans. The United States is currently in a non-international armed conflict with al Qaeda and its associated forces ... Any U.S. operation would be part of this non-international armed conflict, even if it were to take place away from the zone of active hostilities." Barron memorandum, 27. See also Gonzales "Drones."

made it difficult for the public to understand the legal basis for such acts. Perhaps it would have been easier to retain the phrase "the global war on terror" for coherence – however thin an argument it was to designate a series of conflicts or threats from disparate locations as a "war." But to continue the description as war might raise even greater constitutional questions if pursued without further congressional authorization.

War or Criminal Law Model?

The issue of how terrorism is framed further complicates the legal underpinnings for targeted killings in both international and domestic law. The legal analysis of terrorist acts can turn on whether the case is framed as a response to crime or to a war threat, in the formulation of Professors Gabriella Blum and Philip Heymann.[81] If the provocation is construed as a crime, as has been the practice with alleged terrorists in the United States and Europe, then the response is constrained by the due process requirements of peacetime law enforcement. Where terrorism is treated as a crime, the remedy is an effort to extradite the suspect, followed by trial in the United States and, if the suspect is found guilty, punishment. The United States abided by this model in pursuing a number of high-profile terrorists, such as Abu Hamza al-Masri, a radical cleric who was extradited from England to stand trial in New York in 2012, or Sulaiman Abu Ghaith, son-in-law of Osama bin Laden, who was arrested in Jordan in March 2013, extradited, tried by jury in New York, and convicted on March 26, 2014.[82]

---

[81] Gabriella Blum and Philip Heymann, "Law and Policy of Targeted Killing," *Harvard National Security Journal* 1 (June 27, 2010): 145, http://harvardnsj .org/2010/06/law-and-policy-of-targeted-killing/ (accessed December 12, 2014).

[82] Benjamin Weiser, "Jurors Convict Abu Ghaith, Bin Laden Son-in-Law, in Terror Case," *The New York Times*, March 26, 2014, http://www.nytimes .com/2014/03/27/nyregion/bin-ladens-son-in-law-is-convicted-in-terror-trial .html (accessed December 12, 2014). For the Abu Hamza case, see Pervaiz Shallwani, Devlin Barrett, and Evan Perez, "After Long Wait, U.S. Presses Terror Cases against Five," *The Wall Street Journal*, October 6, 2012, http://online .wsj.com/article/SB10000872396390444223104578040482856321890.html (accessed December 12, 2014). For the Abu Ghaith case, see Marc Santora and William K. Rashbaum, "Bin Laden Relative Pleads Not Guilty in Terrorism Case,"

Yet, for targeted killing to be acceptable as a rational, efficient, effective, and legal response that protects more civilian lives in targeted areas and more American military lives than the alternatives of invasion or covert action, terrorism must be construed not as a crime, but rather as war. As Blum and Heymann point out, the United States seems to embrace both models (and some derivatives) simultaneously: terrorists caught within the United States or allied territories are likely to be tried as criminals, while similar suspected terrorists – even if they are U.S. citizens – who happen to be located in areas outside states of established alliances are likely to be treated as combatants or as imminent threats to U.S. security. They are ghost enemies in the amorphous war on terror who are afforded neither the rights of citizens nor the protections given to traditional combatants.

The Obama administration has utilized a criminal law model where feasible, and made efforts to close the Guantanamo prison facilities and incarcerate prisoners on the mainland.[83] The decision to fly a Russian alleged terrorist detained in Afghanistan to the United States for trial in October 2014 was an important move to widen the criminal law model.[84] But the United States has also relied on self-defense and war rationales without hanging its hat on either authority.[85] Clarification could be made about why both approaches might be helpful, and under which circumstances one approach is more apt than another – and why. The current blurring of paradigms, as stated before, gives rise to the accusation that it is easier to kill than to jail suspected terrorists – not a conclusion that reflects well on the American respect for the law.[86]

The New York Times, March 8, 2013, http://www.nytimes.com/2013/03/09/nyregion/sulaiman-abu-ghaith-bin-ladens-son-in-law-charged-in-new-york.html (accessed December 12, 2014).

[83] Erin B. Corcoran, "Obama's Failed Attempt to Close Gitmo: Why Executive Orders Can't Bring about Systemic Change," *University of New Hampshire Law Review* 9 (2010–2011): 207. David J. R. Frakt, "Prisoners of Congress: The Constitutional and Political Clash over Detainees and the Closure of Guantanamo," *University of Pittsburgh Law Review* 74, no. 2 (2012): 181–262.

[84] "'Russian Taliban' Appears in US Court on Terror Charges," *BBC*, http://www.bbc.com/news/world-us-canada-29910022 (accessed December 12, 2014).

[85] Department of Justice White Paper, 3–4.

[86] See Laurie Blank, "Targeted Strikes: The Consequences of Blurring the Armed Conflict and Self-Defense Justifications" *William Mitchell Law Review* 38 no. 5 (2012): 1697. In criticizing the the U.S. justification, the author argues: "[U]sing

Secrecy versus Transparency

Secrecy compounds whatever legal weakness may be inherent in targeting activities. The public is left to rely heavily on journalistic leaks, and correspondingly, journalists become bolder in asserting what they consider to be an obligation to the public.[87] National security suffers even as the public gains important information. The fact that official secrecy was maintained about the al-Awlaki strike for three months after the disclosure of the Department of Justice White Paper increased the contentiousness of that targeted killing. The legal issue had been submitted to the Department of Justice, which, as the White Paper revealed, had supplied legal justification, but classification had prevented informed public debate.[88] Available information about targeted killing in general has only increased slightly, and then sporadically. For example, government debate about whether to target Abdullah al-Shami, an American citizen in Pakistan and a known terrorist, was somehow made known to journalists.[89] But support for the present program does not simply

---

both the armed conflict and self-defense justifications for targeted strikes, whether in Pakistan, Yemen, Somalia, or elsewhere, may be an easy way to communicate to the public that the state is using force to eliminate 'bad guys.' It certainly adds a great deal of flexibility to policy-making and decision-making, which is highly valuable from the perspective of political leaders. The costs of allowing the lines between legal regimes and paradigms to be blurred, however, are far too great."

[87] Jack Goldsmith, *Power and Constraint* (New York: W. W. Norton, 2012), 51–82. But active, investigative journalists, such as James Risen of *The New York Times*, face criminal charges when they refuse to divulge sources, and the pressure on the media to suppress stories is heavy. See Norman Soloman and Marcy Wheeler, "The Government War Against Reporter James Risen," *The Nation*, October 27, 2014, http://www.thenation.com/article/181919/government-war-against-reporter-james-risen (accessed April 17, 2015) and Mark Berman, "The Supreme Court Won't Intervene In the James Risen Case. What's Next?" *The Washington Post*, June 2, 2014, http://www.washingtonpost.com/news/post-nation/wp/2014/06/02/the-supreme-court-wont-intervene-in-the-james-risen-case-whats-next/ (accessed April 17, 2015).

[88] Department of Justice White Paper.

[89] Mark Mazzetti and Eric Schmitt, "U.S. Militant, Hidden, Spurs Drone Debate," *The New York Times*, February 28, 2014, http://www.nytimes.com/2014/02/28/world/asia/us-militant-hidden-spurs-drone-debate.html?emc=eta1&_r=0 (accessed April 17, 2015).

lie with the executive branch. As a recent exposé in *The New York Times* reveals – naming names,

It was two years ago that Mr. Obama gave a speech pledging to pull the targeted killing program from the shadows, and White House officials said they wanted to shift the bulk of drone operations from the C.I.A. to the Pentagon, with the stated intent of making the program somewhat more transparent. But the intelligence committees have resisted the plan, in part because Mr. D'Andrea and other top agency officials have convinced law-makers that the C.I.A. strikes are more precise than those conducted by the Pentagon's Joint Special Operations Command.[90]

Mary Ellen O'Connell remarks that "secret law" is an oxymo-ron: "The rule of law is the basis of our democracy and the founda-tion of international relations. Facts like operational details may properly be kept confidential, but not the law itself."[91] Withholding information about a legal rationale is like classifying the weather report. The public faces a veritable "fog of law" when legal justi-fication is kept classified for a long period of time and not made transparent.[92]

More Oversight?

Serious concerns about legality has given rise to a call for increased oversight. A number of proposals for special oversight, including one modeled on the Foreign Intelligence Surveillance Court (FISC), have been offered. Such a court might be reassuring to the public, but it would be troublesome as a matter of security policy and con-stitutional law for any court to opine on or decide the legality of specific attacks in advance. A deliberative judicial process would only be effective in a post hoc opinion on the legality of a par-ticular strike, or group of strikes. Highly classified and technical

[90] http://www.nytimes.com/2015/04/26/us/politics/deep-support-in-washington-for-cias-drone-missions.html?smprod=nytcore-iphone&smid=nytcore-iphone-share&_r=1 (accessed April 26, 2015).

[91] O'Connell, "Questions Brennan Can't Dodge."

[92] Michael J. Glennon, *The Fog of Law* (Stanford: Stanford University Press, 2010). The Israelis also have issues of disclosure and explanation about the legal-ity of UAV usage. See Amir Oren, "Israeli Military Hiding Targeted Killing Investigative Panel," *Haaretz*, May 31, 2014, http://www.haaretz.com/news/diplomacy-defense/1.596339#.VF5LQfS-IAM.email (accessed November 10, 2014).

information would have to be subject to scrutiny. As Director of Georgetown University's National Security Program and former Justice Department official, Carrie Cordero argues,

[I]f the FISC is used as the model, the Executive Branch must be prepared to explain, in detail, its capabilities, technologies, innovations and compliance vulnerabilities. The intersection of the technological "how" and Court authorization is all the more difficult as technology changes. Just one example to highlight a potential scenario: what if the hypothetical new court becomes interested in collateral deaths? Would a court inquire as to the precision of missile and drone technology to prevent anyone but the identified target from being killed? Is the Defense Department and Intelligence Community prepared to fully inform the court about its equipment, techniques, technologies, designs, prototypes, margin of error and casualty counts? On the other hand, should Congress try to craft a new court that more substantially cabins the authority of the court to request additional information than in the FISA context, it is hard to imagine that federal judges would be comfortable and willing to operate in that more constrained environment. [93]

Furthermore, the record of nearly 99 percent approval of proposed government actions by the FISC calls into question whether such a step would in fact increase effective oversight.[94]

While there are technical, functional, and even structural issues with current oversight mechanisms, the problem with both judicial and congressional oversight may be more a function of unwavering support of the program. Could that be changed by forceful presentation of opposing views?[95] An advocate's voice will only be instituted when there is public demand.

The Privacy and Civil Liberties Oversight Board (PCLOB) as an independent, bipartisan executive agency might provide an alternative route for selective oversight of such issues as targeted killing. Although small and potentially divided along party lines, it has demonstrated its capability and depth in investigation with its

[93] "Carrie Codero on FISA Court Lessons for a Drone Court," *Lawfare* (blog), February 18, 2013, http://www.lawfareblog.com/2013/02/carrie-cordero-on-fisa-court-lessons-for-a-drone-court/ (accessed December 12, 2014).

[94] Andrew Weissman "The Foreign Intelligence Security Court: Is Reform Needed," *Just Security*, June 12, 2014, http://justsecurity.org/11540/guest-post-foreign-intelligence-surveillance-court-reform-needed/ (accessed April 26, 2015).

[95] Ibid

initial "Report on the Telephone Records Program Under Section 215 of the U.S. Patriot Act and on the Operations of the Foreign Intelligence Surveillance Court",[96] which was reinforced by later reports.[97] The PCLOB, with its access to classified materials, as well as its power to hold public hearings, could be a better instrument for airing and analyzing the issues raised here. However, as terrorism metastasizes throughout the world, concerns for effective security will continue to dampen the efforts to provide for more scrupulous oversight. The demand for both greater transparency and oversight waits until public opinion is mobilized. At that point, there are many alternative routes to be explored.[98]

[96] Privacy and Civil Liberties Oversight Board, *Report on the Telephone Records Program Conducted under Section 215 of the USA PATRIOT Act and on the Operations of the Foreign Intelligence Surveillance Court*, January 23, 2014, https://www.pclob.gov/library/215-Report_on_the_Telephone_Records_Program.pdf (accessed on April 18, 2015).

[97] Privacy and Civil Liberties Oversight Board, *Report on the Surveillance Program Operated Pursuant to Section 702 of the Foreign Intelligence Surveillance Act*, July 2, 2014, http://www.pclob.gov/Library/702-Report-2.pdf (accessed December 12, 2014).

[98] For example, there multiple treaty and case law routes for raising the right to life, as Brian Kelly suggests. See, e.g., the Case of Al-Skeini and Others v. The United Kingdom, http://hudoc.echr.coe.int/sites/eng/pages/search.aspx?i=001-105606#{"itemid":["001-105606"]}

9

Opportunities for Stepping Forward

Although the United States seems unlikely to abandon targeted killing in the near future, the focus ought now to be on developing and implementing standards, limits, and safeguards. In addition to the issues of blowback and the potential loss of technological edge already discussed, the United States has lost legitimacy and stature even among its allies. Legal justification, as the late Thomas Franck has written, is a key to legitimacy.[1] There can be little public confidence in the current policy of targeted killing until the legal justification for it is put on firmer ground and strikes are limited to instances in which a sound factual basis for targeting individuals is made to the public. Legal justification, just as the joke about Wagner's music, is better than it sounds. But that justification has not been presented clearly to the public, nor has it been offered in a timely fashion.

Professor Jack Goldsmith relies in part on "accountability journalism," Freedom Of Information Act (FOIA) requests, and litigation to expose conditions that will prompt the public to demand action and Congress to act in response. But he is also ambivalent about the exposure of classified information harmful to national security.[2] And while U.S. Supreme Court rulings during the George W. Bush administration curbed some of the worst prisoner abuses,

[1] Thomas Franck, "Legitimacy in the International System," *American Journal of International Law* 82, no. 4 (October 1988): 705.
[2] Jack Goldsmith, *Power and Constraint* (New York: W. W. Norton, 2012), 205–243.

laid the groundwork for habeas corpus,[3] and spurred improved procedures for trial under the Military Commissions Act of 2009,[4] Guantanamo was not closed, indefinite incarceration has continued, and actual freedom for prisoners has been rare. The broad continuity of policy between the Bush and Obama administrations is notable. Michael Glennon's evidence that a permanent stratum of unaccountable "Trumanites" actually make policy; that a "double government" exists in the United States casts considerable doubt about the effectiveness of the accountability mechanisms suggested by Professor Goldsmith.[5]

It is important now to think ahead about forms of international norms and standards that nations might be willing to live by before we are faced with a crisscrossing of targeted attacks from rogue states and non-state actors who have been able to develop advanced technology. Moreover, the technology may go in a direction of autonomous and miniaturized UAVs presenting even greater problems than the current human-guided ones.[6]

The most desirable outcome for the use of present and future UAVs would be international regulation of drone warfare, as has been achieved slowly with many aspects of war-fighting, such as land mines[7] or cluster bombs.[8] The United States is unlikely to initiate such an international regime, given the fact that it is the

---

[3] Hamdi v. Rumsfeld 542 U.S. 507 (2004); Rasul v. Bush 542 U.S. 466 (2004); Hamdan v. Rumsfeld 548 U.S. 557 (2006); Boumedienne v. Bush 553 U.S. 723 (2008).

[4] See also Jennifer K. Elsea, "The Military Commissions Act of 2009: (MCA 2009): Overview and Legal Issues," Congressional Research Service, August 4, 2014, https://fas.org/sgp/crs/natsec/R41163.pdf (accessed April 22, 2015); Mark Martins, "A Conversation with General Mark Martins, Chief Prosecutor of Military Commissions" (Harvard Law School lecture by Brigadier General Mark Martins, Cambridge, MA, April 14, 2015).

[5] Michael J. Glennon, *National Security and Double Government* (Oxford: Oxford University Press, 2014).

[6] Benjamin Wittes and Gabriella Blum, *The Future of Violence: Robots and Germs, Hackers and Drones: Confronting a New Age of Threat* (New York: Basic Books, 2015).

[7] "Convention on the Prohibition of the Use, Stockpiling, Production and Transfer of Anti-Personnel Mines and their Destruction," United Nations, September 18, 1997, https://www.icrc.org/ihl/INTRO/580 (accessed April 20, 2015).

[8] "Dublin Diplomatic Conference on Cluster Munitions," Dublin, Ireland, May 30, 2008, https://treaties.un.org/pages/ViewDetails.aspx?src=TREATY&mtdsg_no=XXVI-6&chapter=26&lang=en (accessed April 20, 2015).

principal developer and user of UAVs. But circumstances may force the nation to greater openness to international regulation. Even though a binding legal agreement is not feasible politically in the midst of proliferating terrorism, it might not be far-fetched for responsible states to strive for an initial agreement that assures that they will act in ways that specifically uphold the Laws of Armed Conflict, and the UN Charter in the employment of drones.

An imaginative proposal has been made by Professors Allan Buchanan and Robert O. Keohane.[9] They would create a non-legally binding Drone Accountability Regime. Their conception is an informal pledge by nations to adopt internal standards and mechanisms to curb abuses of drone warfare. Their model agreement would rely on states to legislate international common standards. Their model is the Missile Technology Control Regime. Such a pledge is a step beyond internationally agreed codes of conduct. Their proposed nonbinding regime is detailed: it includes an assembly of states to assure transparency and an ombudsperson to settle disputes. It would only provide state enforcement mechanisms to uphold the broad standards of acceptable behavior. Yet the regime would offer the opportunity for civil society to mobilize and pressure the state to implement the agreed standards.[10] A similar model of a nonbinding agreement or pledge is the successful Proliferation Security Initiative, which sets forth broad standards without imposing a regulatory regime.[11] Although these approaches admittedly do not provide for deep regulation, they can represent the beginning steps of a norm-building process.

A 2014 Stimson report, chaired by retired U.S. Army General John Abizaid and Rosa Brooks, offered strong and clear

---

9 Allen Buchanan and Robert O. Keohane, "Toward a Drone Accountability Regime" *Ethics and International Affairs* 29 (Spring 2015), 15–27, http://www.ethicsandinternationalaffairs.org/2015/toward-drone-accountability-regime/ based on their article: "International Institutional Regulation of Lethal Drones" (Unpublished Paper, October 5, 2014).

10 See Beth Simmons, *Mobilization for Human Rights: International Law In Domestic Politics* (New York: Cambridge University Press, 2009).

11 "Proliferation Security Initiative, 10th Anniversary: Joint Statement on Enhancing Interdiction Capabilities and Practices," United States Department of State, http://www.state.gov/t/isn/jtstmts/211498.htm (accessed April 18, 2015).

recommendations for the future U.S. use of lethal UAV technologies.[12] Their methodology, analysis, and eight recommendations carry the weight of a committee distinguished group of former legal, military, and policy officials as well as technical experts. They demand both cost and technological research and analysis. All of the Stimson Report recommendations, including those related to export control, research, and development, and assuring safety through FAA civil aircraft regulation, are worthy of study and support.

The recommendations offered in this book draw from both reports and focus on the most critical issues. They are narrower in scope than those in the Stimson Report, but also are directed toward international action, just as in Buchanan and Keohane's scheme. Many new recommendations will emerge in the years ahead until changes are made. At the very least, the United States might be wise to accept some of the criticism made about its use of lethal UAVs, and move now toward setting internal standards, while demonstrating openness to international agreements.

1. U.S. civil-military roles in UAV warfare should be clarified and made public. Since repetitive and near-routine bombing continues to occur, it is best to make the transition to military operational control without further delay, as President Obama indicated he intended to do.

2. Concerted efforts should be made to gain law enforcement cooperation from nations where terrorist leaders can be found so they are tried, not targeted. The United States should redouble its efforts to bring terrorists who are U.S. citizens through judicial process.

---

[12] John P. Abizaid and Rosa Brooks, *Recommendations and Report on the Task Force on US Drone Policy*, The Stimson Center, June 2014, http://www.stimson .org/images/uploads/research-pdfs/task_force_report_FINAL_WEB_062414.pdf (accessed October 2, 2014). Their recommendations are:

1. Conduct a rigorous strategic review and cost-benefit analysis of the role of lethal UAVs.
2. Improve transparency in targeted UAV strikes.
3. Transfer general responsibility for carrying out lethal UAV strikes from the CIA to the military.
4. Develop more robust oversight and accountability mechanisms for targeted strikes outside of traditional battlefields.
5. Foster the development of appropriate international norms for the use of lethal force outside traditional battlefields.

3. The practice of signature strikes should be ended. The choice of targets should be limited to terrorist leaders who pose a known and imminent threat to the United States and its allies. Stringent standards of imminence should be used. Strikes should be carried out only after positive identification of the targets.[13]

4. Transparency should be increased. Although secrecy may be needed in advance of action, it is not necessary afterwards. Public disclosure about who was targeted and the justification for it would offer civil society and the public the opportunity to raise questions. To the extent that international and domestic publics know what safeguards are in place and what processes have led to the choices made, greater support for policies may be forthcoming.

5. The United States and its allies should display the greatest possible respect for sovereignty. Before a decision is made that national security trumps the sovereign rights of another nation, the kind of intensive civil-military dialogue recommended in Chapter 3 should be institutionalized. Such discourse could be systematized by the various means suggested – by Executive Order, by legislation when feasible, and by such practices as those developed in SOUTHCOM/AFRICOM.[14]

6. If the United States or its allies face imminent attack from ungoverned territories, conditions of the kind proposed by Ashley Deeks should be imposed before reliance on a doctrine of "unable or unwilling." These conditions would help limit intrusions into the sovereignty of a state and offer needed justification when that sovereignty is bypassed.

7. The U.S. government should clarify and further articulate how ongoing threats should be treated (whether they should be

---

6. Assess UAV-related technological developments and likely future trends, and develop an interagency research and development strategy.

7. Review and reform UAV-related export control rules and FAA rules.

8. The FAA should accelerate its efforts to meet the requirements of the 2012 FAA Reauthorization Bill.

[13] If such a standard were implemented under internationally agreed interpretations of Article 51 of the UN Charter and the Laws of Armed Conflict, concerns about reciprocity and mimicking behavior might be lessened.

[14] This is not to say that some such discussions do not now take place, but some results, such as signature strikes in Pakistan, Yemen, and Somalia, suggest either a lack of full discussion or hasty decision making.

considered ongoing war or something lesser), continue to aggressively pursue Congressional support for a new authority to update the Authorization for Use of Military Force (AUMF), and seek the support needed under the War Powers Resolution.

8. A more effective form of supervision should be fashioned to review whether past targeting decisions have met the criteria that have been established. Suggestions for improvement over present Congressional oversight may be forthcoming with the public mobilization that greater transparency might effect. These might include an enhanced PCLOB, as discussed in Chapter 8.

These steps would help allay public and international concern about kinetic actions that many see as lacking sufficient legal or even ethical grounding. Each administration owes to the public its reassurance that the constraints of both international and domestic law are carefully observed. There are no legal doctrines so obscure that they defy explanation in plain language. The first step would parallel a proposal offered in Chapter 13, whose focus is on cyber attacks: developing a formal code of conduct, which might be a prelude to actual international agreements. Codes of conduct and other confidence building measures, as mild as they are, can be an important step forward in counterterrorism activity.

Although America cannot claim to be the "shining city on the hill," American policy still tends to set a standard for the rest of the world. Clarity and transparency are necessary so that people in the United States and the world know that the use of drones complies with legal and humanitarian standards, and that these weapons are used only with the restraint that will encourage other nations to act accordingly.

10

Cyber Attacks and Cyber Warfare

Framing the Issues

Estonia was a highly wired society, but its ability to function as such was nearly brought to a halt in less than a month because of three waves of cyber attacks between April 26 and May 18, 2007, likely carried out by Russian agents. These attacks, more than recent attacks on private noncritical corporations such as Sony Pictures Entertainment, represent another type of gray area between war and peace, raising novel issues about civil-military roles and the inadequacy of the law underpinning this area. Widespread dependence on the internet combined with serious hardware and software flaws and overall system weakness made for a compounded vulnerability of an entire nation.[1] Repeated attacks on banks and other commercial operations in the United States and Europe, and even more serious, cyber attacks on Iran's nuclear facilities, underscore the blurred line between economic crimes and something closer to outright hostilities.

One of the relatively unsophisticated methods used with success during these attacks, Distributed Denial of Service (DDoS), "overloads a victim's server by exploiting communication protocols,"[2] transmitting a false address to a server, which then overloads the

[1] Ian Traynor, "Russia Accused of Unleashing Cyberwar to Disable Estonia," *The Guardian*, May 16, 2007, http://www.theguardian.com/world/2007/may/17/topstories3.russia.

[2] Jason Richards, "Denial-of-Service: The Estonian Cyberwar and Its Implications for U.S. National Security," *International Affairs Review* 18, no. 2 (2009), http://www.iar-gwu.org/node/65.

system by trying to respond, crowding out other legitimate requests. "Ping" attacks were also launched – or attacks that flooded the system with more information than it could handle. The successive waves of attacks crashed Estonia's internet system, leaving the government – including the president, parliament, police, and military – unable to communicate. The country's entire banking system had to shut down. Computers used in the attack were traced to 178 countries. The scope of global participation was breathtaking at the time.[3]

The effects of the attack on Estonia do not appear to be proportional to their cause, which indicates how easily petty disputes can lead to serious consequences in the cyber age. The Estonian government had removed a Russian, Soviet-era statue of the Bronze Soldier from its central location in Tallinn and exhumed an adjacent war grave containing the remains of twelve Soviet soldiers and moved them all to a remote cemetery on the outskirts of the country's capital.[4] Verbal attacks from Russia against the Estonian government followed; the discontent suggested that the source of the cyber attack was from Russia as well. Yet it took longer than the two weeks the attacks lasted to pinpoint their source: most likely the Russian government–sponsored youth group, Nashe.[5]

The ambiguity of the attack on Estonia allows the imagination to create further baffling scenarios. Dr. Herbert Lin[6] has posed several: temporary, reversible interference with military or critical

[3] Charles Clover, "Kremlin-Backed Group Behind Estonia Cyber Blitz," *Financial Times*, March 11, 2009, http://www.ft.com/intl/cms/s/0/57536d5a-0ddc-11de-8ea3-0000779fd2ac.html#axzz3TwGGCf83.
[4] Jari Tanner, "Estonia Reburies Soviet Troops' Remains," *The Washington Post*, July 3, 2007, http://www.washingtonpost.com/wp-dyn/content/article/2007/07/03/AR2007070300490.html.
[5] See Heather A. Conley and Theodore P. Garber, "Russian Soft Power in the 21st Century: An Examination of Russian Compatriot Policy in Estonia," Center for Strategic and International Studies, August 2011; Robert Coalson, "Behind The Estonia Cyberattacks," *Radio Free Europe*, March 9, 2009, http://www.rferl.org/content/Behind_The_Estonia_Cyberattacks/1505613.html; and Charles Clover, "Kremlin-Backed Group Behind Estonia Cyber Blitz," *Financial Times*.
[6] Dr. Herbert Lin was chief scientist at the Computer Science and Telecommunications Board, National Research Council of the National Academies of Science; now Dr. Lin serves as a consulting scholar at the Center for International Security and Cooperation at Stanford University.

infrastructure systems, or introducing a "Trojan Horse" capable of exfiltrating classified data, and more. But while it is useful to imagine hypotheticals to prepare against attacks, there are now real-life examples. Among them since the Estonia attack, are: Georgia (2008), in which a cyber attack on the government's network preceded a hot war, then continued during the war with Russia[7]; and cyber attacks against computer systems that operated Iran's nuclear enrichment facilities.[8] These cases illustrate how crippling and warlike this form of attack can be, even absent wounded or dead. Cyber warfare does not necessarily imply kinetic action, and that fact makes civil-military relationships and the legal framework within which responses must be formulated relatively novel and highly complex.

Yet it is only by using an analogy that the case of Estonia can be characterized as a hostile act approaching war, as there was none of the kinetic action usually associated with a conventional war. Yet, it was certainly a hostile attack. Cyber attacks, based on revolutionary technological innovation, challenge traditional concepts about

---

[7] The 2008 war between Russia and Georgia may represent the first time in history of "a coordinated cyberspace ... attack synchronized with major combat actions in the other warfighting domains." The cyber attacks on Georgia's military and government networks, including DDoS and website defacements, began three weeks before the physical hostilities and continued throughout the war. Linked to Russia's "patriotic hackers/cyber militias," the attacks were timed with the Russian military's ground, air, and naval combat operations and were closely coordinated with the "overall strategic objectives of the Russian government." By disabling Georgia's government and news websites, the attackers sowed panic and confusion among the Georgian civilian population because it was unable to communicate with its government. Cyber warfare also prevented Georgia from sending messages to the outside world, delivering Russia a strategic communications victory. David Hollis, "Cyberwar Case Study: Georgia 2008," *Small Wars Journal*, January 6, 2011, http://smallwarsjournal.com/jrnl/art/cyberwar-case-study-georgia-2008.

[8] Code-named the "Olympic Games," the attacks were allegedly initiated by the administration of George W. Bush and significantly expanded under President Obama. David Sanger, "Obama Order Sped Up Wave of Cyberattacks against Iran," *The New York Times*, June 1, 2012, http://www.nytimes.com/2012/06/01/world/middleeast/obama-ordered-wave-of-cyberattacks-against-iran.html?pagewanted=all; see also David Sanger, *Confront and Conceal: Obama's Secret War and the Surprising Use of American Power* (New York: Broadway Publishers, 2012), 187–207; and P. W. Singer and Allan Friedman, *Cybersecurity and Cyberwar: What Everyone Needs to Know* (New York: Oxford University Press, 2014), 114–120.

war perhaps more than any other type of hostile action. What constitutes an attack? When does an "attack" allow for self-defense? When might an attack be referred to the UN Security Council for response under Chapter 7? What law governs the appropriateness of response? To what extent do political and diplomatic concerns govern – or at least play in the mix? These are the questions now being addressed worldwide.

Cyber attacks and cyber warfare raise issues of self-protection, the ability to fend off (or deny) an attack, issues of attribution about the source of attack, and effectiveness of response. It may be difficult to identify exactly when an "attack" has taken place, who has perpetrated the act, whether more than an internal response to repair and protect is appropriate, and, if so, what response is legal and proportionate. The problem of attribution alone raises novel issues different from those encountered in other gray area conflicts.

Many cyber intrusions are a form of commercial espionage, not an attack that might be a prelude to war. For example, "phishing" – literally requesting information by posing as legitimate organizations[9] – may be a commercial crime, to be dealt with by the domestic criminal justice system, to the extent it has jurisdiction and adequate attribution can be made.[10] Yet economic espionage has been committed by states, and might be a precursor to a system-wide attack to destroy or cripple critical infrastructure such as electric, water, and transportation systems.[11] In fact, the definition

[9] Phishing attacks "use email or malicious websites to solicit personal information by posing as a trustworthy organization. For example, an attacker may send email seemingly from a reputable credit card company or financial institution that requests account information, often suggesting that there is a problem. When users respond with the requested information, attackers can use it to gain access to the accounts." United States Computer Emergency Readiness Team Website, http://www.us-cert.gov/ncas/tips/ST04-014.

[10] According to the U.S. National Conference of State Legislatures, twenty-three states currently have laws specifically against phishing. National Conference of State Legislatures, "State Laws Addressing Phishing," last updated December 30, 2013, http://www.ncsl.org/research/telecommunications-and-information-technology/state-phishing-laws.aspx.

[11] A cyber espionage "toolkit" called Snake, for example, is capable of both collecting information and "manipulating computer networks." David E. Sanger and Steven Erlanger, "Suspicion Falls on Russia as 'Snake' Cyberattacks Target Ukraine's Government," *The New York Times*, March 8, 2014,

of "critical infrastructure" under the Patriot Act of 2001 is very broad: "[T]he term critical infrastructure means systems and assets whether physical or virtual, so vital to the United States that the incapacity or destruction of such systems and assets would have a debilitating impact on security, national economic security, national public health or safety or any combination of those matters."[12]

Nations are acquiring experience and judgment to sort out what kind of response is appropriate to an incident that involves a large-scale, state-sponsored pilfering of data but no shutdown of a system.[13] The waves of attacks on major U.S. banks, such as on Wells Fargo and JP Morgan Chase, are cases in point, with new cases reported weekly.[14]

http://www.nytimes.com/2014/03/09/world/europe/suspicion-falls-on-russia-as-snake-cyberattacks-target-ukraines-government.html?_r=0. In one of the largest intrusions, hackers suspected of having ties with the Russian government infiltrated JPMorgan Chase's computer system in the summer of 2014. The hackers did not demonstrate any profit-seeking intentions but gained "the highest level of administrative privilege to dozens of the bank's computer servers," potentially setting up "vulnerabilities that would allow them re-entry into JPMorgan's systems." Jessica Silver-Greenberg, Matthew Goldstein, and Nicole Persloth, "JPMorgan Chase Hacking Affects 76 Million Households," *The New York Times*, October 2, 2014, http://dealbook.nytimes.com/2014/10/02/jpmorgan-discovers-further-cyber-security-issues/?_php=true&_type=blogs&_r=0.

[12] U.S. Patriot Act of 2001,42 U.S. Code § 5195(e).

[13] One response discussed regarding private-sector protection of intellectual property is allowing a private company to respond to a cyber intrusion, or to "hack back." While doing so is currently illegal under U.S. law, a 2013 report by a private commission addressed the possibility of changing the law to allow companies to respond. Max Fisher, "Should the U.S. Allow Companies to 'Hack Back' against Foreign Cyber Spies?," *The Washington Post*, May 23, 2013, http://www.washingtonpost.com/blogs/worldviews/wp/2013/05/23/should-the-u-s-allow-companies-to-hack-back-against-foreign-cyber-spies/.

[14] See David Henry and Jim Finkle, "JP Morgan Warns 465,000 Card Users on Data Loss after Cyber Attack," *Reuters*, December 5, 2013, http://www.reuters.com/article/2013/12/05/us-jpmorgan-dataexposed-idUSBRE9B405R20131205; Chris Strohm and Eric Engleman, "Cyber Attacks on U.S. Banks Expose Computer Vulnerability," *Bloomberg News*, September 28, 2012, http://www.bloomberg.com/news/2012-09-28/cyber-attacks-on-u-s-banks-expose-computer-vulnerability.html; and E. Scott Reckard, "Cyber Attacks on Banks Resume, Targeting Chase," *Los Angeles Times*, March 13, 2013, http://www.latimes.com/business/money/la-fi-mo-bank-cyber-attacks-chase-20130312,0,1903959.story. In October 2013, Army General Keith Alexander, leading the National Security Agency and the U.S. Cyber Command, noted that "over the last 14 months, we've seen over 350 distributed-denial-of-service attacks on Wall Street, with varying

Factual uncertainty about the origins and nature of a cyber attack almost guarantees legal uncertainty under both international and domestic law. Legal indeterminacy in turn spawns confusion or competition among civilian and military actors about the distribution of roles and relationships. For example, a phishing attack on American telecommunications, if attributed to a private party, might be handled by state law enforcement; if attributed to a nation, might be handled by the FBI; if regarded as part of a series of attacks to bring down critical infrastructure, might be handled cooperatively by the Department of Homeland Security, NSA, and Cyber Command, and perhaps other agencies. The demands for close cooperation, discussed further along, are unprecedented.

Defining Attack

With all these unanswered questions, it is not surprising that so much of the recent literature about cyber exploitation or espionage, cyber crimes, cyber attacks, and cyber war has been devoted to the effort to reach acceptable and widely accepted definitions. Most important is to clarify when a cyber attack constitutes a military attack. Defining and distinguishing among these categories theoretically should help elucidate what law, if any, applies and which government officials are expected to act. Definitions should help determine the allocation of responsibility among civil and military officials and the private sector. But they are only a starting point.

In 2010, the U.S. Joint Chiefs of Staff defined a cyber attack as:

A hostile act using computer or related networks or systems, and intended to disrupt and/or destroy an adversary's critical cyber systems, assets, or functions. The intended effects of cyber attack are not necessarily limited to the targeted computer systems or data themselves – for instance, attacks on computer systems, which are intended to degrade or destroy infrastructure or C2 capability. A cyber attack may use intermediate delivery vehicles including peripheral devices, electronic transmitters, embedded code, or

levels of success." Cheryl Pellerin, "Alexander: Defending against Cyberattacks Requires Collaboration," *American Forces Press Service*, October 30, 2013, http://www.defense.gov/news/newsarticle.aspx?id=121030.

human operators. The activation or effect of a cyber attack may be widely separated temporally and geographically from the delivery.[15]

The definition realistically contemplates a wide temporal distance – lag time – between the action and its impact. But introducing the element of intent, which continues in military doctrinal writing, may complicate the fact-finding process necessary to determine an appropriate response. A standard of proof of "reasonably expected consequences" might be more objective.

Yale Law Professor Oona Hathaway and her colleagues devised a simpler, broader definition of a cyber attack. In their 2012 article, they write: "A cyber attack consists of any action taken to undermine the functions of a computer network for a political or national security purpose."[16] The article goes on to say that "any action" includes "hacking, bombing, cutting, inflecting, and so forth," as long as the action has the objective of undermining or disrupting a computer network.[17] The word "purpose" seems to apply to the intent of the attacking party.

While this definition is not in conflict with that of the Joint Chiefs, its breadth and seeming simplicity seem attractive. At least both definitions help separate cyber attacks that harm the state – even through its private infrastructure – from those that are either commercial theft or espionage. But the very notion of "political purpose" in the Hathaway definition might blur the distinction between crime and war when emanating from a non-state group seeking funding or information.[18]

---

[15] The Vice Chairman of the Joint Chiefs of Staff, Memorandum for Chiefs of the Military Services, Commanders of the Combatant Commands, Directors of the Joint Staff Directorates: Joint Terminology for Cyberspace Operations (2010). http://www.nsci-va.org/CyberReferenceLib/2010-11-joint%20Terminology%20 for%20Cyberspace%20Operations.pdf

[16] Oona Hathaway, Rebeccla Crootof, Philip Levitz, HaleyNix, Aileen Nowlan, willia Perdue &Julia Spiegel, "The Law of Cyber-Attack," *California Law Review* (2012): 9.

[17] Ibid., 10. Presumably this would not include espionage or theft – pulling information from a network without damaging or compromising the network – so long as the ultimate objective was not "undermining or disrupting a computer network."

[18] The International Red Cross definition of cyber warfare is also very broad: "Cyber operations can be broadly described as operations against or via a computer or a computer system through a data stream. Such operations can aim to do

Yet another definition is found in *The Tallinn Manual on the International Law Applicable to Cyber Warfare*, a document developed at the request of NATO's Cooperative Cyber Defense Centre of Excellence. According to the *Manual*, "a cyber attack is a cyber operation, whether offensive or defensive, that is reasonably expected to cause injury or death to persons or damage or destruction to objects."[19]

Drawing a parallel to implanting land mines, the authors of the report conclude that a cyber operation can constitute an attack even before the damaging consequences of such operation become evident. For example, implanting malware that will be activated at a later time but whose "intended consequences meet the requisite threshold of harm" could be defined as an attack "irrespective of whether [the malware] is activated."[20] In a similar vein, a cyber attack that has been launched but defeated still amounts to an attack. The *Manual* does warn that great care should be exercised when identifying the perpetrator of the attack.

different things, for instance to infiltrate a system and collect, export, destroy, change, or encrypt data or to trigger, alter or otherwise manipulate processes controlled by the infiltrated computer system.... It is sometimes claimed that cyber operations do not fall within the definition of 'attack' as long as they do not result in physical destruction or when its effects are reversible. If this claim implies that an attack against a civilian object may be considered lawful in such cases, it is unfounded under existing law in the view of the ICRC. Under IHL, attacks may only be directed at military objectives, while objects not falling within that definition are civilian and may not be attacked.... The definition of military objectives is not dependent on the method of warfare used and must be applied to both kinetic and non-kinetic means; the fact that a cyber operation does not lead to the destruction of an attacked object is also irrelevant." International Committee of the Red Cross, *International Humanitarian Law and the Challenges of Contemporary Armed Conflicts*, Thirty-First International Conference of the Red Cross and Red Crescent, October 2011, http://www.icrc .org/eng/assets/files/red-cross-crescent-movement/31st-international-conference/ 31-int-conference-ihl-challenges-report-11-5-1-2-en.pdf.

[19] Michael N. Schmitt ed., *Tallinn Manual on the International Law Applicable to Cyber Warfare* (Cambridge: Cambridge University Press, 2013), 92. NATO's Glossary of Terms and Definitions describes a computer network attack (CNA) as an "action taken to disrupt, deny, degrade or destroy information resident in a computer and/or computer network, or the computer and/or computer network itself"; see NATO Glossary of Terms and Definitions, http://nuclearenergy .ir/wp-content/uploads/2013/11/tallinn_manual.pdf.

[20] Ibid, 94.

These definitional iterations help refine the issues, although they cannot be expected to answer all questions. They do serve to narrow differences in approach somewhat and to help begin to assure that officials are addressing common issues. However, the lack of internationally accepted distinctions among cyber crime, cyber attack, and cyber war make concerted international action more difficult to achieve. The definitions alone do not delineate civilian and military roles, nor do they designate a legal framework under which to operate, since the issue of whether an attack warrants a military response, even in the military domain, remains ambiguous. Economic attacks may be handled through a variety of international means, both judicial and diplomatic. But crippling economic attacks without serious casualties might not be sufficient to warrant acts in self-defense under Article 51 of the UN Charter or, as in the case of Estonia, a collective response under Article 5 of the North Atlantic Treaty.[21]

Framing a Response

Potential American responses to a cyber attack were outlined in the classified Presidential Policy Directive (PPD) 20, signed in October 2012, revealed by Edward Snowden's leaks of classified documents.[22] The Directive uses a complex vocabulary to describe attacks and potential responses. It described "the manipulation,

---

[21] Article 5 of the North Atlantic (Washington) Treaty states:

The Parties agree that an armed attack against one or more of them in Europe or North America shall be considered an attack against them all and consequently they agree that, if such an armed attack occurs, each of them, in exercise of the right of individual or collective self-defence recognised by Article 51 of the Charter of the United Nations, will assist the Party or Parties so attacked by taking forthwith, individually and in concert with the other Parties, such action as it deems necessary, including the use of armed force, to restore and maintain the security of the North Atlantic area.

Any such armed attack and all measures taken as a result thereof shall immediately be reported to the Security Council. Such measures shall be terminated when the Security Council has taken the measures necessary to restore and maintain international peace and security. http://www.nato.int/cps/en/natolive/official_texts_17120.htm.

[22] PPD 20 further stipulates that both defensive and offensive cyber operation must comply with the U.S. government's obligations under international law, "including with regard to matters of sovereignty and neutrality, and as applicable, the law of armed conflict." The rules expressed in the directive do not seek to affect cyber collection operations unless they are likely to result in "significant consequence." The White House, Presidential Policy Directive 20, October 16, 2012,

disruption, denial, degradation, or destruction of computers, information or communications systems, networks, physical or virtual infrastructure controlled by computers or information systems, or information resident thereon," as a "cyber effect" operation. The Directive defined two types of cyber effects operations: Defensive Cyber Effects Operations (DCEO) and Offensive Cyber Effects Operations (OCEO).[23]

Joint Publication 3–12 (R) titled "Cyber Operations," published by DOD in an unclassified version in February 2013, attempted to clarify military cyber doctrine for the public, even though it is riddled with abbreviations and acronyms. Cyber operations (CO) are divided into three categories: defensive cyber operations (DCO), DOD information networks operations (DODIN), and offensive cyber operations (OCO).[24]

Defensive cyber operations are "intended to defend DOD or other friendly cyberspace." They are described as "passive and active cyberspace defense operations to preserve the ability to utilize friendly cyberspace capabilities and protect data, networks, net-centric capabilities, and other designated systems." DCO include "internal defensive measures" taken within DOD information networks operations (DODIN) as well as "DCO Response Actions" taken outside DODIN to neutralize "ongoing or imminent threats to defend DOD cyberspace." The goal of DODIN operations is to maintain and manage "DOD communications systems and networks" to ensure their protection and sustainability.[25]

http://epic.org/privacy/cybersecurity/#res. See also Ellen Nakashima, "Obama Signs Secret Directive to Help Thwart Cyberattacks," *The Washington Post*, November 14, 2012, http://www.washingtonpost.com/world/national-security/obama-signs-secret-cybersecurity-directive-allowing-more-aggressive-military-role/2012/11/14/7bf51512-2cde-11e2-9ac2-1c61452669c3_story.html.

[23] Both forms of operations are "intended to enable or produce cyber effects outside United States Government networks" and exclude network defense (protection of computers, networks, systems, and the infrastructure under their control, without affecting outside networks) and cyber collection (clandestine intelligence gathering). The purpose of DCEOs is to protect "against imminent threats or ongoing attacks or malicious cyber activity against U.S. national interests from inside or outside cyberspace."

[24] Department of Defense, *Cyberspace Operations*, Joint Publication 3–12(R) (unclassified version, February 5, 2013).

[25] Ibid.

The U.S. military's interest in offensive cyber capabilities has continued to grow.[26] Military doctrine incorporates offensive operations (OCO) into its repertoire, but the content of, and guidance for, offensive cyber operations remains classified. The 2015 Cyber Strategy, in less opaque language, made the choices clearer.

There may be times when the President or the Secretary of Defense may determine that it would be appropriate for the U.S. military to conduct cyber operations to disrupt an adversary's military-related networks or infrastructure so that the U.S. military can protect U.S. interests in an area of operations. For example, the United States military might use cyber operations to terminate an ongoing conflict on U.S. terms, or to disrupt an adversary's military systems to prevent the use of force against U.S. interests. United States Cyber Command (USCYBERCOM) may also be directed to conduct cyber operations, in coordination with other U.S. government agencies as appropriate, to deter or defeat strategic threats in other domains.

But the strategy also emphasized "Any decision to conduct cyber operations outside of DoD networks is made with the utmost care and deliberation and under strict policy and operational oversight, and in accordance with the law of armed conflict."[27] Many geopolitical and domestic political and economic factors would have to be considered when calculating and making an effective response. But leaving uncertainty about the nature of a U.S. response is itself useful as a deterrent.

Denial and punishment – another way of characterizing defensive and offensive action – is a familiar analysis, drawn from nuclear deterrence,[28] although that analogy should be approached

---

[26] "U.S. military spending, depending on the measure, is 2.5 to 4 times as much on cyberoffense research and development as cyberdefense research." P. W. Singer and Allan Friedman, "Cult of the Cyber Offensive," *Foreign Policy*, January 15, 2014, http://www.foreignpolicy.com/articles/2014/01/15/cult_of_the_cyber_offensive_first_strike_advantage.

[27] U.S. Department of Defense *Cyber Strategy* April 2015 http://www.defense.gov/home/features/2015/0415_cyber-strategy/Final_2015_DoD_CYBER_STRATEGY_for_web.pdf

[28] See, e.g., Bernard Brodie, *Strategy in the Missile Age* (Princeton: Princeton University Press, 1959); Thomas Schelling, *Arms and Influence* (New Haven: Yale University Press, 1966); Alexander George and Richard Smoke, *Deterrence in American Foreign Policy: Theory and Practice* (New York: Columbia University

with caution. Several scholars offer a more comprehensive frame-work.[29] The approach is triadic: (1) denial, (2) punishment, and (3) international cooperation.

The first leg of the triad is prevention. Essential to prepared-ness, it is addressed in part by the Joint Staff in its discussion of DCO. The ability to deny the success of a probable attack is a time-honored deterrent from the dawn of nuclear weapons. Effective prevention against cyber incursions is important in civil domains, and especially in critical infrastructure, but also for all cyber incursions that would seriously disrupt the ability of a nation to function normally. Reducing vulnerability in order to create effective prevention is one form of deterrence, and would seem to be the wisest course to follow initially. Hardening systems to make them less vulnerable is optimal. Fast-changing technol-ogy makes such an approach challenging, though not impossible. Improved defenses and system updates must be constant, so that a high degree of resilience can be achieved. These efforts deter by communicating that an attack will not achieve its objective. But government efforts are complicated by the fact that critical infrastructure is in the hands of private industry that remains in control of its preventive measures.[30] By contrast, nuclear weapons are controlled by the state, which controls their storage, safety from theft, reliability, and resiliency to attack.

Press, 1974); Thomas Schelling, *The Strategy of Conflict* (Cambridge, MA: Harvard University Press, 1980); Ashton B. Carter, John D. Steinbruner, and Charles A. Zraket, eds., *Managing Nuclear Operations* (Washington, DC: The Brookings Institution, 1987); and Keith Payne, *The Great American Gamble: Deterrence Theory and Practice from the Cold War to the Twenty-First Century* (Fairfax, VA: National Institute Press, 2008).

[29] Christopher Wrenn, "Strategic Cyber Deterrence" (PhD dissertation, Fletcher School of Law and Diplomacy, Tufts University, July 2012); Herbert Lin, "A Virtual Necessity: Some Modest Steps toward Greater CyberSecurity," *Bulletin of the Atomic Scientists* 68, no. 5 (2012): 68–87.

[30] The possibility of removing some functions to local or meshed systems is now under experiment. The possibility of creating closed systems has also been raised but has gained no traction thus far. Carlotta Gall and James Glanz, "U.S. Promotes Network to Foil Digital Spying," *The New York Times*, April 20, 2014, http:// www.nytimes.com/2014/04/21/us/us-promotes-network-to-foil-digital-spying .html?ref=us.

The second leg of a triadic model is the capability to punish, for which credible offensive capability is needed. The concept of "punishment" is part of classical nuclear deterrence, and the same pitfalls of vast expenditures of funds to assure balance with an opponent may come into play with offensive cyber capability as it has with nuclear prowess. The consequences of punishment by the use of offensive cyber operations are not so disastrous as the use of nuclear weapons, and thus punishment is a more realistic response to attack to contemplate – but the deterrent effect might be weaker. Punishment in cyber warfare might, but would not necessarily involve military measures that raise legal issues under the UN Charter and issues of proportionality under the law of armed conflict. Response to attack might involve trying to develop regional or fully international sanctions if the facts warranted it and a coalition could be mounted. Alternatively, it might involve treating the cyber exploitation as a criminal offense and pursuing law enforcement responses under the Budapest Convention, which provides measures to strengthen interstate cooperation in pursuit of cyber crimes.[31]

On the other hand, if the controls of a nuclear plant were undermined so that radiation killed people for miles around, that would certainly be the equivalent of an armed attack, and military measures might well be taken if attribution were assured. But there are less immediate forms of lethal attack. If critical infrastructure systems were destroyed or crippled, death and illness might result – quickly or slowly. A full-scale attack on critical infrastructure theoretically could prove as much a military attack with kinetic effects over time as are bombing raids on industrial production in traditional wars. It is not a stretch to treat a situation in which people are wounded or die as a consequence of a cyber attack as worthy of military response.[32]

---

[31] Council of Europe, "Convention on Cybercrime," http://conventions.coe.int/Treaty/en/Treaties/Html/185.htm. See Articles 16–17 on the storage and preservation of data including traffic data, Articles 18–19 on the production of data, Articles 23, 25 on international cooperation, and Article 24, which provides for extradition.

[32] Harold Koh, "International Law in Cyberspace" (speech, USCYBERCOM Inter-Agency Legal Conference, September 18, 2012), http://www.state.gov/s/l/releases/remarks/197924.htm.; and Michael Schmitt, "International Law

Although thus far hostile cyber events have not risen to the level of killing people, it is plausible that a cyber attack might do so. But attribution is always essential to response. A false accusation could trigger a diplomatic crisis, and one would hope no cautious leader would take retaliatory action without firm knowledge of the source of an attack.

The third and perhaps most promising element of the triadic construct is international cooperation, discussed at greater length in Chapter 13. The scope of attacks already crosses many state boundaries, and international cooperation is likely to be needed for a response to a cyber attack, as the Estonia case revealed. Post hoc cooperation was effective there, even though the restorative efforts were not only post hoc but also very much ad hoc. Experts from Finland, Slovenia, and Germany happened to be in Estonia and joined the effort to undo the damage in a dramatic all-night session, countering the flaws that had left the Estonian system so vulnerable.[33] Of course, advance collaborative planning for a cooperative response is far preferable to reliance on post hoc efforts: NATO and the EU have moved in that direction. Yet, further moves toward international agreements that restrain aggressive cyber action will likely be far in the future given states' reluctance to relinquish potential weapons in the face of a threatening security climate.[34]

---

in Cyberspace: The Koh Speech and Tallinn Manual Juxtaposed," *Harvard International Law Review* 54 (2012): 13.

[33] Wrenn, "Strategic Cyber Deterrence," 220–221.

[34] The United States still has not acceded to the Biological Weapons Protocol, for example, nor is there much movement toward a Comprehensive Test Ban Treaty. A Fissile Material Cut-Off Treaty has not been accomplished since first proposed in 1993 G.A. Res. 48/75L, http://www.acronym.org.uk/official-and-govt-documents/un-general-assembly-4875l-consensus-resolution-prohibition-production-fissile-materials-nuclear-weap.

See also http://www.nti.org/treaties-and-regimes/proposed-fissile-material-cut-off-reaty/.

11

Implications for Civil-Military Relations in Cyber Attacks and Cyber Warfare

Both civilian and military actors are needed to prevent and respond to cyber exploitation and cyber attacks. Unlike other gray areas, any effort to respond involves cooperation of the private sector, since 85–90% of the critical infrastructure, by any definition, is privately owned and operated. Critical infrastructure is known to be vulnerable, including the electric grid, utilities – especially those fueled by nuclear energy – transportation, and all forms of communication.[1] Public reports indicate that most cyber intrusions and putative attacks have been against privately held critical infrastructure, both in America and Europe.[2]

Three distinct types of novel problems emerge from the demands that will be placed on civil-military relationship in the event of a cyber attack. The first is the fact of private ownership of most critical infrastructure. The need to secure cooperation between government and the private sector presents serious obstacles. In the United States,

[1] In the United States, the private sector "owns and operates approximately 85% of the nation's critical infrastructure." Department of Homeland Security, "Critical Infrastructure Sector Partnerships," http://www.dhs.gov/critical-infrastructure-sector-partnerships. Likewise, in Europe, "approximately 85% [of the critical infrastructure] are owned by the private sector." Bernard Haemmerli and Andrea Renda, *Protecting Critical Infrastructure in the EU*, Regulatory Policy, CEPS Task Force Reports, December 16, 2010, http://www.ceps.be/book/protecting-critical-infrastructure-eu.

[2] According to Verizon's Data Breach Investigations Report, there were 511 cyber espionage incidents in 2013. Cyber espionage incidents "include unauthorized network or system access linked to state-affiliated actors and/or exhibiting the motive of espionage." Verizon Wireless, *Data Breach Investigations Report 2014*, http://www.verizonenterprise.com/DBIR/2014/.

efforts to legislate standards for the private sector, discussed in Chapter 12, have been thwarted.[3] However the issues are not simply industrial reluctance to cooperate with all of government: fear of antitrust prosecution also plays a role. Moreover, resistance to NSA overreach in monitoring telecommunications and the internet have helped create deep concerns about government regulation within the private sector and civil liberties groups alike.[4] The same issue arises in Europe, where cooperation across state lines is even more important given the interdependence of much of its critical infrastructure. Lack of resilience in one nation's infrastructure immediately affects its neighbors: a failure of the electric grid in Germany triggered power outages in France, Italy, and parts of Spain.[5]

The second problem is the joinder of the intelligence and military domains, and the potential intertwining of operations. U.S. Cyber Command is co-located with the NSA, and headed by the same person. This has led to questions about oversight and control of both intelligence activities and military responses.[6] In cyber war, as in targeted killing, intelligence services may be performing essentially military operations. The President's Independent Review Group recommended separating the agencies and their leaderships, with the NSA clearly designated as a foreign intelligence agency, but as of this writing, leadership is still shared.[7] U.S. Cyber Command

[3] "Banks Say Efforts to Bolster U.S. Cyber Defenses Should Complement Industry Practices," *American Banker*, April 12, 2013, http://www.americanbanker.com/issues/178_70/banks-say-efforts-to-bolster-u-s-cyber-defenses-should-complement-industry-1058220-1.html.

[4] Privacy and Civil Liberties Oversight Board, *Report of the Surveillance Program Operated Pursuant to Section 702 of the Foreign Intelligence Surveillance Act*, July 2, 2014, http://www.pclob.gov/library.html. See also Ellen Nakashima, "NSA Thwarted in Cybersecurity Initiative," *The Washington Post*, February 28, 2012, http://www.washingtonpost.com/national/major-internet-service-providers-cooperating-with-nsa-on-monitoring-traffic/2011/06/07/AG2dukXH_story.html.

[5] Bernard Haemmerli and Andrea Renda, *Protecting Critical Infrastructure in the EU*, Regulatory Policy, CEPS Task Force Reports, December 16, 2010, http://www.ceps.be/book/protecting-critical-infrastructure-eu, 3.

[6] Richard A. Clarke, Michael J. Morell, Geoffrey R. Stone, Cass R. Sunstein, and Peter Swire, *Liberty and Security in a Changing World: Report and Recommendations of The President's Review Group on Intelligence and Communications Technologies*, December 12, 2013, http://press.princeton.edu/titles/10296.html.

[7] Ellen Nakashima, "White House to Preserve Controversial Policy on NSA, Cyber Command Leadership," *The Washington Post*, December 13, 2013,

reports through Strategic Command to the Secretary of Defense. NSA, a critical (and much criticized) part of America's intelligence network, reports both to the Secretary of Defense and to the Director of National Intelligence.[8]

The third problem is to secure effective and timely collaboration of the essential civil departments and levels of government below the federal level in the United States. In the event of a crippling attack, an effective response will require all levels of government and industry to function together smoothly and with unprecedented speed. In both the United States and Europe, many departments and agencies have only partial responsibility.

Efforts are under way in the U.S. government to develop effective collaboration, and to deal with the three types of civil-military problems outlined here. Presidential Policy Directive (PPD) 21 of February 2013[9] (together with Executive Order 13636)[10] requires "a national unity of effort pursuant to strategic guidance from the Secretary of Homeland Security."[11] A documentary review indicates government awareness of the complexity of coordinating the many relevant agencies and departments sprawled over the federal system. As indication of the difficulties, the President created a Cyber Threat Intelligence Integration Center under the auspices of the Director of National Intelligence to connect and coordinate the

---

http://www.washingtonpost.com/world/national-security/white-house-to-preserve-controversial-policy-on-nsa-cyber-command-leadership/2013/12/13/4bb56a48-6403-11e3-a373-0f9f2d1c2b61_story.html.

[8] National Security Agency, "Frequently Asked Questions, Oversight," https://www.nsa.gov/about/faqs/oversight.shtml#oversight1.

[9] White House, Presidential Policy Directive 21 (PPD 21), "Critical Infrastructure Security and Resilience," February 12, 2013, http://www.whitehouse.gov/the-press-office/2013/02/12/presidential-policy-directive-critical-infrastructure-security-and-resil.

[10] Executive Order 13636, "Improving Critical Infrastructure Cybersecurity," February 12, 2013.

[11] According to PPD 21, the primary responsibility for the security of the nation's critical infrastructure belongs to the Secretary of Homeland Security, who is appointed to "provide strategic guidance, promote a national unity of effort, and coordinate the overall Federal effort to promote the security and resilience of the Nation's critical infrastructure." Various sectors of critical infrastructure benefit from the expertise of the Sector-Specific Agencies, which among other duties "provide, support, or facilitate technical assistance and consultations for that sector to identify vulnerabilities and help mitigate incidents." White House, PPD 21.

intelligence gathered by other agencies, rather than to engage in programmatic efforts.[12] But whether such coordination will work in a cyber crisis remains to be proven.

Wide Array of Civil and Military Actors

PPD 21 allocated important cyber responsibilities to many departments and agencies.[13] The State Department is given the lead in securing foreign cooperation and in negotiating formal or informal international agreements.[14] The Department of Justice is given responsibility for counterterrorism investigation and law enforcement activities pertaining to infrastructure, although its investigatory relationship to the intelligence community is unclear in PPD 21.[15] The Department of Treasury is also essential both for the banking area and for imposing financial sanctions on any offending state.[16] Other agencies, such as the departments of Commerce and Interior, also have designated roles, as does the Nuclear Regulatory Commission.[17] Federal unclassified spending on cybersecurity in fiscal year 2014 totaled $12.7 billion, which was a 23 percent increase

---

[12] Presidential Memorandum, "Establishment of the Cyber Threat Intelligence Integration Center," February 25, 2015, https://www.whitehouse.gov/the-press-office/2015/02/25/presidential-memorandum-establishment-cyber-threat-intelligence-integrat

[13] White House, PPD 21.

[14] The State Department has created the Office of the Coordinator for Cyber Issues to encourage "global diplomatic engagement." Its website is available at http://www.state.gov/s/cyberissues/.

[15] Ibid. See also "U.S. Department of Justice Overview," http://www.justice.gov/sites/default/files/jmd/legacy/2014/08/25/fy13-bud-summary-request-performance.pdf; and PPD 21, no 36.

[16] The Department of Treasury "works with other Federal agencies, including the intelligence community and DHS, to assess physical and cyber threats that are identified as specifically directed at the sector or at an asset on a national, regional, or local level. Relationships with DHS, the intelligence community, and other [sector-specific agencies] provide real-time information regarding these threats. Additionally, when threats are identified, frequent communications between the FBIIC and the private sector facilitate efficient and effective transfer of potential threat information, permitting the sector to mitigate the associated vulnerabilities." Department of Homeland Security, *Banking and Finance Sector: Specific Plan and Annex to the National Infrastructure Protection Plan*, 2010.

[17] White House, PPD 21.

TABLE 11.1 *Wide Array of Government Actors*

Civil	Military
President (National Command Authority [NCA])	NCA, Secretary of Defense
DHS	Combatant Commands (esp. Cyber Command)
State Department	Military Services
Treasury	Reserves and National Guard
Interior	Coast Guard
Intelligence Community (NSA, CIA)	
Justice Department: FBI Plus	
Commerce	
Nuclear Regulatory Commission	
States and Cities	

from fiscal year 2013.[18] The intelligence community has a major role, especially in determining the origin of an attack.

To this wide array of governmental actors (Table 11.1), many other civil actors would be affected by a cyber attack, and many would have to be involved in reconstitution efforts, just as they should be involved in preventive efforts: providers of internet technology (IT) products and services, internet service providers (ISP), security services, and IT-dependent providers of goods and services, to name a few.[19] In addition to the many layers of collaboration within the United States, international cooperation will certainly be required to prevent attacks and to repair damage.

The Department of Homeland Security (DHS) is responsible for coordinating all government efforts in protecting infrastructure and coordinating efforts with state and local government organizations. It has primary responsibility for securing cooperation with the private industry that controls critical infrastructure.[20] However, without the legislative authority to require compliance, DHS can

[18] "Fiscal Year 2014 Federal Cyber Security Spending Update," The Soter Group, March 2015, http://www.scribd.com/doc/259935090/The-Soter-Group-Fiscal-Year-2014-Federal-Cyber-Security-Spending-Update (accessed April 20, 2015).

[19] Thanks to Dr. Herbert Lin for these additions.

[20] "Presidential Policy Directive/PPD-21 – Critical Infrastructure and Security Resilience," The White House, February 12, 2013.

only "jawbone" – urge cooperation, assist and advise.[21] Moreover, increasing foreign private ownership of American infrastructure further complicates efforts at government-business collaboration.[22]

The effort made by PPD 21 and Executive Order 13636 to create a "whole of government" approach did not provide a blueprint for the complex collaboration required, leaving it to DHS to develop a model and to evaluate its progress.[23] DHS has been implementing its mandate, starting with an Integrated Task Force, to coordinate the disparate elements within it, and to involve other departments and state and local governments.[24] Numerous studies and recommendations have been made. It is a work in progress of ongoing bureaucratic and organizational efforts, which may change over time with experience and different personnel.[25]

[21] By contrast, the state of Israel has instituted its "CERT-IL" program, which provides for government management of critical infrastructure in case of cyber attack. But its infrastructure is largely publicly held. Even in the case of banking, however, the government sets cybersecurity standards through its banking regulators. Lecture by Professor Isaac Ben Israel at the Fletcher School, April 24, 2015.

[22] Committee on Foreign Investment in the United States, *Annual Report to Congress*, December 2013; William R. Vigdor and Adrianne L. Goins, *Trends in U.S. National Security Review: A More Active CFIUS*, Vinson & Elkins LLC, March 2011; James A. Lewis, "New Objectives for CFIUS: Foreign Ownership, Critical Infrastructure, and Communications Interception," *Federal Communications Law Journal* 57, no. 3 (May 1, 2005): 458–478.

[23] PPD 21 directs the Secretary of Homeland Security to lead the effort of developing "Critical Infrastructure Security and Resilience Functional Relationships" and to evaluate the public-private model. PPD 21; Exec. Order 13636, *Federal Register* 78, no. 33 (February 19, 2013), https://www.whitehouse.gov/the-press-office/2013/02/12/presidential-policy-directive-critical-infrastructure-security-and-resil.

[24] Robert Kolasky, Director, Integrated Task Force, United States Department of Homeland Security (statement for the record before the United States House of Representatives Committee on Homeland Security Subcommittee on Cybersecurity, Infrastructure Protection and Security Technologies, July 18, 2013), http://docs.house.gov/meetings/HM/HM08/20130718/101151/HHRG-113-HM08-Wstate-KolaskyR-20130718.pdf; see also Department of Homeland Security, "Integrated Task Force," http://www.dhs.gov/sites/default/files/publications/EO-PPD%20Fact%20Sheet%202018March13.pdf.

[25] Department of Homeland Security Integrated Task Force, *Executive Order 13636: Improving Critical Infrastructure Cybersecurity*, Incentives Study Analytic Report, June 12, 2013, http://www.dhs.gov/sites/default/files/publications/dhs-eo13636-analytic-report-cybersecurity-incentives-study.pdf; see also Michael Daniel, "Incentives to Support Adoption of the Cybersecurity Framework," *The White House Blog*, August 6, 2013, http://www.whitehouse.gov/blog/2013/08/06/incentives-support-adoption-cybersecurity-framework.

Implementation of PPD 21 and Executive Order 13636 has been
under way, but its effectiveness has yet to be tested.[26] Sequestration,
stringent budgets, and staff turnover have strained the capability
of DHS.[27] According to the Center for Strategic and International
Studies, for FY2015, DHS requested $1.25 billion for "cybersecu-
rity activities, an increase from the $792 million enacted in the 2014
Consolidated Appropriations Act." By contrast, "the Department of
Defense (DoD) request includes $5.1 billion, or about four times
the DHS request, to support cyber operations."[28] In the event of an
attack on critical infrastructure, it seems likely that DoD's capacity
will lead to its predominant role in managing the problems.

Early reports on implementation of PPD 21 and Executive
Order 13636 by the DHS Infrastructure Advisory Council (NIAC)

[26] See the detailed report prepared by the Global Institute for Cyber Security
and Research, Global Situation Awareness Center, http://www.nhisac.org/
wp-content/uploads/NH-ISAC-Advisory-Report-201.13_National-Critical-
Infrastructure-Resilience.pdf

[27] Jerry Markon, Ellen Nakashima, and Alice Crites, "Top-Level Turnover Makes It
Harder for DHS to Stay on Top of Evolving Threats," *The Washington Post*, September
21, 2014, http://www.washingtonpost.com/politics/top-level-turnover-makes-it-
harder-for-dhs-to-stay-on-top-of-evolving-threats/2014/09/21/ca79192a6-39d7-
11e4-9c9f-ebb47272e40e_story.html.

[28] Stephanie Sanok Kostro and Garrett Riba, "Major Takeaways from the President's
FY 2014 Budget Request for DHS," Center for Strategic and International Studies,
March 13, 2014, http://csis.org/publication/major-takeaways-presidents-fy-
2015-budget-request-dhs. Peter Singer, in a public lecture at the Fletcher School,
stated that the budget of the DoD and the NSA combined, not counting the clas-
sified budget, was twelve times that of the DHS.
  In 2014, the Cyber Command budget doubled to $447 million (U.S. million).
Brian Fung, "Cyber Command's Exploding Budget, in 1 Chart," *The Washington
Post*, January 15, 2014, http://www.washingtonpost.com/blogs/the-switch/
wp/2014/01/15/cyber-commands-exploding-budget-in-1-chart/. The suggested
2015 defense budget allocates $5.1 billion to cyber defense. Department of Defenses,
"DoD Releases Fiscal 2015 Budget Proposal and 2014 QDR," news release, March
4, 2014, http://www.defense.gov/releases/release.aspx?releaseid=16567. According
to U.S. Chief Information Officer Steven VanRoekel, "the 2014 President's Budget
devotes over $13B to cyber-related programs and activities." White House,
"Federal Information Technology FY 2014 Budget Priorities."
  The DHS FY2015 budget request includes $1.25 billion for safeguarding
and securing cyberspace. Department of Homeland Security, "Budget-in-Brief
Fiscal Year 2015." The Department of Justice FY 2015 budget "provides a total
of $722 million" for cyber security. Department of Justice, "FY 2015 Budget
Summary," http://www.justice.gov/jmd/2015summary/pdf/fy15-bud-sum.pdf#p4.

Report,[29] composed primarily of business and outside counsel, suggested the need to set priorities and provide milestones for measuring outcomes. It criticized redundancy and overclassification.[30] The report also reiterated the search for a "safe harbor" against antitrust violations, adding a request for limiting liability in case of a cyber event. It discussed the need for training funds for smaller business entities to respond to cyber exploitation. Although couched in a bland vocabulary, the report suggests to the reader that the desired collaboration between government and business was far from achieved. Greater federal-state cooperation was called for in the sixteen "lifeline" areas identified as critical infrastructure, as different geographic areas had different priorities. The report emphasized the general need for modernization and the lack of capital investment made, suggesting vulnerability not only to cyber attacks but also to major weather events. Over time, advisers and researchers may be more satisfied with the complex structure that is constantly being adjusted under a snowstorm of memoranda, department directives, and organizational changes, but lack of investment is a persistent theme.

How Good Are the Precedents for Collaboration?

A look at the history of interagency and intergovernmental cooperation during a crisis is not very encouraging. To illustrate, consider the impossibly slow, clumsy governmental response to Hurricane Katrina in 2005 and the complex interagency, intergovernmental, private sector management issues following the Deepwater Horizon oil spill of 2010. Hurricane Katrina was one of the most tragic environmental disasters the United States has ever suffered. Predictable and predicted, the break in the levies that flooded parts of New Orleans killed between 1,500 and 1,800 people, resulted in 1.2 million evacuees, and caused many more thousands of displaced persons and $100 billion in damage.[31] Despite a new National Incident

---

[29] See the National Infrastructure Advisory Council (NIAC), *Final Report and Recommendations*, November 21, 2013, http://www.dhs.gov/publication/national-infrastructure-advisory-council-strengthening-regional-resilience.

[30] Ibid.

[31] Lise Olson, "Five Years after Katrina, Storm's Death Toll Remains a Mystery," *Houston Chronicle*, August 30, 2010, http://www.chron.com/news/nation-world/article/5-years-after-Katrina-storm-s-death-toll-remains-1589464.php.

Management System, the worst-hit states – Louisiana, Mississippi, and Alabama – were unused to collaboration, nor was the Federal Emergency Management Agency (FEMA) or the Coast Guard – despite their co-location within DHS. The National Guard of three states also attempted to help, but the lack of unified command precluded timely and useful cooperation.[32] The human disasters mounted while the government agencies floundered.

By April 2010, when the Deepwater Horizon explosions and oil spill occurred, there was improvement in coordination, at least in the U.S. Coast Guard's ability to respond to the largest marine spill in the history of the petroleum industry – nearly five million barrels spread across the waters of many states.[33] Many of the same problems of interagency and intergovernmental collaboration had to be faced as after the Katrina landfall. The circumstances were different, and the toll in human lives vastly lower, but it was evident that five years of practice with the National Response System[34] did somewhat improve collaborative efforts.

However, another important difference was a twenty-year experience with federal legislation. The Oil Pollution Act of 1990 (OPA90) – created after the Exxon Valdez spill, firmly established that the federal government had supreme authority over oil spills (primarily delegated to the Coast Guard), and provided severe penalties for failure to meet prescribed standards.[35] Although commentators disagree about the effectiveness of the law's implementation,

Eric Iverson, "Networked Resilience: Achieving Inter-Organizational and Intergovernmental Collaboration" (PhD dissertation, Fletcher School of Law and Diplomacy, Tufts University, January 6, 2013).

[32] Ibid. See recommendations made in Department of Homeland Security, Office of Inspector General, *A Performance Review of FEMA's Disaster Management Activities in Response to Hurricane Katrina*, March 2006, http://www.oig.dhs.gov/assets/Mgmt/OIG_06-32_Mar06.pdf.

[33] "BP Oil Spill," National Oceanic and Atmospheric Administration, http://www.gulfspillrestoration.noaa.gov/oil-spill/ (accessed April 20, 2015).

[34] The National Response System is the federal mechanism developed to prepare for and respond to environmental disasters. It is designed to coordinate the resources of federal, state, and local authorities and to organize an efficient and effective response to such a disaster – i.e., to seek improvement over past responses.

[35] Summary of Key Provisions of the Oil Pollution Act of 1990, U.S. Environmental Protection Agency, Pub. L. No. 101–380, 104 Stat. 484 (1990), http://www.epa.gov/oecaagct/lopa.html.

it does appear that oil spills were reduced after its passage, and that potential punishment helped create a somewhat higher standard of care.[36] Although there was an improvement in performance over the period between the two crises, both examples suggest the complexity of developing collaboration when responsibilities must be divided among so many agencies and levels of government.

Disputes and mistakes may be inevitable. In 2010, U.S. Central Command dismantled an online forum created by the CIA and the Saudi government as part of an intelligence-gathering effort to identify dangerous terrorists because they had concluded that extremists' use of the site constituted a threat to the United States. The journalist Ellen Nakashima quoted a former national security official: "The point of the story is it hasn't been sorted out yet in a way that all the persons involved in cyber-operations have a clear understanding of doctrine, legal authorities and policy, and a clear understanding of the distinction between what is considered intelligence activity and wartime [Defense Department] authority."[37] Such inter-agency conflicts need sorting out before, not after, an attack.

Other examples cast doubt on achieving a smooth "whole of government" response. Hurricane Sandy in 2012 left many residents homeless for a long time, with some plaudits and many complaints about the responses.[38] And the inconsistent federal-state and civil-military response to the travellers from Liberia, Guinea, and Sierra Leone who might be carrying the Ebola virus in October 2014 also serves warning about the difficulties of collaboration.[39]

---

[36] Jeffery D. Morgan, "The Oil Pollution Act of 1990: A Look at Its Impact on the Oil Industry," *Fordham Environmental Law Review* 2, VI (1994): 10–12.

[37] Ellen Nakashima, "Dismantling of Saudi-CIA Web Site Illustrates Need for Clearer Cyberwar Policies," *The Washington Post*, March 19, 2010, http://www .washingtonpost.com/wp-dyn/content/article/2010/03/18/AR2010031805464 .html.

[38] Tim Starks, "Katrina's Lessons Seen in Response to Sandy," *Congressional Quarterly*, December 29, 2012, http://public.cq.com/docs/weeklyreport/ weeklyreport-000004197197.html (accessed April 20, 2015).

[39] See Jon Swaine and Dan Roberts, "New Federal Ebola Guidelines Issued in US After Criticism from UN," *The Guardian*, October 27, 2014, http://www .theguardian.com/world/2014/oct/27/ban-ki-moon-concerned-ebola-restrictions (accessed May 14, 2015); Ellen Wulfhorst and David Morgan, "U.S. CDC Says Returning Ebola Medical Workers Should Not be Quarantined," Reuters,

Many obstacles remain before an effective response to a cyber attack against public or private assets can be assured. First, one can only speculate how long – if ever – it will take to assess whether the intrusion is more likely to be espionage (commercial or political) or a precursor to attack against the state. Problems with attribution will continue to complicate response potential. Pinpointing Chinese intrusions into U.S. infrastructure to a physical location and specific officials in the Chinese military in Shanghai is encouraging in that sources of intrusion may not be permanently elusive.[40] Even when attribution is certain, the United States wisely has not yet treated intrusions into critical infrastructure as a prelude to a system shutdown. Although it is conceivable that significant tensions might alter the diplomatic calculus, at least there should be reliable, tested interagency and intergovernmental mechanisms that would allow for rapid reconstitution.

The assessment process itself requires a system of collaboration to avoid agencies tripping over each other, waiting for another to make an assessment, or performing the task separately and competitively. The issues of resources, experience, and capability apply even more strongly to attribution, and thus it is likely that Cyber Command and NSA would take the lead.[41]

Second, once there is adequate certainty about attribution – and that might take months, not days – a course of action must be determined. Since a decision to act or refrain from acting is highly political, a collaborative recommendation to the president would presumably be made about the choices available for action. This is

October 27, 2014, http://www.reuters.com/article/2014/10/27/us-health-ebola-usa-newyork-idUSKBN0IG12920141027 (accessed May 14, 2015); Abby Phillip, "Why Hasn't the U.S. Closed Its Airports to Travelers from Ebola-ravaged Countries," *The Washington Post*, October 4, 2015, http://www.washingtonpost.com/news/to-your-health/wp/2014/10/01/why-hasnt-the-u-s-closed-its-airports-to-travelers-from-ebola-ravaged-countries/ (accessed May 14, 2015).

[40] "Hello, Unit 61398," *The Economist*, February 2013, http://www.economist.com/blogs/analects/2013/02/chinese-cyber-attacks.

[41] Richard A. Clarke et al., *Liberty and Security in a Changing World*. See also Ellen Nakashima, "White House to Preserve Controversial Policy on NSA, Cyber Command Leadership," *The Washington Post*, December 13, 2013, http://www.washingtonpost.com/world/national-security/white-house-to-preserve-controversial-policy-on-nsa-cyber-command-leadership/2013/12/13/4bb56a48-6403-11e3-a373-0f9f2d1c2b61_story.html.

a cumbersome process requiring inputs from all relevant agencies to offer viable options. The process changes as administrations change, but it has involved options developed for the Deputies' Committee, then rehashed and refined in the Principals' Committee, and finally honed for NSC with the President.[42] Hopefully, a process would be accelerated in an emergency. But a further element – collaboration with allies for attribution, response, and repair – will also take time and effort.

In a 2012 article, Professor Mary Ellen O'Connell notes her concern about overmilitarization of cyber issues that could well be handled by civilian authorities, with a different formulation of the problem – a reliance on economic regulation. She argues that instead of drawing on analogies from nuclear deterrence, the government should rely on international legal norms of nonintervention and countermeasures. She suggests the danger from cyber attacks be treated much as chemical weapons were handled – by an international agreement that reduces stockpiles and gradually eliminates the threat of chemical warfare by international regulation of universal proportions, or by actions against piracy.[43] She argues:

In the USA and other States where the thinking is in conventional military terms respecting responses to cyber problems, the advocates of such thinking appear to be trapped by an ideology of militarism. The vast majority of cyber security incidents are carried out not by government-sponsored hackers causing deaths and brick and mortar destruction. The major challenge to Internet security is by private criminals interested in private gain. International law supports cyber security that is achieved through law enforcement cooperation, supported by shared legal norms governing the use of the Internet.[44]

Professor O'Connell's worry about overmilitarization is one that deserves consideration, given budgetary disparities between DoD

---

[42] "An NSC Deputies Committee (NSC/DC) shall serve as the senior sub-Cabinet interagency forum for consideration of policy issues affecting national security." The principals' committee involves the cabinet members, specifically agency heads. The Organization of the National Security Council, "Presidential Decision Directive PDD2," http://www.fas.org/irp/offdocs/pdd/.

[43] Mary Ellen O'Connell, "Cyber Security without Cyber War," Journal of Conflict & Security Law (2012): 190, http://jcsl.oxfordjournals.org/content/17/2/187.full.pdf?ijkey=T6J6KDRCRcHM4A0&keytype=ref%2520.

[44] Ibid., 191.

and other government agencies, especially the combination of Cyber Command with NSA. The President's initial decision to continue joint control perpetuates the imbalance with DHS, but even if those agencies were separated, the budgetary imbalance would exist.[45]

A move toward broad regulation of cyber exploitation that includes military and nonmilitary offenses is an important ultimate approach. But Professor O'Connell's suggested analogy to piracy does not take into account the difficulties of securing deep regulatory regimes. The Convention for the Suppression of Unlawful Acts against Safety of Maritime Navigation (SUA) came into force in a somewhat more treaty-friendly era,[46] but today, the SUA protocol of 2005 that bans transport of such dangerous materials as nuclear, chemical, and biological precursors to weapons lacks signatories from critical nations such as the United States, China, and Russia.[47] The Chemical Weapons Convention, which came into force in 1997, created a robust international organization, the Organization for the Prohibition of Chemical Weapons (OPCW), that is the instrument of intrusive verification. As discussed later in the book, many steps will have to precede deep regulation, even if that could ultimately be accomplished. Meanwhile, with attacks on critical infrastructure numbering in the hundreds in 2013 and growing, security concerns must be addressed quickly and effectively.[48]

Simulations and Exercises

In the absence of international regulation, and even should it be developed, nations will still be responsible for internal agency collaboration to deal with a disastrous cyber event. Without many rehearsals and clear delineation of roles, critical departments are

---

[45] Richard A. Clarke et al., *Liberty and Security in a Changing World.*

[46] SUA came into force in 1988.

[47] https://imo.amsa.gov.au/public/parties/sua05prot.html.

[48] According to a DHS industrial control systems cyber emergency response team (ICS-CERT) annual report, in the fiscal year 2013, 257 incidents were reported to ICS-CERT. This is an increase from both fiscal years 2012 (197 incidents reported) and 2011 (140 incidents reported). The largest percentage (56 percent) of sector-specific incidents was in the energy sector. Department of Homeland Security, *ICS-CERT Year in Review, 2013,* http://ics-cert.us-cert.gov/sites/default/files/documents/Year_In_Review_FY2013_Final.pdf.

unlikely to collaborate effectively with instant and effective communication in a crisis. As Hurricane Katrina demonstrated, the existence of a government-wide alert or management system is not sufficient without experience in using it.[49] Effective collaboration has to be planned for, and exercised, especially where the private sector is not compelled by legislation to cooperate.

Some issues may arise in exercises, and their identification and careful joint planning for correction is necessary. Constant and penetrating exercises are needed that test suspected weakness in interagency, intergovernmental, and public-private cooperation. Exercises have been conducted to test the effectiveness of the National Cyber Incident Response Plan (NCIRP), whose purpose is to provide "a blueprint for cybersecurity incident response,"[50] to deal with cyber incidents. The National Cyber Security Division (NCSD), an arm of DHS, has conducted a number of simulations in recent years.[51] One exercise was an attempt by the administration

---

[49] Eric Iverson, "Networked Resilience."

[50] Department of Homeland Security, "Cyber Storm: Securing Cyber Space," http://www.dhs.gov/cyber-storm-securing-cyber-space.

[51] In 2006, DHS initiated a series of biennial exercises aptly named "Cyber Storm" to test and monitor public- and private-sector preparedness in the event of a cyber attack. The fourth installment concluded in 2012, but the final report was unavailable at writing. See Department of Homeland Security, "Cyber Storm: Securing Cyber Space," http://www.dhs.gov/cyber-storm-securing-cyber-space.

Attack exercises included the 2012 National Level Exercise (NLE), which simulated a cyber attack on critical infrastructure systems that had a physical impact. As part of the exercise, President Obama held a cabinet meeting to discuss "with his leadership team the time-sensitive decisions that would have to be made if a significant cyber event affected critical infrastructure systems." See White House Press Secretary, "Statement on the 2012 National Level Exercise," June 5, 2012, http://www.whitehouse.gov/the-press-office/2012/06/05/statement-press-secretary-2012-national-level-exercise. Additionally, the National Cyber Security Division (NCSD), a DHS agency, plans and conducts cyber exercises to protect the critical infrastructure on state, federal, regional, and international levels. These exercises involve a diverse array of actors, from "emergency managers, homeland security advisors, state and local government officials, to law enforcement, private sector owners and operators as well as academia, media outlets, and community groups." See US-CERT, "National Cyber Security Division Cyber Exercise Program."

On July 18, 2013, the financial service sector carried out a cyber attack simulation, Quantum Dawn 2, to "test incident response, resolution and coordination processes." The exercise involved some fifty financial service and government entities and gave participants the opportunity to run through their crisis response procedures, practice information sharing, and refine their protocols

to demonstrate to senators the vulnerability of the nation's critical infrastructure and to persuade them to pass the Cybersecurity Act of 2012 that set performance standards for all industry. The senators were shown how the attack on the electrical grid could be initiated by a phishing e-mail. The scenario included deaths and billions of dollars in losses. According to accounts, close to fifty senators attended, but apparently were not convinced enough to pass the proposed legislation.[52]

A number of CyberStorm Exercises continue to be held by DHS involving relevant partners, including foreign governments. The published critiques, however, seem to "paper over" problems with such statements as "[a]lthough public–private interaction around cyber response is continually evolving and improving, it can be complicated by the lack of timely and meaningful shared situational awareness; uncertainties regarding roles and responsibilities; and legal, customer, and/or security concerns."[53]

DoD is engaged in a parallel effort to test concerted government approaches to cyber defense. In February 2014, General Keith B. Alexander, who then headed the U.S. Cyber Command, described its exercises in testimony before the Senate Armed Services Committee, emphasizing the focus on military services and National Guard units, although many other agencies and international partners were included. General Alexander indicated Cyber Command's goal of developing strong working relationships among DOD/NSA, DHS, and FBI in defending critical infrastructure, including water treatment facilities, gas pipelines, and electrical grids.[54]

relating to a systemic cyber attack. See SIFMA, "Statement on Quantum Dawn 2 Cybersecurity Exercise," July 18, 2013, http://www.sifma.org/newsroom/2013/sifma-statement-on-quantum-dawn-2-cybersecurity-exercise/.

[52] Brendan Sasso, "White House Simulates Cyberattack for Senators in Push for More Regulation," *The Hill* (blog), March 8, 2012, http://thehill.com/blogs/hillicon-valley/technology/214951-white-house-simulates-cyber-attack-for-senators-as-part-of-push-for-legislation; Jennifer Martinez, "White House Tries Cyber Scare Demonstration to Spur Senate," *Politico*, March 8, 2012, http://www.politico.com/news/stories/0312/73800.html.

[53] Department of Homeland Security, *CyberStorm III, Final Report*, July 2011, http://www.dhs.gov/sites/default/files/publications/CyberStorm%20III%20FINAL%20Report.pdf.

[54] Colonel Rivers Johnson, "Cyber Guard Exercise Focuses on Defensive Cyberspace Operations," U.S. Army, August 16, 2012, http://www.army.mil/article/85786/.

Both departmental exercises seem to be useful. The DHS Cyber Storm exercise series involved a wider variety of participants including more than a dozen federal government entities, state authorities, and a large number of private companies.[55] Cyber Command simulations, with a more inclusive military cast, are equally important, especially because they include the National Guard, which has long been important in disaster relief.[56]

The fact that the EU is also engaged in biannual detailed exercises means that the chance for more effective civil-military multilevel and multinational response might be enhanced.[57] NATO has held a large exercise in Estonia.[58] All of these exercises contribute to experience in handling a real crisis, but greater transparency in exercise evaluations would help the U.S. Congress and the public in both the United States and allied nations better understand how effective the current response system is likely to be and what kind of improvements might be made.

In 2014, the same actors exercised their support for DHS and FBI responses to foreign-based attacks on simulated critical infrastructure networks to further promote collaboration and critical information sharing. Department of Defense, "Cyber Guard Exercise Tests People, Partnerships," July 17, 2014, http://www .defense.gov/news/newsarticle.aspx?id=122696. The exercises brought together DHS, FBI, USCYBERCOM, state government officials, the National Guard, Information Sharing and Analysis Centers, and private industry participants. General Keith B. Alexander, Commander of United States Cyber Command (statement before the Senate Committee on Armed Service, February 27, 2014), http://www.armed-services.senate.gov/imo/media/doc/Alexander_02-27-14.pdf.

[55] See Department of Homeland Security, *Cyber Storm III Final Report*, annex A, "Participant List."

[56] These simulations focus on how DoD/NSA and the National Guard interact in cyberspace to support DHS and the FBI. The role of nongovernmental participants in Cyber Guard was unclear. On the one hand, they were described as "partners" who "completed" the exercise. On the other hand, it was suggested that they took part as observers.
See Department of Defense, "Cyber Guard Exercise Tests People."

[57] http://www.enisa.europa.eu/media/press-releases/biggest-eu-cyber-security-exercise-to-date-cyber-europe-2014-taking-place-today.

[58] Sam Jones, "NATO Holds Largest Cyber War Games," *Financial Times*, November 20, 2014, http://www.ft.com/intl/cms/s/0/9c46a600-70c5-11e4-8113-00144feabdco.html#axzz3TwGGCf83.

12

Legal Implications of Cyber Attacks and Cyber Warfare

Since the very concept of cyber attacks as a form of warfare is so novel, it is unsurprising that legal guidance has not caught up with technological possibilities. In the absence of international agreements and domestic legislation in the United States and Europe, creative attempts have been made to bring cyber attacks under the umbrella of existing international and domestic legal doctrines. Yet analogies, however creative and persuasive, are not infinitely elastic.

The Tallinn Manual represents an important international step in attempting to state current international treaty and customary law that pertains to cyber exploitation. In 2009, the NATO Cooperative Center of Excellence commissioned a broad international group of legal and technical experts to explain the relevant law and practice as it stood at the time. Under the leadership of its editor, Professor Michael N. Schmitt, it chose the format of rules with explanations, not unlike the judicious approach taken by the American Law Institute in its Restatements of Law in various fields. It is not meant to express an official interpretation, as a disclaimer makes clear,[1] but it is an influential document toward that end, and it has been treated as such. It did not create new law, nor suggest possible international agreements that might be adopted. It did create a consensus, nonbinding document that could form the basis for future negotiations. However, the process has not stimulated

---

[1] Michael Schmitt, Gen Ed. Tallinn Manual on the International Law Applicable to Cyber Warfare, http://www.knowledgecommons.in/wp-content/uploads/2014/03/Tallinn-Manual-on-the-International-Law-Applicable-to-Cyber-Warfare-Draft-.pdf

perceptible international movement since its completion in 2012. Unfortunately, a life raft that is being constructed very slowly – one nail at a time – may not be finished before the storm hits.

U.S. Domestic Legal Issues

While questions of international law and use of force may be at the forefront of scholarly discussion, domestic steps to cope with cyber incidents are of immediate importance in view of the vulnerability of critical infrastructure in the United States. The U.S. president has war powers to deal with an unmistakable cyber attack with kinetic effects under the AUMF of 2001[2], limited to those responsible for 9/11, and under Article II of the U.S. Constitution. In the event of a cyber attack on critical infrastructure, what powers would an American president have to intervene to step in to restore and manage the problem if the private company were not cooperating?

Any president must be mindful of the caveats of the "Steel Seizure" case (Youngstown Sheet & Tube Co. v. Sawyer)[3] and its progeny. The U.S. Supreme Court decided that the president lacked the power, absent congressional authorization, to do so. The precedent of that case, decided when Harry Truman was president, still looms large. In 1952, the United States was in the middle of the Korean War, and steelworkers unions were about to go on strike. The President, concerned that a work stoppage in such a critical industry would adversely affect the conduct of the war, decided to place the steel mills under government control by drafting the workers and having them continue production. In the most cited concurring opinion, Justice Jackson offered a three-part test for determining the scope of presidential powers.[4] The third situation,

---

[2] Authorization for the Use of Military Force, Public Law 107–40, 107th Congress, which states "[t]hat the President is authorized to use all necessary and appropriate force against those nations, organizations, or persons he determines planned, authorized, committed, or aided the terrorist attacks that occurred on September 11, 2001, or harbored such organizations or persons, in order to prevent any future acts of international terrorism against the United States by such nations, organizations or persons."

[3] Youngstown Sheet & Tube Co. v. Sawyer, 343 U.S. 579 (1952).

[4] First, the strongest case for permitting the president's intervention, he argued, is government seizure under facts supported by legislation. A seizure executed by the

which fit the facts of the Youngstown case, Justice Jackson stated, was "when the President takes measures incompatible with the expressed or implied will of Congress, his power is at its lowest ebb, for then he can rely only upon his own constitutional powers minus any constitutional powers of Congress over the matter." He argued that in seizing the steel mills, presidential power was exercised, "not because of rebellion but because of a lawful economic struggle between industry and labor," and thus "it should have no such indulgence."[5] Congress had prescribed a method for resolving labor disputes in the Taft-Hartley law,[6] and as Justice Black's opinion of the court stated, "When the Taft-Hartley Act was under consideration in 1947, Congress rejected an amendment which would have authorized such governmental seizures in cases of emergency." Instead, it prescribed detailed methods for dispute resolution by "customary devices" such as mediation and conciliation.

If a future president should determine that it is necessary for the government to interfere with or even partly manage and operate privately owned infrastructure that has been crippled by a cyber attack, government counsel would need to review both the legislative history of all legislation then on the books and any proposed bills to see whether Congress had considered and rejected government assumption of management to any degree. Counsel also would have to closely examine the facts to opine on inherent presidential commander-in-chief powers. In that way, counsel could advise the

president pursuant to an act of Congress would be supported by the strongest of presumptions and the widest latitude of judicial interpretation, and the burden of persuasion would rest heavily on any who might attack it. A second situation in which government seizure might be permissible involved presidential action without legislative support or expression of congressional direction. That situation would turn on the facts. In Justice Jackson's words, "[W]hen the President acts in absence of either a congressional grant or denial of authority, he can only rely upon his own independent powers, but there is a zone of twilight in which he and Congress may have concurrent authority, or in which its distribution is uncertain. Therefore, congressional inertia, indifference or quiescence may sometimes, at least as a practical matter, enable, if not invite, measures on independent presidential responsibility." 343 U.S. 579 (1952), 636–637.

[5] Id at 646
[6] National Labor Relations Act of 1947, http://www.nlrb.gov/resources/national-labor-relations-act (accessed December 11, 2014).

president whether any government seizure would likely be upheld.[7] The composition of the Supreme Court at the time would also be crucial. Prediction is so fraught with uncertainty that few people would venture a definitive answer. Judicial precedents, even during a war, offer limited guidance. Nevertheless, without a specific congressional mandate, and short of a national emergency, the Supreme Court might not support government seizure and operation of critical infrastructure. Even though the "tests" of Justice Jackson have already been somewhat modified with time and new case facts,[8] it would take a major cyber catastrophe for a president to take control of critical infrastructure.[9]

Thus, absent congressional action, and before a crippling cyber attack on critical infrastructure, the government needs to heighten

[7] See *Hamdan v. Rumsfeld*, where the Court held, inter alia, that absent specific congressional authorization, not offered by the AUMF, the defendant could not be tried by military commission. 548 U.S. 557, 586 ff (2006), http://ccrjustice.org/files/2006-CCR-Hamdan-v-Rumsfeld-Amicus.pdf.

[8] An interesting comment was made by Justice Rehnquist in his majority opinion in Dames v. Moore v. Regan, a case about government seizure of Iranian assets: "Although we have in the past found and do today find Justice Jackson's classification of executive actions into three general categories analytically useful, we should be mindful of Justice Holmes' admonition, quoted by Justice Frankfurter in Youngstown, supra, at 597 (concurring opinion), that '[t]he great ordinances of the Constitution do not establish and divide fields of black and white.'" Springer v. Philippine Islands, 277 U.S. 189, 209 (1928) (dissenting opinion). Justice Jackson himself recognized that his three categories represented "a somewhat over-simplified grouping," 343 U.S., 635, and it is doubtless the case that executive action in any particular instance falls, not neatly in one of three pigeonholes, but rather at some point along a spectrum running from explicit congressional authorization to explicit congressional prohibition. This is particularly true as respects cases such as the one before us, involving responses to international crises the nature of which Congress can hardly have been expected to anticipate in any detail." 453 U.S. 654, 669(1981),

[9] That, of course, leaves ordinary federal action under criminal law. See "Prosecuting Computer Crimes," Office of Legal Education Executive Office for United States Attorneys, Department of Justice, http://www.justice.gov/criminal/cybercrime/docs/ccmanual.pdf; "Kaspersky Lab publishes an article entitled 'Cybercrime and the Law: a review of UK computer crime legislation,'" Kapersky Lab, May 29, 2009, http://securelist.com/analysis/36253/cybercrime-and-the-law-a-review-of-uk-computer-crime-legislation/ (accessed April 20, 2015); "United Kingdom of Great Britain and Northern Ireland Cybercrime legislation-country profile," Council of Europe, May 2011, http://www.coe.int/t/dghl/cooperation/economiccrime/cybercrime/Documents/CountryProfiles/cyber_cp_United_Kingdom_2011_May.pdf (accessed April 20, 2015).

its efforts to achieve a degree of civilian-military and private-sector cooperation and coordination that has yet to be reached.

The Cybersecurity Act of 2012, introduced by Senators Lieberman, Collins, Feinstein, and Rockefeller, would have provided for risk assessment, set standards for critical infrastructure such as energy, transportation, water, food, and dealt with both private industry and public agencies.[10] Unlike earlier proposed legislation, internet freedom and civil liberties advocates raised few objections to this piece of draft legislation.[11] Their opposition had provided impetus to shelving the Protecting Cyberspace as a National Asset ("Kill-Switch") Act of 2010.[12] But their concerns were addressed by the creation of an oversight board in the 2012 bill.

The original Cybersecurity Act of 2012, and less so its revised version, was not aggressive. The later version mandated the creation of a cybersecurity council and reinforced the provisions of PDD 21 and Executive Order 13636 deepening its effect and making reversibility more difficult.[13] The second version required the Council to develop an inventory of critical infrastructure.[14] The second version even softened the provision providing that the Department of Homeland Security (DHS) set sector performance standards by allowing industry to set standards voluntarily, but while technical assistance and even security clearance would also be offered, the standards had to be approved by the Council.[15] It provided oversight through required reporting.

The original legislation and its revision suggested that in times of "national cyber emergency," the president would retain the

---

[10] S. 2105 (112th): Cybersecurity Act of 2012. An amended version, s-3414 was introduced July 19, 2012

[11] Adi Kamdar, "EFF Opposes California's Cell Phone 'Kill Switch' Bill," Electronic Frontier Foundation, June 18, 2014, https://www.eff.org/deeplinks/2014/06/eff-opposes-californias-cell-phone-kill-switch-bill (accessed April 20, 2015); George Skelton, "Smart Phone 'Kill Switch' Bill Mugged By Telecom Industry," *The Los Angeles Times*, April 30, 2014, http://www.latimes.com/local/politics/la-me-cap-kill-switch-20140501-column.html (accessed April 20, 2015).

[12] S. 3480 (111th): Protecting Cyberspace as a National Asset Act of 2010.

[13] S-3414 introduced July 19, 2012; Section 102, and new section 3553.

[14] Ibid., Sec 102.

[15] Ibid., Sec. 103–105.

power to require providers of critical infrastructure to implement emergency response plans. But neither version of the bill provided strong enforcement powers. Although its supporters asserted that the legislation did not give the president power to completely shut down the internet, the vagueness in defining a "cyber emergency" and the measures flowing from that declaration alone were enough to defeat the bill.[16] Given the potential chaos that a cyber incident could cause, the Cybersecurity Act of 2012 was far from draconian in its requirements. Nevertheless, Republican senators led by Senator McCain, with pressure from business interests,[17] prevented its passage. Even its moderate requirements were regarded as too burdensome.[18]

---

[16] Ibid. Note that Section 249 of the Cybersecurity and Internet Freedom Act of 2011 bill provided that the "President may issue a declaration of a national cyber emergency to covered critical infrastructure" empowering "measures or actions necessary to preserve the reliable operation, and mitigate or remediate the consequences of the potential disruption, of covered critical infrastructure." The bill did include safeguards in a governmental body and time limits – all of which could have been strengthened and clarified; Cybersecurity and Internet Freedom Act of 2011, http://www.gpo.gov/fdsys/pkg/BILLS-112s413is/html/BILLS-112s413is.htm.

[17] Siobhan Gorman, "Cybersecurity Plan Faulted," *The Wall Street Journal*, May 27, 2011, http://online.wsj.com/article/SB1000142405270230365480457634577235236525258.html.

The U.S. Chamber of Commerce, in rejecting S-3414, stated: "Cybersecurity relies on the business community and the federal government working collaboratively. The regulatory approach provided in S. 3414 would likely create an adversarial relationship, which should be unacceptable to lawmakers. The Chamber urges Congress to not complicate or duplicate existing industry-driven security standards with government mandates and bureaucracies, even if they are couched in language that would mischaracterize these standards as 'voluntary.'"

"The Chamber believes Congress can move the needle in a meaningful way on cybersecurity by approving the SECURE IT Act. The Chamber urges you to support amendments expected to be offered that would strike the text of S. 3414 and replace it with the SECURE IT Act of 2012. The Chamber strongly opposes S. 3414, the Cybersecurity Act of 2012 and may consider votes on, or in relation to S. 3414 in our annual How They Voted scorecard." Key Vote letter on S. 3414, the "Cybersecurity Act of 2012," https://www.uschamber.com/letter/key-vote-letter-s-3414-cybersecurity-act-2012%E2%80%9D. See also Ken Dilanian, "U.S. Chamber of Commerce Leads Defeat of Cyber-Security Bill," *Washington Bureau*, August 3, 2012, http://articles.latimes.com/2012/aug/03/nation/la-na-cyber-security-20120803.

[18] Michael S. Schmidt, "Senators Force Weaker Safeguards Against Cyberattacks," *New York Times*, July 27, 2012, http://www.nytimes.com/2012/07/28/us/politics/new-revisions-weaken-senate-cybersecurity-bill.html?pagewanted=all.

An even weaker legislation than the Cyber Security Act of 2012 was introduced in 2013 to strengthen research efforts and to cement the efforts made under PPD21 and Executive Order 13636.[19] Although such legislation would have greater permanence than an executive order, it did not amount to effective regulation. Legislative efforts have continued to improve government capability to work with privately-held critical infrastructure, but as of this writing, they do not provide for regulation of standards.[20] Ironically, progress has been made with bills that provide information-sharing measures that permit the government access to private information, while limiting corporate liability.[21]

Without legislation and the uncertainty of presidential powers, the American people must rely on progress made in voluntary compliance. It is hard not to be skeptical of an effort that can do no more than seek to persuade reluctant industry to implement the standards and procedures on a voluntary basis that they worked so hard to defeat as a statutory requirement. Only the experience of a crippling attack will reveal whether the voluntary measures and exercised collaboration will prove sufficient to obviate the need for legislation. And without legislation that at least has the power to set and implement standards, the constitutionality of presidential seizure in a cyber crisis affecting infrastructure remains in doubt.

International Legal Issues

A key international legal question in cybersecurity is whether and when a cyber attack should be treated as a move toward war or as something else – an economic crime, or political or commercial espionage. Although under many circumstances characterization of

---

[19] The bill had been reported by committee in the Senate. For further action, see: S.1353 (113th): Cybersecurity Act of 2013, https://www.govtrack.us/congress/bills/113/s1353. Later, the Chamber of Commerce wrote a detailed letter in support of S. 1353, the Cybersecurity Act of 2013, yet the bill did not become law.

[20] For example, the National Cyber Security Protection Advancement Act of 2015 (H.R. 1731) https://www.congress.gov/bill/113th-congress/house-bill/1731. (accessed April 27, 2015).

[21] The Cyber Security Information Sharing Act of 2015 https://www.congress .gov/bill/114th-congress/senate-bill/754; See http://www.wired.com/2015/03/cisa-cybersecurity-bill-advances-despite-privacy-critiques/

cyber exploitation turns on the facts, any characterization is likely to be speculative, until next moves occur. Thus far, just as with targeted killing, doctrinal thinking has wavered between legal alternatives. Since ambiguity is likely to continue, definitive allocation of governmental responsibility among civilian and military agencies will remain a question in many situations, mandating collaboration regardless of the characterization.

Professor Mary Ellen O'Connell, in the article mentioned in Chapter 11, argues that the balance has tipped in favor of militarization, although remedies, such as countermeasures, are available through existing international legal means. She suggests augmentation by "dual use" treaties, patterned on the Chemical Weapons Convention or the Nuclear Proliferation Treaty.[22] No such deep international regulatory treaties dealing with cyber attacks exist to clarify international law, nor are any under serious negotiation in the west.

The same issues of imminence of attack and legality of response are present as in the other new gray areas of warfare. International legal doctrine is understandably in the process of formation since there are few, if any, examples thus far of cyber attacks that resulted in death or permanent destruction. Harold Koh, former State Department Legal Adviser, in speaking to Cyber Command in 2012, noted that a cyber operation would constitute a use of force if damage were done that approximated damage by the use of weapons – in other words, if death or significant destruction resulted from cyber activities. He stated:

In assessing whether an event constituted a use of force in or through cyberspace, we must evaluate factors: including the context of the event, the actor perpetrating the action (recognizing challenging issues of attribution in cyberspace), the target and location, effects and intent, among other possible issues. Commonly cited examples of cyber activity that would constitute a use of force include, for example: (1) operations that trigger a nuclear plant meltdown; (2) operations that open a dam above a populated area causing destruction; or (3) operations that disable air traffic control resulting in airplane crashes. Only a moment's reflection makes you realize that this is common sense: if the physical consequences of a cyber attack work the kind of physical damage that dropping a bomb

---

[22] Mary Ellen O'Connell, "Cyber Security without Cyber War," *Journal of Conflict & Security Law* (2012), 190, esp. pp. 203, 205.

or firing a missile would, that cyber attack should equally be considered a use of force.[23]

But as Professor Jack Goldsmith points out, the cyber attack that causes deaths is not the hard case:

The challenges arise mainly because the [UN] Charter focuses its prohibitions on military means of inflicting damage on another state, but does not prohibit economic or political means of inflicting damage on another state.[24]

But that may be the case that ultimately will have to be addressed. It is not an easy matter to find a current legal basis to treat an economic attack as an armed attack when no loss of lives has occurred. Nor can the concept of imminence be stretched to include intrusions that might result in physical harm at some future date.[25] The full impact of a cyber attack may not be easy to ascertain just after it occurred. Thus far, the United States has not treated intrusions into critical infrastructure as a prelude to a shutdown. Some of the novel legal questions that cyber attacks pose can only reach by tortured interpretations – or creative lawyering.

To redefine attack under the UN Charter in order to treat an economic attack as a prelude to an attack with kinetic consequences would create enormous political as well as legal problems. It is not

[23] Harold Koh, "International Law in Cyberspace," remarks made at USCYBERCOM Inter-Agency Legal Conference, September 18, 2012, http://www.state.gov/s/l/releases/remarks/197924.htm.

[24] Jack Goldsmith "How Cyber Changes the Laws of War," *European Journal International Law* (2013)24 (no.1), 129–138 http://ejil.oxfordjournals.org/content/24/1/129.short?rss=1.

[25] For an extended discussion of the legal analogies, see Michael Gervais, "Cyber Attacks and the Laws of War," *Berkeley Journal of International Law* 30, No. 2 (2012), 525-579. http://scholarship.law.berkeley.edu/cgi/viewcontent.cgi?article=1422&context=bjil; also see Michael N. Schmitt, "Cyber Operations in International Law: The Use of Force, Collective Security, Self-Defense, and Armed Conflicts," Proceedings of a Workshop on Deterring Cyber Attacks: Informing Strategies and Developing Options for U.S. Policy, http://www.lawfareblog.com/wp-content/uploads/2012/02/schmitt.pdf; Estonian Defense Minister Jaak Aaviksoo has compared the effects of cyber warfare to the effects of economic blockades. "The analogy raises questions about whether cyber attacks should now be categorized amongst conventionally regarded acts of war," Sverre Myrli, "173 DSCFC 09 E BIS-NATO and Cyber Defense," http://www.nato-pa.int/default.asp?SHORTCUT=1782. Alison Lawler Russell Cyber Blockades (Washington D. C.: Georgetown University Press, 2014).

clear, out of a specific context, what response would be legally or politically appropriate. Harold Koh left the issue of response deliberately open: "A State's national right of self-defense, recognized in Article 51 of the UN Charter, may be triggered by computer network activities that amount to an armed attack or imminent threat thereof." He added, "[a]s the United States affirmed in its 2011 International Strategy for Cyberspace, 'when warranted, the United States will respond to hostile acts in cyberspace as we would to any other threat to our country.'"[26] Potential use of offensive cyber operations and an insistence on legality were equally emphasized by Secretary of Defense Ash Carter in 2015 in announcing a new cyber strategy: "[A]dversaries should know that our preference for deterrence and our defensive posture don't diminish our willingness to use cyber options if necessary. And when we do take action – defensive or otherwise, conventionally or in cyberspace – we operate under rules of engagement that comply with international and domestic law.[27]

In May 2014, the United States unveiled charges of economic cyber espionage against five officers from the Chinese People's Liberation Army for infiltrating six American firms and stealing trade secrets to provide a competitive advantage to their Chinese counterparts.[28] Treating such acts as crimes when there is neither

---

[26] Koh, "International Law in Cyberspace."

[27] Secretary of Defense, Ash Carter; Address to Stanford School of Business, April 23 2015; http://www.defense.gov/Transcripts/Transcript.aspx?TranscriptID=5621. Previous policy was expressed in Department of Defense Strategy for Operating in Cyberspace, July 2011, http://www.defense.gov/home/features/2011/0411 %5Fcyberstrategy/docs/DoD_Strategy_for_Operating_in_Cyberspace_July_2011 .pdf. See also David E. Sanger "Pentagon Announces a New Strategy for Cyberwarfare" New York Times, April 23, 2015, http://www.nytimes.com/2015/04/24/us/politics/ pentagon-announces-new-cyberwarfare-strategy.html?_r=o

[28] Attorney General Eric Holder described the indictment as "the first ever charges against a state actor" for economic espionage through hacking; see Department of Justice, "U.S. Charges Five Chinese Military Hackers for Cyber Espionage Against U.S. Corporations and a Labor Organization for Commercial Advantage," May 19, 2014, http://www.justice.gov/opa/pr/2014/May/14-ag-528.html. This case demonstrates the enormous legal complexity of responding to cyber attacks. Hackers who work for the Chinese military (state actor) attack commercial entities (non-state actors) in the United States to steal trade secrets for the benefit of the Chinese businesses. At the same time, some of the Chinese companies receiving

a treaty nor working arrangements for extradition provides public relations value rather than concrete value as punishment.[29] However, the U.S. Executive Order "Blocking the Property of Certain Persons Engaging in Significant Malicious Cyber-Enabled Activities" (Cybersanctions Order) of April 1, 2015, may offer a serious deterrent for states, companies, or individuals whose assets could be frozen on the basis of an executive finding alone. [30] Whether that would include acts by states using non-state surrogates, as Russia reportedly did with Nashe in the Estonia attack of 2007, remains to be seen. Where state responsibility is unclear, diplomatic issues may prove of greater importance than retaliation. Cyber attacks by terrorist organizations are the most elusive of all. In those cases, what form of punishment can be fashioned, and against whom?

The Tallinn Manual addresses the question of what constitutes a threat or use of force in its detailed discussion in Rules 10 through 12,[31] and provides guidance for appropriate countermeasures in Rules 13 and 14. It states that countries can implement cyber "countermeasures" when exercising the right to self-defense, in accordance with the principle of proportionality, only for the purpose of compelling the attacking state to adhere to its international legal obligations, and those measures should "have temporary or reversible effects."[32]

Proportionality, as used in the Manual and more generally in the threshold before war (*jus ad bellum*), remains a guide to legitimate action, although that issue has not been tested in a cyber attack at present. Should the most appropriate or "proportionate" Iranian response to Stuxnet have been a cyber attack, as a retaliation in kind? That route portends escalating tit-for-tat. The borrowed concepts of *jus ad bellum* and *jus in bello* for response to an economic

---

the stolen information are owned by the Chinese state. The case combines the elements of both commercial espionage and national security.

[29] "U.S. Charges Five Chinese Military Hackers for Cyber Espionage Against U.S. Corporations and a Labor Organization for Commercial Advantage," Department of Justice, May 19, 2014, http://www.justice.gov/opa/pr/2014/May/14-ag-528 .html (accessed April 20, 2015).

[30] https://www.whitehouse.gov/the-press-office/2015/04/01/executive-order-blocking-property-certain-persons-engaging-significant-m

[31] Tallinn Manual, supra no. 1 Rules 10–12.

[32] Tallinn Manual, supra no. 1, Rule 9, Paragraph 6.

cyber attack need much further articulation through exercises that play out countermeasures. By 2016, when the Talinn Manual is to be updated, perhaps more international experience may sharpen the international legal analogies now relied upon.

Dispute settlement through existing treaty mechanisms may offer some possibilities for clarification about incursion and harm done to aviation, telecommunication, or international trade.[33] Sanctions under Chapter VII of the UN Charter offer a politically difficult but sound international legal avenue for punishment of non-life-threatening cyber attacks. However until international agreements alter the law, or the International Court of Justice should rule on such issues, many of the novel legal questions that cyber attacks pose will be answered by creative, if contrived, adaptation of historic doctrines.

---

[33] "Understanding the WTO: Settling Disputes," WTO Website, http://www
.wto.org/english/thewto_e/whatis_e/tif_e/disp1_e.htm; Jon Bae, "Review of the Dispute Settlement Mechanism Under the International Civil Aviation Organization: Contradiction of Political Body Adjudication," *Journal of International Dispute Settlement* 4, No. 1 (2013), 65–81. "Dispute Resolution in the Telecommunications Sector: Current Practices and Future Directions," World Bank Working Paper, February 2006.

13

International Cooperation on Training Wheels

Efforts to institutionalize international cooperation are rudimentary. In 2011 the Department of Homeland Security negotiated a memorandum of understanding with India on cyber attack cooperation, and in 2012 negotiated a cooperative arrangement with the Canadian government to integrate "respective national cyber-security activities and improved collaboration with the private sector."[1] This is a bare beginning.[2]

The attacks on Estonia prompted some interesting beginnings in NATO's cooperative effort, not only for cooperation after an attack but also for attack prevention. Both Estonia and NATO treated those attacks under Article 4, which provides for member state consultations after an attack: no action is promised.[3] In contrast, Article 5 of the NATO charter states that "the Parties agree that

[1] "United States and India Sign Cybersecurity Agreement," Department of Homeland Security, July 7, 2011, https://www.dhs.gov/news/2011/07/19/united-states-and-india-sign-cybersecurity-agreement; Cybersecurity Action Plan: Between Public Safety Canada and the Department of Homeland Security, http://www.publicsafety.gc.ca/cnt/rsrcs/pblctns/cybrscrt-ctn-plan/index-eng.aspx.

[2] For example, in June 2013, the State Department hailed the achievement of an international "landmark consensus" on cyber security issues. The United Nations Group of Government Experts on cyber security agreed to advance stability and transparency in cyberspace. They also agreed "that existing international law should guide state behavior with regard to the use of cyberspace." "Statement on Consensus Achieved by the UN Group of Governmental Experts on Cyber Issues," Press Statement, U.S. Department of State Website, June 7, 2013, http://www.state.gov/r/pa/prs/ps/2013/06/210418.htm.

[3] "Building a Secure Cyber Future: Attacks on Estonia, Five Years On," Atlantic Council, May 23, 2012, http://www.atlanticcouncil.org/news/transcripts/building-a-secure-cyber-future-transcript-5-23-12

an armed attack against one or more of them in Europe or North America shall be considered an attack against all."[4] The potential for NATO collective action does exist if a cyber attack were part of a traditional attack, or produced similar kinetic effects, which was not arguably the case in Estonia, where the damage was economic and relatively short term.

At the Wales summit in September 2014, NATO announced an enhanced cyber strategy recognizing that a cyber attack might be as harmful as a conventional attack. It affirmed that cyber defense "is part of NATO's core task of self defense,"[5] but added that the decision to intervene would be made on a case-by-case basis. Thus it was left ambiguous what kind of attack might prompt NATO to respond under Article 5, and left unaddressed the issue of widespread economic harm.

At present, NATO has put in place an institutional structure to deal with cyber attacks: the Cyber Defense Management Board, creating, inter alia, a Computer Incident Response Capability (NCIRC) to protect its own systems,[6] and the NATO Cooperative Cyber Defense Center of Excellence in Tallinn. The Cyber Defense Policy is now integrated into the NATO Defense Planning Process. There are conferences and membership training to defend against cyber attack including NATO training the Jordanian army to defend against ISIS cyber attacks.[7] It is not clear yet how effective any of these developments may turn out to be, but they are part of a developing institutional framework.[8]

---

[4] "Article 5 of the North Atlantic (Washington) Treaty," (1949) NATO Website, http://www.nato.int/terrorism/five.htm

[5] NATO official text, http://www.nato.int/cps/en/natohq/official_texts_112964 .htm, paragraph 72

[6] NATO Cyber Defense Center website, http://www.nato.int/cps/en/SID-856984FF-06F9E6E7/natolive/topics_78170.htm. See James Andrew Lewis, "Thresholds of Uncertainty: Collective Defense and Cybersecurity," *World Politics Review*, June 11, 2013, http://www.worldpoliticsreview.com/articles/13009/thresholds-of-uncertainty-collective-defense-and-cybersecurity. See also Marcin Terlikowski and Jozef Vyskoč, "Coming to Terms with a New Threat: NATO and Cybersecurity," February 17, 2013, http://www.cepolicy.org/publications/coming-terms-new-threat-nato-and-cyber-security

[7] "NATO helps Jordan fend off ISIL cyber threat," NATO YouTube Channel, https://www.youtube.com/watch?v=-TpIouWHNLA

[8] However, of NATO's twenty-eight countries, the Cyber Defense Center only includes eleven: Estonia, Latvia, Lithuania, Germany, Hungary, Italy, Poland,

The European Union issued a proposal for a EU-wide directive on February 7, 2013, in order to improve cooperation on cyber-security. The European Parliament adopted the Directive in March 2014.[9] The proposal unsurprisingly notes that the "current situation in the EU, reflecting the purely voluntary approach followed so far, does not provide sufficient protection" against cyber attacks. Therefore, the Directive would (1) require EU states to: "ensure that they have in place a minimum level of national capabilities by establishing competent authorities ... setting up Computer Emergency Response Teams (CERTs)," and adopting national strategies; (2) encourage national authorities "to cooperate within a network enabling secure and effective coordination, including coordinated information exchange as well as detection and response at EU level"; and (3) "ensure that a culture of risk management develops and that information is shared between the private and public sector."[10] These provisions may do little more than urge member states to reach a minimum level of sensible cyber defense capabilities, but it is a beginning. Moreover, if and when a more robust regulatory scheme might be adopted, the EU has strong monitoring capabilities to ensure adequate implementation.

The Council of Europe's Budapest Convention on Cybercrime, which came into force in 2004, bans a wide variety of criminal activity such as illegal interception, system and data interference,

Slovakia, Spain, the Netherlands, and the United States, although France and the United Kingdom have indicated they will join. See NATO Cooperative Cyber Defence Centre of Excellence website, https://www.ccdcoe.org/.

[9] "Great news for cyber security in the EU: The EP successfully votes through the Network & Information Security (NIS) directive," European Commission, March 13, 2014, http://europa.eu/rapid/press-release_STATEMENT-14-68_en.htm. "Network & Information Security Directive," http://www.europarl.europa.eu/sides/getDoc.do?pubRef=-//EP//TEXT+TA+P7-TA-2014-0244+0+DOC+XML+V0//EN&language=EN

[10] "Proposal for a Directive of the European Parliament and of the Council Concerning Measures to Ensure a High Common Level of Network and Information Security Across the Union," Brussels, February 7, 2013, COM(2013) 48 final, http://ec.europa.eu/dgs/home-affairs/what-is-new/news/news/2013/docs/1_directive_20130207_en.pdf. See also Bernard Haemmerli and Andrea Renda, *Protecting Critical Infrastructure in the EU*, Regulatory Policy, CEPS Task Force Reports, December 16, 2010, http://www.ceps.be/book/protecting-critical-infrastructure-eu.

and a range of other acts including child pornography and intellectual property theft. It does not deal with cyber attacks amounting to an act of war.[11] Its structure, requiring signatories to create domestic legislation to criminalize the defined activities, is a less threatening model to potential state signatories than a treaty that would set clear standards internationally and provide an international body to assure implementation.[12] It provides for retention of data and methods for cooperation among its signatories. The Budapest Convention permits member states to define and enforce the enumerated cybercrimes by its provisions that begin with the phrase: "each party shall adopt such legislative and other measures." Thus variations might undermine the collective flavor of the treaty regime. Moreover, the potential for member state reservations to certain provisions appear in the treaty.[13] The Convention has also been criticized for lack of enforcement mechanisms and, thus far, lacking the accession of major states such as Russia and China.[14] It is too early to tell whether permitted variations in crime definition and state enforcement procedures will impede the development of an effective international regime. Even though the Convention does not provide for a dedicated international organization to monitor compliance of the states parties, it is under the aegis of the Council of Europe, which has considerable persuasive power. And it is a binding treaty. Though far from universal, the Budapest Convention has the potential to grow in strength, cementing the norms it created. Nevertheless, it may simply remain a weak treaty that only partially develops cooperative behavior.

Regional organizations have cooperated in developing some form of association to prevent cyber intrusions and attacks. The efforts seem piecemeal and, in some cases, more conversational than

---

[11] "Convention on Cybercrime," Council of Europe Website, http://conventions.coe
.int/Treaty/en/Treaties/Html/185.htm
[12] Ibid, Article 13.
[13] Ibid, e.g., Chapter II, Articles 6(3), 9(4), 10(3).
[14] Jack Goldsmith, "Cyber Security Treaties: A Skeptical View," http://media.hoover
.org/sites/default/files/documents/FutureChallenges_Goldsmith.pdf; Proceedings
of a Workshop on Deterring CyberAttacks: Informing Strategies and Developing
Options for U.S. Policy, http://www.nap.edu/catalog/12997.html. In fact, more
than 40 Council of Europe states have become signatories and a number of
non-Council members.

operational.[15] The 2007 Association of Southeastern Asian Nations (ASEAN) Convention on Counter-Terrorism (ACCT) includes "cyber terrorism" as an "area of cooperation."[16] ASEAN and Japan issued a ministerial-level statement emphasizing the importance of "strengthening [their] collective efforts in cyber security" and encouraging further cooperation.[17] The Asia-Pacific Economic Group (APEC) has a telecommunications and information working group.[18] In Central and Latin America, the Organization of American States (OAS) members have adopted the Inter-American Comprehensive Strategy for Cybersecurity.[19] The African Union has produced drafts of its Convention on Cyber Security.[20]

The Shanghai Cooperation Organization's (SCO) treaty on cooperation in cyber space provides the "legal and organizational framework"[21] for information security cooperation and has taken

[15] Caitríona H. Heinl, "Enhancing ASEAN-Wide Cybersecurity: Time for a Hub of Excellence? – Analysis," *Eurasia Review*, July 19, 2013, http://www.eurasiareview.com/19072013-enhancing-asean-wide-cybersecurity-time-for-a-hub-of-excellence-analysis/.

[16] ASEAN Convention on Counter Terrorism, http://www.iom.int/pbmp/PDF/ASEAN_Convention_Counter_Terrorism_2007.pdf.

[17] "Joint Ministerial Statement of the ASEAN-Japan Ministerial Polity Meeting on Cybersecurity Cooperation,"ASEAN, September 13, 2013, http://www.asean.org/images/Statement/final_joint_statement%20asean-japan%20ministerial%20policy%20meeting.pdf.

[18] APEC's Telecommunication and Information Working Group (TEL) is to support security efforts associated with the information infrastructure of member countries through activities designed to strengthen effective incident response capabilities, develop information security guidelines, combat cybercrime, monitor security implications of emerging technologies, and foster international cooperation on cyber-security. According to APEC, the working group has pursued some of these activities by collaborating with other international organizations, such as the Association of Southeast Asian Nations, the International Telecommunication Union, and the Organization for Economic Cooperation and Development. United States Government Accountability Office, United States Faces Challenges in Addressing Global Cybersecurity and Governance, August 2, 2010, http://www.gao.gov/products/GAO-10-606.

[19] Organization of American States, "A Comprehensive Inter-American Cybersecurity Strategy: A Multidimensional and Multidisciplinary Approach to Creating a Culture of Cybersecurity," http://www.oas.org/juridico/english/cyb_pry_strategy.pdf.

[20] African Union, "Draft African Union Convention on the Establishment of a Credible Legal Framework for Cyber Security in Africa," http://au.int/en/cyberlegislation (accessed April 20, 2015).

[21] "Agreement between the Governments of the Member States of the Shanghai Cooperation Organization on Cooperation in the Field of International Information

significant steps toward cooperation and to understand the scope of the threat pose by cyber attacks.[22] A treaty served as a basis for the International Code of Conduct for Information Security that China, Russia, Tajikistan, and Uzbekistan submitted to the General Assembly in 2011.[23] However, SCO may include some serious cyber offenders, and the organization's efforts may seem cynical to other nations, or as efforts to control information flows internally. All these efforts provide beginning models for wider measures that should include all the nations who might suffer cyber attacks or initiate them. Due to the wide gaps in both political systems and similar gaps in trust across so many nations, any beginnings will be slow to spread and to gain effectiveness even within a regional compass.[24]

Any such efforts must address the question: Are major powers such as the United States, China, and Russia ready to relinquish offensive cyber capabilities?[25] No regulation is politically realistic so long as offensive capabilities are being employed as an instrument of policy. While there is growing interest in international

Security," June 16, 2009, http://media.npr.org/assets/news/2010/09/23/cyber_treaty.pdf.

[22] Oona Hathaway, Rebeccla Crootof, Philip Levitz, HaleyNix, aileen Nowlan, willia Perdue &Julia Spiegel, "The Law of Cyber-Attack," *California Law Review* (2012).

[23] "Letter dated 12 September 2011 from the Permanent Representative of China, the Russian Federation, Tajikistan and Uzbekistan to the United Nations addressed to the Secretary General," September 14, 2011, http://cs.brown.edu/courses/csci1800/sources/2012_UN_Russia_and_China_Code_o_Conduct.pdf.

[24] James Andrew Lewis, "Thresholds of Uncertainty: Collective Defense and Cybersecurity," *World Politics Review*, June 11, 2013, http://www.worldpoliticsreview.com/articles/13009/thresholds-of-uncertainty-collective-defense-and-cybersecurity.

[25] The *Washington Post* reported that in 2011 the intelligence community conducted 231 offensive cyber operations. The newspaper argued that the large numbers of operations signaled that the Obama administration did not show as much interest in working to "preserve an international norm against acts of aggression in cyberspace" as it did toward engaging in offensive cyber operations against potential adversaries: China, Russia, Iran, and North Korea. Barton Gellman and Ellen Nakashima, "U.S. Spy Agencies Mounted 231 Offensive Cyber-Operations in 2011, Documents Show," *Washington Post*, August 30, 2013, http://www.washingtonpost.com/world/national-security/us-spy-agencies-mounted-231-offensive-cyber-operations-in-2011-documents-show/2013/08/30/d090a6ae-119e-11e3-b4cb-fd7ce041d814_story.html.

cooperation, corresponding interest has not been expressed in curbing offensive power.

Even before the publication of military doctrine in Joint Publication 12–3, which provides for offensive operations, as indicated, American interest in offensive action was its putative involvement in offensive cyber action in the "Olympic Games." One element of the Olympic Games was a complex computer worm, "Stuxnet," designed to obstruct the operation of Iran's centrifuges at the uranium enrichment facility in Natanz.[26] In the summer of 2010, Stuxnet had moved to an Iranian engineer's computer due to programming error and subsequently was spread around the world through the internet, causing embarrassment to the United States and Israel and dislocation for many users.[27] While the full impact of the first known cyber weapon on Iran's nuclear program remains largely unknown, it appears to have achieved only limited success.[28]

It remains a question how long resisting regulation of offensive acts will continue to be effective policy. Even now, American offensive cyber capabilities may not be superior to those of potential rivals, despite vast expenditures.[29] Russia and China have already

[26] Stuxnet was developed with the assistance of NSA's Israeli counterpart, Unit 8200, and tested at Israel's nuclear facility in Dimona. Stuxnet had two variants. The older version infiltrated the system that operated the valves, which regulated the outflow of gas from the cascades of centrifuges. Blocking the outflow of gas increased the pressure on centrifuges, causing them damage. The second variant harmed the centrifuges by controlling their operating speed and causing them to crash. Sanger, *Confront and Conceal*, 190, 197. See also Ralph Langner, "Stuxnet's Secret Twin," Foreign Policy, November 19, 2013, http://www.foreignpolicy.com/articles/2013/11/19/stuxnets_secret_twin_iran_nukes_cyber_attack.

[27] David E. Sanger, "Obama Order Sped Up Wave of Cyberattacks Against Iran," *New York Times*, June 1, 2012, http://www.nytimes.com/2012/06/01/world/middleeast/obama-ordered-wave-of-cyberattacks-against-iran.html?pagewanted=all&_r=0.

[28] Langner, "Stuxnet's Secret Twin." See also Joby Warrick, "Iran's Natanz nuclear facility recovered quickly from Stuxnet cyberattack," *Washington Post*, February 16, 2011, http://www.washingtonpost.com/wp-dyn/content/article/2011/02/15/AR2011021505395.html?sid=ST2011021404206; Ivanka Barzashka, "Are Cyber-Weapons Effective?," *The RUSI Journal*, 48–56, http://www.tandfonline.com/doi/pdf/10.1080/03071847.2013.787735.

[29] According to David Sanger, the U.S. government's annual spending on offensive cyber weapons amounts to billions. See Sanger, supra no. 8, 191.

demonstrated their cyber prowess. Attacks range from crime to commercial and political espionage, launched by hackers for thrills or for hire, by terrorists, or by states. As one commentator has observed, our conceptual frameworks have not developed sufficiently to grasp the full implications of this global domain; how to deal with the threats it poses, nor the potential for its regulation.[30] Nevertheless, it may be too politically difficult to make the case for self-limitation of such an efficient instrument until a catastrophe has occurred on native soil. Further, despite the many intrusions into commercial sites and acts of espionage through 2014, neither the United States nor Europe has suffered a crippling infrastructure attack. Even the computer virus that destroyed data on 30,000 computers belonging to the world's largest oil producer, Saudi Aramco, in 2012 was not close to a crippling event. Corporate records were affected, but oil production was not seriously disrupted.[31]

In general, the American political climate has not been conducive to the ratification of treaties, particularly those curbing offensive capabilities, especially since 9/11. Recent arms control

---

[30] Observation of Col. Michael Sullivan.

[31] The United States blamed Iran, describing the attack as "a significant escalation of the cyber threat." Nicole Perlroth, "In Cyberattack on Saudi Firm, U.S. Sees Iran Firing Back," *New York Times*, October 23, 2012, http://www.nytimes .com/2012/10/24/business/global/cyberattack-on-saudi-oil-firm-disquiets-us .html?pagewanted=all. According to Aramco, the attack was a failed attempt to disrupt oil production. See "Aramco Says Cyberattack Was Aimed at Production," *New York Times*, December 9, 2012, http://www.nytimes.com/2012/12/10/ business/global/saudi-aramco-says-hackers-took-aim-at-its-production.html. Iran was also blamed for hacking into the U.S. Navy Marine Corps Internet – an "unclassified network used by the Department of the Navy to host websites, store non-sensitive information and handle voice, video and data communication" – and compromising communications on the network. See Siobhan Gorman and Julian R. Barnes, "Iranian Hacking to Test NSA Nominee Michael Rogers," *Wall Street Journal*, February 18, 2014, http://online.wsj.com/news/articles/SB10001424052702304 8997045793894028266814 52?mg=reno64-wsj&url=http%3A%2F%2Fonline .wsj.com%2Farticle%2FSB10001424052702304899704579389402826681452 .html. In Israel, a cyber attack took down cameras at the Carmel Tunnels Toll Road, shutting down one of the country's most important highways for two days. See Daniel Estrin, "AP Exclusive: Israeli tunnel hit by cyber attack," *USA Today*, October 17, 2013, http://www.usatoday.com/story/tech/2013/10/27/ ap-exclusive-israeli-tunnel-hit-by-cyber-attack/3281133/.

failures, such as American reluctance to ratify the Bioweapons Protocol and the Ottawa Land Mine Treaty,[32] suggest high barriers beyond the supermajority required for a Senate vote to ratify.[33] Even ratification of the New START Treaty 2011[34] revealed powerful political obstacles. Facing strong opposition within the Senate, President Obama was forced to increase spending on costly nuclear weapons–related modernization programs in exchange for reductions in the U.S. arsenal.[35]

Nevertheless, the history of nuclear arms control negotiations and agreements with the Soviet Union is not a totally discouraging precedent, even if developments were slow and included high levels of mutual suspicion between the two cold war adversaries. Interest in nuclear arms limitation and creating a test ban treaty was kindled when the Soviet Union developed threatening nuclear capability in the 1950s. The interest grew as it became clear that even numerical superiority was not de facto superiority. Both superpowers had the capability to effectively wipe out large swaths of the adversary's populations. The reductions – to the present – in nuclear weapons have only marginally curbed effective destructive capability, but the ongoing process of dialogue and efforts to continue to reduce weapons have been as important

---

[32] The Protocol would have strengthened the Bioweapons Convention by creating an implementation structure similar to that of the Chemical Weapons Convention. http://www.un.org/disarmament/WMD/Bio/; The Convention on the Prohibition of the Use, Stockpiling, Production and Transfer of Anti-Personnel Mines and on their Destruction, September 18, 1997, 2056 U.N.T.S 211, http://www.icrc.org/ihl.nsf/385eco82b509e76c41256739003e636d/d111fff4b9c85b0f41256585003caec3.

[33] Although the Obama administration has taken steps in mid-2014 to sign the Ottawa Treaty, including production and acquisition limits, ratification is a remote goal. Rick Gladstone, "U.S. Lays Groundwork to Reduce Land Mines and Join Global Treaty," *New York Times*, June 27, 2014, http://www.nytimes.com/2014/06/28/us/us-to-cut-its-land-mine-stockpile.html?_r=0.

[34] New Strategic Arms Reduction Treaty (New START), signed April 8, 2010, http://www.state.gov/t/avc/newstart/c44126.htm.

[35] Hearing before the Committee on Foreign Relations of the U.S. Senate, June 12, 2010, "Implementation of the New Start Treaty and Related Matters," Statement of Senator Richard Lugar, http://fas.org/irp/congress/2012_hr/implement.pdf; Nicolai Sokov and Miles A. Pomper, "New Start Ratification: A Bittersweet Success," Monterey Institute of International Studies, December 22, 2010, http://cns.miis.edu/stories/101222_new_start_ratified.htm.

as the physical reductions themselves.[36] As McGeorge Bundy said in 1988, "[T]here is work enough in smaller steps toward safety. Good choices are not easy but the record shows that they are not impossible."[37]

That ongoing dialogue, as difficult as it has been, has led to the evolution of norms that discourage use of nuclear weapons. It is true, however, that existing binding arms control agreements depend on verification for reassurance. The Chemical Weapons Convention[38] and the various nuclear arms agreements with the former Soviet Union[39] provide demanding technical means of verification – even intrusive verification – by a robust treaty organization such as the Organization for the Prohibition of Chemical Weapons (OPCW). One of the stated objections to the bioweapons protocol, if not decisive, was that it could not be verified by traditional means such as intrusive inspections or technical means that provide visibility. The demands for adequate verification cannot be met in such an easily concealed means of attack as cyber offers. Moreover, the numbers of non-state actors who could act on behalf

---

[36] Many writers in the midst or toward the end of the Cold War were moving toward the idea that the ongoing process of negotiation itself lessened danger. Some, like McGeorge Bundy relied on the fact of reduction, more than the scope of reduction of nuclear weapons as lessening danger. He said, in discussing U.S.-Soviet relations in 1988: " Both great governments have learned to respect the nuclear danger and to practice, if not preach coexistence. They have been slow about arms control and still have much to learn about it, but both are now doing better than they were. We are in danger still, but the risk of catastrophe at the end of the 1980s is much lower than in earlier decades." McGeorge Bundy, *Danger and Survival: Choices About the Bomb in the First Fifty Years* (New York, Random House (1988), 616.

   See also T. V. Paul, Richard J. Harknett, and James J. Wirtz. *The Absolute Weapon Revisited: Nuclear Arms and the Emerging International Order* (Ann Arbor, MI: University of Michigan Press, 2000).

[37] Bundy, *Danger and Survival*, 617.

[38] "Convention on the Prohibition of the Development, Production, Stockpiling and Use of Chemical Weapons and on their Destruction (Chemical Weapons Convention)," Organization for the Prohibition of Chemical Weapons, http://www.opcw.org/chemical-weapons-convention/.

[39] "Interim Agreement between the United States of America and the Union of Soviet Socialist Republics on Certain Measures with Respect to the Limitation of Strategic Offensive Arms," Federation of American Scientists, http://www.fas.org/nuke/control/salt1/text/salt1.htm; "Strategic Arms Limitation Talks (SALT II) Texts," Federation of American Scientists, http://www.fas.org/nuke/control/salt2/text/index.html.

of a state – such as Russia's Nashe in Estonia – or on their own behalf further compound the verification problem.[40]

Professor Michael Glennon sees the situation differently, in looking at the conditions that are necessary for regulation of cyber attacks:

Law is a form of cooperation. Certain conditions normally exist when cooperative mechanisms like law emerge and function properly. Actors within the system, for example, are relatively equal. Future dealings are expected. Trust is high. A consensus exists concerning foundational values. The cost of non-cooperation is high. Individual and collective interests align. Underlying social norms reinforce legal norms. Free riders and trans- gressors are easily spotted and penalized. For better or worse, however, these and other conditions necessary to promote the emergence and development of legalist constraints are not present in sufficient degree to support further international rules governing cyber conflict – any more than those conditions have been present, in the past, to support the emergence of rules governing clandestine or covert intelligence operations of which cyber activity normally is a part.[41]

Professor Jack Goldsmith, in expressing doubt about the feasibility of cyber arms control, states: "One prerequisite to a treaty – at least among powerful nations – is the possibility of mutual gain. Otherwise, there is no incentive to enter into the contract or to comply with it. For most cyber-security issues, it is not clear that a mutually beneficial deal is possible in theory, even assuming that the massive verification problems … can be overcome."[42] Yet if many nations persistently suffer from cyber exploitation and feel threatened by cyber attacks, they may come recognize the potential for mutual gain.

How then to enter a dialogue about restraint and reduction? Given the long (and bumpy) history of the evolution of norms in preventing the spread and use of dangerous weapons, attempts at cooperation are worth making, even before a disastrous event. Voluntary nonbinding efforts (or "pledges") might begin to create confidence that other nations share concerns about intrusive

[40] See Herbert Lin, "A Virtual Necessity: Some Modest Steps Toward Greater Cybersecurity", *Bulletin of Atomic Scientists* 68(5) 75–87 (2012), 82–85.
[41] Michael J. Glennon, "Gaps, Leaks, and Drips: The Road Ahead" 89 International Legal Studies, 362–386; at 379 (2013).
[42] Jack Goldsmith, "Cybersecurity Treaties: A Skeptical View," Hoover Institution Task Force on National Security and Law, March 2011.

attacks.[43] Such confidence-building measures (CBMs) might develop as the discomfort of intrusiveness and potential harm from attack begin overshadowing the desirability of maintaining offensive capability. CBMs, however mild, can move toward shifting norms until there is a "cascade" that creates an environment in which binding agreements can be developed. Herbert Lin suggests one approach to CBMs: a group of nations might trade hacking devices that may have but a single use before a defense is possible – a trade in perishable devices – what has come to be known as "zero day vulnerability." These perishable devices now often are bought and sold by hackers.[44]

Another model is a Code of Conduct, or a CBM of the kind that the Fletcher School of Law and Diplomacy students and faculty have been working on for Lincoln Laboratories. Its preamble sets forth its objectives:

The purpose of this Code is to help facilitate unimpeded access to cyberspace, based upon principles enshrined in the UN Charter and the International Convention (sic) on Civil and Political rights, subject to appropriate international and domestic legal requirements. Cyberspace should be reserved for peaceful purposes. This Code is further designed to establish a widely accepted norm that States shall refrain from the threat or use of force consistent with the principles of international law, subject to the international law of self-defense. It further provides that States shall cooperate with each other in assisting in the defense of states threatened by cyber exploitation or under cyber attack. Adherence to this Code of Conduct is voluntary and open to all states.[45]

The draft Code of Conduct includes provisions concerning unimpeded access, prevention of harm, mutual cooperation, measures for domestic protection and privacy, and procedures for peaceful dispute settlement.

If such a CBM were accepted by the United States and even a small core group of nations, it might signal a shift in norms that would begin to attract more nations. A somewhat stronger move would be an agreement of like-minded states providing for specific

---

[43] Raustiala, Kal, "Form and Substance in International Agreements," February 2004, http://www2.law.ucla.edu/raustiala/publications/Form%20and%20Substance%20in%20International%20Agreements.pdf

[44] Interview with Herbert Lin, notes on file with the author, May 3, 2014.

[45] Unpublished Code: on file at Fletcher School.

restraints and actions to protect collective cybersecurity, in addition to a collective code of conduct. This was the approach of the nonbinding Proliferation Security Initiative (PSI). The PSI began in 2003 with eleven like-minded nations and, as of 2013, expanded to 102, with its binding additional ship-boarding agreements bringing some success in preventing trafficking in items designed to facilitate nuclear weapons development and proliferation. Admittedly, even weak measures such as those embodied in CBMs or nonbinding pledges may take a long time, and much pain may be suffered before the potential of norm development can be achieved. But strong and ongoing diplomatic presence and dialogue, together with improving civil-military collaboration within democratic nations, offer the most constructive and rational approach.

14

Conclusion

The End Is the Beginning

The law hath not been dead though it hath slept.
Shakespeare, *Measure for Measure*, 2.2.90

Any current analysis is likely to fade away with time, the way children's sandcastles do when the tide rises, leaving behind their vague shapes. New episodes eclipse the old, and they are treated as novel problems, not merely new examples of familiar unsolved issues.

The three areas discussed in this book will remain relevant even after a new administration is in charge of the country and after the past dozen years of war have become a distant memory. Different versions of similar problems will plague government agencies. Insurgencies with different names and faces will challenge governments and terrorize civilians. America or Europe might well suffer a crippling cyber attack.

Yet, as difficult and enduring as the problems discussed in this book may be, they are not impervious to ingenuity. The United States has always been an innovative, problem-solving nation, and those skills are sorely needed now to deal with the gray space between war and peace. Other rising nations will also show resilience and find imaginative approaches.

Counterinsurgency

Counterinsurgency in the form laid out in the *U.S. Army/Marine Corps Counterinsurgency Field Manual* may not be repeated for a decade or more, after its unfulfilled promises in both Iraq and Afghanistan. Moreover, the pattern of retreat into national isolationism after a period of aggressive military effort is well established.[1] But when the international community becomes engaged in asymmetric ground warfare once again, we should finally recognize that supporting governments that cannot gain the trust of their people is a poor investment. Why were we surprised by ISIS gains when the United States had accepted the al-Maliki government's exclusion of Sunnis from all forms of political and economic advancement in Iraq?[2] Surely we could have predicted Taliban gains in Afghanistan when police and the courts routinely demanded bribes and two elections were fraught with corruption. In each case there were democratic alternatives.[3]

Before the next such intervention, mechanisms must be institutionalized through legislation and otherwise so that a whole-of-government approach is not just a hollow phrase. An effective, international civil-military planning effort is needed before intervention occurs. Institutionalizing such planning will allow for the process to occur even under time pressure.

Ambitious goals of reconstructing and transforming a war-torn society should be scaled back until both resources and donor governments are able to support a sufficient cadre of competent civilians to work long-term with local populations. No single nation can support such an effort alone. Without robust alliance participation, fatigue and inconsistent policy will erode any gains made. Long-term goals need to be articulated; steps along the way measured, and manifestly failing approaches adjusted. The military have improvised – often brilliantly – to make up for civilian deficiencies, but lack of role distinction only creates tension and resentment.

Counterterrorism

When an innocent hobby drone lands on the White House lawn, we must ask questions about the risks of technological catch-up

---

[1] The swings in policy are well described by Stephen Sestanovich, *Maximalist: America in the World from Truman to Obama* (New York: Knopf, 2014).
[2] Emma Sky, *The Unraveling: High Hopes and Missed Opportunities* (New York: Public Affairs 2015), 317–342.
[3] Sarah Chayes, *Thieves of State: Why Corruption Thretens Global Security* (New York: W. W. Norton, 2015), 58–66.

and proliferation. Have we begun to limit drone targeting to those people who actually threaten the homeland? We may be spawning new generations of terrorists when we kill innocent people in signature strikes of anonymous large groups of young men. Such blowback is a serious risk.

Are civil-military roles being clarified, explained, and made transparent? Have we worked through the moral issues and social risk to civilians who pilot drones safely so far from battle? Is it clear that our civilian leadership is in knowledgeable control? With all the criticism, surely governments must realize that transparency is needed to reassure people in the United States and throughout the world that the actions taken are in accordance with the law.

A firm legal basis for action would do more than help clarify roles and missions. The United States must evolve its thinking about the legality of drone killings at the very least to maintain the sturdiness of our most important alliances. Borderless wars and sectarian conflicts may seem to erode sovereignty, but some of the fiercest battles – even recent ones – have been fought to maintain state sovereignty, as the battle for Ukraine has underscored.

Borders deserve respect, and transgressing them, even for self-protection, requires strong justification. All of the strictures of *jus ad bellum* and *jus in bello* must be honored to restore and preserve the integrity of the United States. While due process may be sacrificed in wartime, safeguards can be erected to make sure that it is a rare occurrence.

Cyber Attacks and Cyber Warfare

Civil and military roles are not easily sorted out in the area of cyber attacks and cyber warfare. Continuing simulations will no doubt sharpen the response system, and a fair degree of cooperation is more likely than chaos. But the military has the lion's share of funds, personnel, and capability in an emergency, and that capability will be needed and probably will be called upon. The private sector-owners of critical infrastructure will not easily submit to government control of response to an attack. But rapid restoration after a crippling attack will be required for the health of the people and the economy. The overwhelming economic and political power of the corporations that control private infrastructure has hindered even mild regulation. It is only sensible for them to moderate their stance before a crippling attack occurs in order to allow necessary government action thereafter. Legislation is needed in the United States and its allies to provide for rapid reconstruction.

Turning outward, to the world so dependent on internet connectivity, it will ultimately be necessary to find ways to restrain nations (if not non-state actors) from using offensive cyber capabilities. Existing international law has been shoehorned into novel situations where the fit is bad.

What is needed is a move toward international regimes that modify the norms of acceptable behavior in the use of both UAVs and offensive cyber attacks. Skeptics of arms limitation dismiss the notion of international regulation that cannot provide as much reassurance as verification measures in nuclear agreements and the Chemical Weapons Convention afford. But many steps can be taken in the run-up to effective controls. Confidence-building measures, such as codes of conduct or agreements to create parallel domestic legislation, can introduce norms of behavior. After a period of time, these measures might encourage self-restraint, and states may be willing to enter into more effective regulation and deeper agreements. The development of norms and their internalization is a very slow process, as we have learned with state restraint in the use of nuclear weapons.

The United States can best exercise leadership by example. It has not acknowledged the concerns voiced throughout the world that our nation was operating outside the bounds of international law with its invasion of Iraq in 2003. Further erosion of trust occurred after grisly facts of torture emerged. Worldwide perceptions of the United States have been descending from "the shining city on the hill" to a point where the term "American Exceptionalism" has become a pejorative. Likewise, domestic critics have expressed deep concern that the American Constitution was ignored and undermined. Indeed, even a conservative Supreme Court found that many actions to stem terrorism were impermissible and in violation of long-standing constitutional practices. Although the Obama administration corrected some of the worst legal abuses, such as torture by waterboarding and extreme rendition, pervasive secrecy has left a residue of suspicion that the U.S. government has engaged in covert action using civilian intelligence agencies that operate beyond the law. Whether or not the suspicion is fair, such a perception lends credence to the concern that appropriate civilian and military roles have been scrambled to avoid scrutiny or to avoid legal strictures or both. Shakespeare, in a different context – a plea for mercy – said:

O it is excellent to have a giant's strength; but it is tyrannous
To use it like a giant.[4]

Democratic societies have the resources and the skills to engage collectively in curbing the brutality of the twenty-first century. Their "giant's strength" is needed in the effort to protect against violent criminality while upholding democratic decency.

---

[4] William Shakespeare, *Measure for Measure*, 2.2.107.

Index

Abbas, Hassan, 108n49
Abbaszadeh, Nima, 52n64
Abdulimutallab, Umar Farouk, 116
Abizaid, John P., 40, 126, 127n12
Abrams, Creighton, 26–27
Abu Ghaith, Sulaiman, 118
Abu Ghraib prison, 44–45, 118
Ackerman, Spencer, 73n5
Additional Protocol of 1977, Article 48,
 Geneva Convention, 110–113
Afghanistan
 contractor accountability,
  44–45, 44n40
 counterinsurgency, 29, 67–69
 government corruption, 32–35
 international support for invasion of,
  105–106
 Joint Interagency Task Force, 77
 long-term commitment, 52–54
 National Solidarity Program
  (NSP), 39n26
 objectives, policy issues in, 52–54
 Provincial Reconstruction Teams
  (PRTs), 51–52
 reconstruction, kinetic action
  simultaneity, 37–41
 reforms, local customs in, 32–35
 targeted killing, 99–100
 trust building by host
  government, 31–37
Africa Command (AFRICOM), 65–67
African Union, 175–177

Al Alawi v. Panetta, 1–2, 92n1
Al Awlaki, A., 1–2, 87–89, 99–100,
 115–118, 117n79, 120–121
al-Qaeda in the Arabian Peninsula
 (AQAP), 100–103, 116–118
al-Qaeda, 99–104, 107–108
al Shaba'ab, 100–103
Al-Aulaqi v. Panetta, 93n2
Al-Aulaqi, Anwar, 1, 11, 88, 92, 92n1,
 95n9, 100n20, 117n79
Alexander, General Keith B., 158, 159
Alexander, Keith B., 158
Allison, Graham T., 20, 20n17
al-Mazri, Abu Hamza, 118n82
al-Saiedi, Abdulrazzaq, 35n13
Al-Shami, Abdullah, 120
Alston Report on Extrajudicial,
 Summary, or Arbitrary Executions,
 78–79, 85
"American Civil-Military
 Relations," 23–24
Anbar Province, 29, 35
Anderson, Kenneth, 99n19
Andrade, Dale, 37n20
Arkin, William M., 76n18, 76n19
Article 51, UN Charter
 cyber attacks, cyber war, 168–169
 targeted killing, 97–98, 108–109
 terrorist classification, 10–11
Ashkenas, Jeremy, 82n3
Asia-Pacific Economic Group (APEC),
 175–177, 176n18

191